D1592909

POETIC THINKING

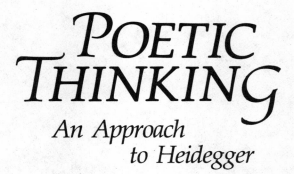

POETIC THINKING

An Approach
to Heidegger

David Halliburton

The University of Chicago Press ● Chicago and London

B
3279
.H49
H26

The University of Chicago Press, Chicago 60637
The University of Chicago Press, Ltd., London

©1981 by The University of Chicago
All rights reserved. Published 1981
Printed in the United States of America
88 87 86 85 84 83 82 81   5 4 3 2 1

Library of Congress Cataloging in Publication Data

Halliburton, David.
  Poetic thinking.

  Includes index.
  1. Heidegger, Martin, 1889–1976. 2. Literature—
Philosophy. 3. Poetry. I. Title.
B3279.H49H26   700'.1   81–7542
ISBN 0-226-31372-7   AACR2

DAVID HALLIBURTON is chairman of the Modern
Thought and Literature Program and professor of
English, Comparative Literature, and Modern
Thought and Literature at Stanford University.
His other publications include *Edgar Allan Poe: A
Phenomenological View.*

Contents

Preface

Among modern thinkers no one has made higher claims for art or
for poetry than Martin Heidegger. It also appears that no one has
provoked more discussion of the relation between literary and philosophical issues—between, on the one hand, issues of the sort we call
metaphysical, epistemological, or ontological, and, on the other hand,
issues of artistic presentation, form and content, and aesthetic values.
To speak in this way of issues, disciplines, and the like is, of course,
misleading insofar as Heidegger leaves the field of philosophy early on,
and insofar as he never really enters the field of literary criticism.
Rather, he undertakes poetic thinking, which is not so much a field
as a self-defining enterprise with its own manner and momentum. To
those made uneasy by any questioning of boundaries or established
forms—and poetic thinking is supremely interrogative—such an enterprise is, undoubtedly, disturbing. And even those who count Heidegger among the great modern minds find themselves, when immersed
in his discourse, at times strangely stirred, at times stopped short.
For poetic thinking transpires in an unfamiliar zone, making its own
course as it proceeds, speaking all the while in peculiar accents. Rigorous in its own way, it is at once playful and sober, innovative and
traditional, carefully argued and arbitrarily avowed.

This thinking has drawn the interest not only of fellow philosophers
such as Theodor Adorno, Oskar Becker, Jacques Derrida, Mikel Dufrenne, Michel Foucault, Karl Jaspers, Emmanuel Levinas, Maurice
Merleau-Ponty, and Jean-Paul Sartre, but of cultural critics such as
Max Bense, sociologists such as Alfred Schütz and Lucien Goldmann,
and writers such as Maurice Blanchot, Antonio Machado, John Nollson,
Octavio Paz, and Walker Percy.

On the Continent Heidegger has received attention from readers as
diverse as Hans-Georg Gadamer, author of *Truth and Method*, and

members of the French *Arguments* group, especially the "Heideggerian
Marxists" Kostas Axelos and Pierre Fougeyrollas. A variety of scholars,
including K. O. Apel, Walter Biemel, Alphonse De Waelhens, Ludwig
Landgrebe, Karl Löwith, Julián Marías, Werner Marx, Otto Pöggeler,
and Erasmus Schöfer, have examined Heidegger's ontology, his relation to philosophical tradition, his use of language, and his relevance to
the contemporary world. John H. Cobb, Jr., John Macquarrie, Gerhard
Noller, Heinrich Ott, and James M. Richardson, among others, have
speculated on Heidegger's significance for theology.

If Heidegger has influenced Anglo-American literary and aesthetic
practice, this has been partly due to the mediation of philosophically
oriented commentators such as William Barrett, Ronald Bruzina, Edward S. Casey, Hubert L. Dreyfus, James M. Edie, Stephen Erickson,
Marvin Farber, Michael Gelven, Marjorie Grene, Karsten Harries,
Albert Hofstadter, David Couzens Hoy, Magda King, Joseph J. Kockelmans, Thomas Langan, Michael Murray, J. L. Mehta, William J.
Richardson, Stanley Rosen, John Sallis, Richard Schmitt, Reiner
Schürmann, Calvin O. Schrag, Hugh J. Silverman, Herbert Spiegel-
berg, Charles Taylor, David White, Bruce Wilshire, and John Wild.

Because of the relative esteem in which psychology and psycho-
analysis have been held in the United States, another important mediating service has been provided by psychoanalytic interpreters, including Ludwig Binswanger, Medard Boss, F. J. J. Buytendijk, Eugen Kahn,
Rollo May, Erwin Straus, and Irvin Yalom.

To a greater extent, perhaps, Heidegger's influence in literary and
aesthetic fields can be traced to the work of such readers as Beda
Allemann, Else Buddeberg, Albert Cook, Stanley Corngold, Paul de
Man, L. L. Duroche, Frances C. Ferguson, Alexander Gelley, Vernon L.
Gras, F. W. Kaufmann, Hans Jaeger, Donald G. Marshall, Kurt Mueller-
Vollmer, Richard Palmer, Johannes Pfeiffer, Joseph N. Riddell, John
Carlos Rowe, Alvin H. Rosenfeld, Hans Joachim Schrimpf, William
V. Spanos, Theophil (and to a lesser extent Theodor) Spoerri, James
F. Swearingen, Emil Staiger, and George Steiner. Joseph P. Fell, *Heideg-
ger and Sartre: An Essay on Being and Place* (New York: Columbia Uni-
versity Press, 1979), and Paul A. Bové, *Destructive Poetics: Heidegger
and Modern American Poetry* (New York: Columbia University Press,
1980), are among the publications which appeared after the present
book was completed.

Meanwhile, the later writings of Kenneth Burke reveal the imprint of
Heidegger's thinking; Heidegger has been linked to American blues
music by John J. Moody; to electronic music by Gerry Stahl; and to
architecture by Christian Norberg-Schulz. I might also mention the

influence of Heidegger on my *Edgar Allan Poe: A Phenomenological View* (Princeton: Princeton University Press, 1973).

English translations of Heidegger have also played a crucial role. The 1927 masterpiece *Sein und Zeit (Being and Time)* appeared in 1962, three years after *Einführung in die Metaphysik (An Introduction to Metaphysics)*. As early as 1949, Werner Brock had edited *Existence and Being*, containing four essays by Heidegger. The introduction to *Was ist Metaphysik? (What is Metaphysics?)* appeared in 1957, *Zur Seinsfrage (The Question of Being)* and *Was ist das—die Philosophie? (What is Philosophy?)* in 1958, while 1962 saw not only the publication of *Sein und Zeit* but the publication of *Kant und das Problem der Metaphysik (Kant and the Problem of Metaphysics)*, the "Brief über den Humanismus" ("Letter on Humanism"), and *Platons Lehre von der Wahrheit (Plato's Doctrine of Truth)*. The period from 1966 to 1972 bore witness to the appearance in English of *Gelassenheit (Discourse on Thinking)*, *Die Frage nach dem Ding (What Is a Thing?)*, *Was heisst Denken? (What Is Called Thinking?)*, *Vom Wesen des Grundes (The Essence of Reasons)*, *Zur Sache des Denkens (On Time and Being)*, and *Identität und Differenz (Identity and Difference)*. In the 1970s appeared several volumes of writings previously untranslated, including *The End of Philosophy*, *Early Greek Thinking*, *The Piety of Thinking*, and *The Question Concerning Technology and Other Essays*. A list of English translations appears in Michael Murray, ed., *Heidegger and Modern Philosophy: Critical Essays* (New Haven: Yale University Press, 1978), pp. 357–64.

More directly significant for literary studies were the translation of the two lectures on Hölderlin in the Brock volume, the translation by Joan Stambaugh and Peter D. Hertz of all but one of the essays in *Unterwegs zur Sprache (On the Way to Language)*, and the publication, as *Poetry, Language, Thought*, of Albert Hofstadter's translations of *Der Ursprung des Kunstwerkes*, "Wozu Dichter?", " . . . dichterisch wohnet der Mensch," and "Die Sprache" (to name the pieces of particular literary and aesthetic interest).

Yet it is still hard to find in English detailed studies of Heidegger aimed mainly at persons outside the discipline of philosophy, and even harder to find discussions of that peculiar phenomenon—of such great potential interest to the "literary world," especially in the United States—which I am calling poetic thinking. The present volume is intended to address this need.

I hope to accomplish several aims: to improve the access of English-speaking readers, in particular those concerned with literary interests, to the Heideggerian canon; to explore the concept and practice of poetic thinking in relation to Heidegger's preoccupation with Being and related issues; and to compare Heidegger's work, where feasible, to the work of other thinkers. Space limitations have prevented me from treating at length Heidegger's relation to Nietzsche, his interest in Eastern thought, and his inquiries into technology.

Although my comments are based on my reading of the work in the original German, I have made extensive use of several excellent and readily available translations (for which bibliographical data are furnished in the List of Abbreviations); other translations are my own.

I have often retained the term *Dasein*, since it has taken on a life of its own, though the need for variety and clarity has prompted me to supplement it from time to time with "Being-there," "human being," and with two additional synonyms from Heidegger's later usage, "man" and "mortals."

Where Heidegger employs *Seiende*, meaning any entity that is, such as a book or a tree (more on this in the pages that follow), I have employed "being" or occasionally "entity." Where Heidegger employs *Sein*, *In-der-Welt-Sein*, and related constructions, I have employed "Being," "Being-in-the-world," and the other English compounds provided by Macquarrie and Robinson's translation of *Being and Time*. These practices vary at times from the usage in a quotation (as in the case of Manheim's choice of "essent" for *Seiende* in *An Introduction to Metaphysics*, or the use of lowercase "being" in other translations). Context clarifies the matter in most cases; where it does not—or in places where the original presents difficulties—I have provided explanatory remarks.

I have reproduced the manner in which translators supply words from the original German texts. Generally, Macquarrie and Robinson make insertions, sometimes italicized but usually not, within square brackets. Manheim makes unitalicized insertions within angle brackets. When the translations are mine, and also when I supply terms in translations not my own, insertions appear italicized within parentheses.

List of Abbreviations

As a convenience to the reader, parenthetic references indicate, first, the page number in the original and then, after the virgule, the page number in the translations.

E = *Erläuterungen zu Hölderlins Dichtung,* 4th ed. (Frankfurt: Klostermann, 1971).

EM = *Einführung in die Metaphysik* (Tübingen: Niemeyer, 1973). *An Introduction to Metaphysics,* trans. Ralph Manheim (1959; rpt. New York: Doubleday, 1961).

G = *Gesamtausgabe,* vol. 24: *Die Grundprobleme der Phänomenologie* (Frankfurt: Klostermann, 1975).

H = *Holzwege,* 4th ed. (Frankfurt: Klostermann, 1963). *Poetry, Language, Thought,* trans. Albert Hofstadter (New York: Harper & Row/Colophon, 1975). The translation of "Die Zeit des Weltbildes" appears in *The Question Concerning Technology,* trans. William Lovitt (New York: Harper & Row, 1977).

KK = *Gesamtausgabe,* vol. 25: *Phänomenologische Interpretation von Kants Kritik der reinen Vernunft* (Frankfurt: Kolstermann, 1977).

SG = *Der Satz vom Grund* (Pfüllingen: Neske, 1957).

SZ = *Sein und Zeit,* 11th ed. (Tübingen: Niemeyer, 1967). *Being and Time,* trans. John Macquarrie and Edward Robinson (New York: Harper & Row, 1962).

U = *Unterwegs zur Sprache,* 4th ed. (Pfüllingen: Neske, 1971). *On the Way to Language,* trans. Peter D. Hertz and Joan Stambaugh (New York: Harper & Row, 1971).

VA = *Vorträge und Aufsätze,* 3 vols. (Pfüllingen: Neske, 1971). The translation of "Die Frage nach der Technik" appears in *The Question Concerning Technology* (see H, above).

W = *Gesamtausgabe*, vol. 9: *Wegmarken* (Frankfurt: Klostermann, 1976).
WHD = *Was heisst Denken?* (Tübingen: Niemeyer, 1954).

POETIC THINKING

1

Introduction

The present study is primarily concerned with the shape that Heidegger's thinking began to take in the decade following *Being and Time*
(1927); with the way it developed after that; with his approach to art
and, in particular, poetry; with the role of poetry, as language in the
primordial sense, in relation to the constitution of the world; and with
the concept and practice of play. A full exposition of issues treated in
the earlier works, while of much intrinsic interest, therefore lies outside
the scope of this book. It will be helpful, however, to pick up from these
works some threads that are relevant to my discussion of the later writings.

The Heidegger of 1927 wishes to raise anew the question of the
meaning of Being, a question as elusive as it is decisive. In the words of
Plato (*Sophist* 244a): "For manifestly you have long been aware of what
you mean when you use the expression 'being' *(seiend)*. We, however,
who used to think we understood it, have now become perplexed *(in
Verlegenheit gekommen)*" (SZ, 1/19). Perplexity is a condition that accompanies, to a greater or lesser degree, all of Heidegger's inquiries,
which rarely achieve the closure of traditional philosophical discourse.
Part of what perplexes is the fact that we are no longer perplexed: we
"know" what Being "is"; yet the basis of that knowing, obscured by its
own "clarity," remains unexamined. Metaphysics perpetuates the
obscurity by its constant recourse to what is supposedly self-evident:

> Greek ontology and its history—which, in their numerous filia-
> tions and distortions, determine the conceptual character of phi-
> losophy even today—prove that when *Dasein* understands either
> itself or Being in general, it does so in terms of the "world," and
> that the ontology which has thus arisen has deteriorated [verfällt]
> to a tradition in which it gets reduced to something self-evident—
> merely material for reworking, as it was for Hegel. [SZ, 22/43]

Statements such as this—and they are numerous in Heidegger's writings, early and late—are not meant to denigrate investigations carried out along the lines laid down in Greek ontology but to question the extent to which they have held themselves open to what remains, for Heidegger, the paramount question: "In the course of this history certain distinctive domains of Being . . . have served as the primary guides for subsequent problematics: the *ego cogito* of Descartes, the subject, the 'I,' reason, spirit, person. But these all remain uninterrogated as to their Being and its structure, in accordance with the thoroughgoing way in which the question of Being has been neglected" (SZ, 22/44).

Throughout the history of Western metaphysics, Heidegger suggests, thinkers have tried to take hold of their own tradition, so as to build upon it, without realizing that all the while the tradition has been taking hold of them, preventing them from perceiving that on which the tradition itself is already built: the forgetting of the question of Being. Having lost sight of this ground, one "naturally" concentrates on whatever comes down through time as so self-evident that we have only to chart the multiplicity of forms it takes in this or that culture or period (hence Heidegger's skepticism about comparative studies); but the one history that does not get transmitted is, inevitably, the one that matters most because it is essentially prior to any other kind of history, and that is the history of Being. Heidegger concludes that if we are ever to uncover that history the concealed and concealing metaphysical tradition must be broken apart: "We understand this task as one in which by taking *the question of Being* as our clue, we are to *destroy* the traditional content of ancient ontology until we arrive at those primordial experiences in which we achieved our first ways of determining the nature of Being—the ways which have guided us ever since" (SZ, 22/44). Like other Heideggerian terms, "destruction" seems slightly skewed, even forced, a characteristic that can perhaps be traced to a desire for a diction with shock value; in any case, destroying tradition, as Heidegger understands that process, does not mean annihilating the past or putting it aside, any more than the synonymous phrase "overcoming metaphysics" means taking a position without reference to what is being overcome. The process works, rather, from within: "We must . . . stake out the positive possibilities of that tradition, and this always means keeping it within its *limits*; these in turn are given factuality in the way the question is formulated at the time, and in the way the possible field for investigation is thus bounded off" (SZ, 22/44).

The "world" to which Heidegger alludes, above, denotes what is given to experience in the immediate form of actual, present beings: this page in this book, that office building, a pencil, a rabbit, a street. These are the things we encounter and live with; they matter to us; and it is hardly surprising that thinkers have based their sense of truth and their sense of "what is" upon the apprehension of just such beings as these. Beings thereby become universally normative for ontological inquiry; Being means the Being of things, quite apart from any meaning Being might have in itself. *Whether* it has such a meaning—and in the event that it has, *what* that meaning is—become hidden issues, or, rather, they remain the hidden issues they were fated to be from the time that ancient ontology located the decisive question in the intersection between beings and the Being of beings.

Notwithstanding this omission, there is immense value, Heidegger insists, in the understanding we do have. Indeed, if we could not operate intelligently in the "world," if we did not grasp beings in their presence, we could not carry out any inquiries at all. The very fact that we do inquire entails the presupposition that the beings inquired about actually are; hence we proceed on *some* understanding of what Being is:

> Inquiry, as a kind of seeking, must be guided beforehand by what is sought. So the meaning of Being must already be available to us in some way. As we have intimated, we always conduct our activities in an understanding of Being. Out of this understanding arise both the explicit question of the meaning of Being and the tendency that leads us towards its conception. We do not *know* what 'Being' means. But even if we ask, 'What *is* "Being"?', we keep within an understanding of the 'is', though we are unable to fix conceptually what that 'is' signifies. We do not even know the horizon in terms of which that meaning is to be grasped and fixed. *But this vague average understanding of Being is still a Fact.* [SZ, 6/25]

The "we," referring to the type of being Heidegger calls *Dasein* or Being-there, is privileged in *Being and Time* insofar as any inquiry must regard "what is" from the way it is lived by *Dasein* as such—a procedure at odds with metaphysical tradition, which employs everyday present beings as touchstones for defining everything, including the world of *Dasein.* Thus in Cartesian metaphysics, the world is discovered through the *cogito* as a substance derived from a kind of being found in "nature," not from the phenomenon of the world as it is primordially lived.

The inquiries carried out in *Being and Time,* by contrast, demonstrate that the kinds of Being that belong to various entities are distinctively different and, further, are incommensurate with the kind of Being we call human. In our everyday experience, for example, we encounter things that are just there, before us, such as trees or hills or birds or rivers or rocks. Because such things are indubitably present, are really "right there," and because they are so without necessary orientation toward human interests, Heidegger calls their mode of Being "presence-at-hand" *(Vorhandenheit)*.

A different kind of Being is found in entities that do have such an orientation. These are, for example, *Zeuge*—tools (or equipment)—which are handled this way or that way in order to attain some human end. This kind of Being is *Zuhandenheit*, or "readiness-to-hand"; that is, tools are prepared for us, prepared by us, and we are prepared for their being prepared, whereas things that are present-at-hand are inherently and wholly "just there."

It does not follow that we normally focus on the traits that a tool has when we use it, least of all that we draw the distinctions of the sort that interest philosophy. Indeed, the less we focus and the more we just wield the hammer we find ready, "the more primordial does our relationship to it become, and the more unveiledly is it encountered as that which it is—as equipment" (SZ, 69/98). Our interest centers on what Heidegger calls "the 'in-order-to,'" indicating the direction in which the manipulation of the tool seems almost autonomously to lead; because our action is clearly purposeful and its purpose is clear, we move along in this direction without stopping to think about—or as Heidegger prefers to say, to stare at—the tool. We so move because all dealings with equipment accommodate themselves to our *Umsicht*, or circumspection, a concept that entails the sense of looking around before moving ahead but also the sense of "looking around for a way to get something done" (SZ, 69/98n.). If the description thus amounts to a definition of one kind of practice, it carries implications for a concept of theory, as Heidegger is well aware. Thus one might be said to turn theoretical as soon as one stops hammering and stares at the hammer: "Theoretical behaviour is just looking, without circumspection" (SZ, 70/99). In other words, as we cease looking around for a way to get something done, the "in-order-to," the direction and the process, give way to an act of attention wherein the tool becomes an object of scrutiny. In this way Heidegger distinguishes between what are sometimes called operational and thematic modes. In the first, a practice is carried out or a project put forth transparently, so that we go about our doing, or point ourselves toward our doing, without cognizing the process. In the second, what is transparent turns opaque; we see what we are about and make it a "theme" of our reflection. In other words, the "in-order-to" is seen as such. At this juncture circumspection becomes a distraction, the point of our behavior now being to discover the very nature of what we are staring at. We get at readiness-to-hand more directly, it seems, when the tool does not work: a *broken* hammer is a broken *hammer*, which I recognize as equipment rather as if, after a wind that I have been half-hearing suddenly ceases, I suddenly hear it as having blown. "The tool turns out to be damaged, or the material unsuitable. In each of these cases *equipment* is here, ready-to-hand. We discover its unusability, however, not by looking at its properties, but rather by the circumspection of the dealings in which we use it. When its usability is thus discovered, equipment becomes conspicuous" (SZ, 73/102).

At this point we appreciate the extent to which the kind of Being called present-at-hand continues in the tool, for if we stare at a broken hammer we can conceive not only its renewable future (it can be repaired and used again); we can also see that its past (part of it was once a tree) is still there. Once repaired, the tool assumes its character of Being-ready-at-hand; or as Heidegger puts it, pure presence-at-hand withdraws to Being-ready-at-hand, whereupon the hammer returns, as tool, to the assignment it has for circumspection.

With this background, we gain insight into Heidegger's consternation over the fact that metaphysics, from antiquity through Christianity and into the modern period, unthinkingly defines *Dasein* in terms of what is present-at-hand. According to the venerable concept of "man" as *zōon logon echon* or *animal rationale*, the animal capable of reason, "the kind of Being which belongs to a *zōon* is understood in the sense of occurring and Being-present-at-hand" (SZ, 48/74). Such a definition, besides being inappropriate, is strikingly incomplete, Heidegger argues, because its decisive feature—the attribute of possessing *logos*—is left hanging, there having been no effort at all to determine *its* kind of Being. In this instance, at least, traditional metaphysics hands down a mystery bound to a mistake.

Heidegger's inquiry, for its part, necessitates inquiry into the Being of the inquirer:

> Looking at something, understanding and conceiving it, choosing, access to it,—all these ways of behaving are constitutive for our inquiry, and therefore are modes of Being for those particular entities which we, the inquirers, are ourselves. Thus to work out the question of Being adequately, we must make an entity—the inquirer—transparent in his own Being. The very asking of this question is an entity's mode of *Being;* and as such it gets its essential character from what is inquired about—namely, Being. This entity which each of us is himself and which includes inquiring as one of the possibilities of its Being, we shall denote by the term 'Dasein.' [SZ, 7/26–27]

In contrast to the notion of world described above, Heidegger's concept of world is inseparable from his concept of *Dasein*. For Heidegger the world is not a designation for all the things that surround us, such as things that are present-at-hand. It is, rather, a characteristic of that very *Dasein;* or, to borrow another term, it is that "wherein" *Dasein* lives. Yet some of the things discussed above—tools, for example—are intelligible only in terms of that Being-in-the-world that is the essential state of Being-there. Something ready-to-hand, for instance, is ready because it has been given an assignment, which means in turn that "there is an involvement which it has *in* something" (SZ, 84/115):

> *with* this thing, for instance, which is ready-to-hand, and which we accordingly call a "hammer," there is an involvement in hammering; with hammering, there is an involvement in making something fast; with making something fast, there is an involvement in protection against bad weather; and this protection 'is' for the sake of [um-willen] providing shelter for *Dasein*—that is to say, for the sake of a possibility of *Dasein*'s Being. [SZ, 84/116]

Being-there understands all this through giving itself an assignment as well, an assignment aiming toward some goal it aspires to achieve. Because Being-there is, by Heidegger's definition, the kind of Being for which its Being is at issue, such an assignment may be said to be "for the sake" of that potentiality; and the direction in which the assigning moves is from this toward some involvement, as described above, which, for its part, operates for the sake of Being-there. *"The 'wherein' of an act of understanding which assigns or refers itself . . . is the phenomenon of the world"* (SZ, 86/119). Although the language is difficult and abstract, the phenomenon at issue is simple and concrete. If I exist, I exist somewhere, in some world, which, insofar as I am in it and experience it myself, is *my* world. But this world is also the place in which I find some things present-at-hand, such as trees, and other things ready-to-hand, such as hammers, and in which I live with other persons. Because world is a characteristic of Being-there, Being-in-the-world is *a priori.*

> We, as human beings, have relationships both with things and with other human beings. They are relationships of which we are *aware* and which change us. In *this* sense, inanimate objects do not have relationships. Now suppose one is asked: What is the capacity by which one has such relationships? There must be some *a priori* capacity within us that allows us to relate in the first place. This prior capacity is the *a priori* existential Being-in-a-world.[1]

On such a basis it is quite proper to speak, as Heidegger does in *The Basic Problems of Phenomenology,* of the priority of world in relating understandingly to things, and especially equipment. Each item of

---

1. Michael Gelven, *A Commentary on Heidegger's "Being and Time"* (New York: Harper & Row, 1970), pp. 54–55.

equipment, each tool, makes sense to us only in relation to all of the equipment belonging to what might be called the relevant scene. Borrowing instances from *Being and Time,* we could say that, when I am writing, the pen I use makes sense within the scene of the room, which is also composed of paper and ink and blotting pad, of windows and doors, of a lamp and other furnishings.

Such a scene, it should be said, is only one aspect of the fuller scene in which Being is disclosed; the phenomenon of world also includes, *inter alia,* Being-one's-self and Being-with-others (more on these below). It is nonetheless an important aspect, since time and again Heidegger's interpretations, as in this stage of his quest for a fundamental ontology, use their hermeneutic leverage to best effect by prying between *Dasein* and the beings around it.

Since world is *a priori* and hence the very medium in which we live, it is necessarily the condition of my understanding anything within-the-world:

> Because we, as those who exist, already understand world in advance . . . we are continually able to understand and meet one another in terms of the entities within-the-world that we encounter. . . . The shoemaker is not the shoe, but the shoemaking equipment, belonging to the totality of equipment in his environment, is understandable only in relation to the actual world which belongs to the existential conception of Being-there as Being-in-the-world. . . . In his manner of existing [the shoemaker] *is* his world, which first makes it possible to disclose a totality of equipment as within-the-world. . . . [G, 243–44; italics mine]

In an uncharacteristic move, Heidegger asks himself to what extent his conception of world would apply to children. Such a world is "primitive," he surmises, and the things the child meets with are not fully encountered or understood; and yet "perhaps," he says, all of these things are laden with world in the same way as the things that are within-the-world for the adult. The issue, then, it would seem, is not so much the scope of the child's world as the broader question of a fundamental capacity to bring the phenomenon of the world from "background" to "foreground," this capacity depending upon how primordial one is toward one's existential possibilities. If one is primordial enough—or if one is original enough, for the issue is how to generate, as it were, the movement in question—then possibilities are actualized, meaning that the world, which was already disclosed by one's very existence, is, first, distinctly seen, then put into words so as to become "explicitly visible for others" (G, 244).

This is, of course, what Heidegger as thinker is trying to do in his own discourse. But why should it be necessary for him, or for anyone

else, to *see* world instead of simply living it? Is world something that
has to be spelled out? The answer furnished by *Being and Time* is no;
Being-in-the-world is also Being-with others, as revealed by the fact
that the shoemaker's work, for example, is shaped to size and hence
contains "an essential assignment or reference to possible wearers" (SZ,
118/153) or the fact that the book I am reading was purchased from a
shop owned by one person and was then given to me by another. All
these other persons are thus within the same *world* as things, and they
are in it in the same basic *way* as I am.

Because communication belongs to the phenomenon of Being-in-the-
world, one does not have to make utterances in order to be understood
by someone else: just because that other is in the world as I am in the
world, we already have an understanding, and what we understand
most fundamentally is *the fact that we are both in the world, along with
everyone else:* "Communication is never anything like a conveying of
experiences, such as opinions or wishes, from the interior of one subject into the interior of another. *Dasein*-with is already essentially manifest in a co-state-of-mind and a co-understanding" (SZ, 162/205). *Rede*,
discourse, is for the early Heidegger the very foundation of language
and a basic condition of Being-in-the-world. In discourse the act of
utterance is not decisive: if I am dealing with you in a social situation,
language as discourse transpires as long as I understand you, whether
or not either of us speaks aloud, because my understanding depends
upon my hearing, and I can perfectly well "hear what you are saying" in
the sense of understanding what you "really" mean, even if you remain
silent. The novels of Henry James abundantly demonstrate this remarkable ability of discourse to communicate without recourse to utterance.
On the other hand, if I am not hearing, you may speak *without* my
understanding you, the degree of hearing precisely reflecting the degree of understanding.

In talking to one another it is not that we change our basic condition
of Being-with but that we experience it as *our* condition, not merely
yours or merely mine: "In discourse Being-with becomes 'explicitly'
shared; that is to say, it *is* already, but it is unshared as something that
has not been taken hold of and appropriated" (SZ, 162/205).

The position Heidegger assumes in *The Basic Problems of Phenomenology* is related but a little different. Here what is to be communicated is
the entire phenomenon of the world, and this phenomenon is conceived of as invisible until brought to discourse. It would appear from
this that, whereas Being-with is shared by the very fact of counderstanding and discourse, the totality of the world is not. Hence, though
Heidegger is not explicit on the issue, the fact that the world is my own

involves the possibility that it can be so "personal" that others do not see it, or it can become "interpersonal" in that others are then able to see it. A valuable dimension is added when, above and beyond disclosure, the world can be *looked-upon* as disclosed. The same applies, evidently, to existence itself: "In 'poetical' discourse, the communication of the existential possibilities of one's state-of-mind *(Befindlichkeit)* can become an aim in itself, and this amounts to a disclosing *(Erschliessen)* of existence" (SZ, 162/205).

Most readers of *Being and Time* are probably surprised that, in a book little concerned with art of any kind, the author should make so high a claim for the poetic. If I am not mistaken, the brevity of the remark, also surprising at first, results not from casual interest but from a deep conviction of poetry's ability to illuminate, in its own way, the phenomena that Heidegger is exploring in his own discourse. When he wants to illustrate the preontological way in which Being-there interprets itself, Heidegger quotes an ancient Latin fable he came across in an article on *Faust,* supplements his commentary on it with a footnote on a poem by Herder, and, in another footnote, cites Tolstoy's "The Death of Ivan Ilyich" as an account of how we watch others die. If in *Being and Time* the significance of literature remains on the level of the implicit, it moves nearer the center of concern in a section of *The Basic Problems of Phenomenology* dealing, again, with the phenomena of the world. There, Heidegger provides a lengthy quotation from Rilke's novel *The Notebooks of Malte Laurids Brigge,* prefacing it with the statement that "Poetry is nothing other than the elemental way in which existence as Being-in-the-world is discovered *(Entdecktwerden der Existenz als des In-der-Welt-seins)*, that is, comes into words. Through what is expressed the world becomes visible to the others, who before this are blind" (G, 244). Here as elsewhere Heidegger uses the term "poetry" as a generic term for heightened authentic discourse, whether in verse or in prose (though in practice most of his examples are drawn from verse). Such discourse, deemed in *Being and Time* to possess the capacity to disclose existence, now discovers it, the difference between the two verbs being far from accidental. The reader will recall that in our dealings with equipment, we rely on circumspection, looking for a way to get something done, and (as Heidegger explains in another part of *Being and Time*) this means discovering the appropriate referential contexts for our tools. Such an orientation directs us toward entities but not toward seeing what they are *for* or what they are ready-to-hand *with,* the latter features having already been disclosed to circumspection. Disclosure therefore means laying open "as implicit in what is given" (SZ, 75/105–6n.). In other words, we understand but do not explicitly see what the tool is for or what it is ready with, this understanding being based on disclosure, and we employ the tool through circumspection's discovery of the contexts to which its appropriate employment is referred. Now, when a tool is broken, as we saw in the case of the hammer, we observe the assignment which it no longer carries out, which is to say that it becomes explicit. Similarly, when a tool is missing, "this makes a *break* in those referential contexts which circumspection discovers. Our circumspection comes up against emptiness, and now sees for the first time *what* the missing article was ready-to-hand *with,* and *what* it was ready-to-hand *for*" (SZ, 75/105).

Although Heidegger does not name such seeing, it is evidently more like another phase of discovering than another phase of disclosing. In any case, discovering—in many instances one might equally say uncovering—is closely related to language, as Heidegger conceives it in *Being and Time,* and it is this relation, I believe, that underlies the shift from stating that poetical discourse discloses to stating that poetry discovers. When we judge an assertion *(Aussage)* to be true, we mean that it discovers or uncovers the being it is directed toward: "Such an assertion asserts, points out, 'lets' the entity 'be seen' *(apophansis)* in its uncoveredness" (SZ, 219/261). More fundamentally, this capacity inheres in the very concept of *logos:* "The *logos* lets something be seen *(phainesthai),* namely, what the discourse is about . . ." (SZ, 32/56). Truth or *alētheia* consists in being brought forth from hiddenness: "The 'Being-true' of the *logos* as *alētheuein* means that in *legein* as *apophainesthai* the entities *of which* one is talking must be taken out of their hiddenness; one must let them be seen as something unhidden *(alēthes);* that is, they must be *discovered*" (SZ, 33/56–57).

With this context in mind, the reader may be less surprised that Rilke's text (which is reproduced below in part) makes the world visible by evoking an experience analogous to the experience, described above, of achieving vision through absence:

> Houses? But to be precise, they were houses that were no longer there. Houses that had been pulled down from top to bottom. What *was* there was the other houses, those that had stood alongside of them, tall neighboring houses. Apparently these were in danger of falling down, since everything alongside had been taken away; for a whole scaffolding of long, tarred timbers had been rammed slantwise between the rubbish-strewn ground and the bared wall. I don't know whether I have already said that it is this wall I mean. But it was, so to speak, not the first wall of the existing houses (as one would have supposed), but the last of those that had been there. One saw its inner side. One saw at the different storeys the walls of rooms to which the paper still clung,

and here and there the join of floor or ceiling. The stubborn life of these rooms had not let itself be trampled out. It was still there; it clung to the nails that had been left, it stood on the remaining handsbreadth of flooring, it crouched under the corner joints where there was still a little bit of interior. . . . There stood the middays and the sicknesses and the exhaled breath and the smoke of years, and the sweat that breaks out under armpits and makes clothes heavy, and the stale breath of mouths, and the fusel odor of sweltering feet. There stood the tang of urine and the burn of soot and the grey reek of potatoes, and the heavy, smooth stench of ageing grease. The sweet, lingering smell of neglected infants was there, and the fear-smell of children who go to school, and the sultriness out of the beds of nubile youths. To these was added much that had come from below, from the abyss of the street, which reeked, and more that had oozed down from above with the rain, which over cities is not clean. And much the feeble, tamed domestic winds, that always stay in the same street, had brought along; and much more was there, the source of which one did not know. I said, did I not, that all the walls had been de-molished except the last—? It is of this wall I have been speaking all along. One would think I had stood a long time before it; but I'm willing to swear that I began to run as soon as I had recog-nized that wall. For that is the terrible thing, that I did recognize it. I recognize everything here, and that is why it goes right into me: it is at home in me.[2]

In a remark following the quotation Heidegger states that, in our relation to things, the things "leap against us" (G, 246), in which case Rilke's discovering consists in letting that process be seen. Rilke's readers now explicitly recognize the world of Malte; but because Being-in-the-world involves Being-with-others and counderstanding, at the same time they recognize their own world in his and—what is not the same thing—they further recognize that, because they have the same kind of Being as all other persons, world is a pervasive phenomenon—what Heidegger calls an "existential"—to be met with everywhere in human experience. Given the relation between *logos* and *alētheia* described above, Rilke's depiction must be true: what Rilke describes "is not put into the wall through his writing (*hineingedichtet*) but, on the contrary, the depiction is only possible as interpretation and illumination of what 'really' is in the wall . . ." (G, 246). After putting quotation marks around the adverb, Heidegger, as if to emphasize the ambiguity of the issues he is raising, goes on to use a term, *erfinden*,

2. Rainer Maria Rilke, *The Notebooks of Malte Laurids Brigge*, trans. M. D. Herter Norton (1949; rpt. New York: Capricorn, 1958), pp. 47–48.

which can mean either "discover" or "create," as in making up a fiction: "The poet is able not only to see this primordially but unthinkingly *(unbedachte)* and not at all theoretically discovered *(erfundene)* world—but Rilke also understands the philosophical meaning of the concept of life which Dilthey already adumbrated and which we laid hold of by the concept of existence" (G, 246–47). The use of quotation marks around "really" suggests ambivalence concerning the manner in which the author achieves his revelation. If Heidegger makes the depiction a mere representation, he loses the connection between *logos* and *alētheia* as well as the view that the work of art provides an elemental way of discovering existence or, better, *is* that way. But if, on the other hand, he goes too far in the opposite direction, he risks implying that the world thus presented is an independent phenomenon, one that is, in effect, its own origin. As later writings attest, the latter is the idea Heidegger will work toward, and his unwillingness to move toward it here is what marks this treatment of literary art as an early endeavor. At this juncture, Heidegger is not yet thinking, in the sense of the term that applies to later writings; he is performing the tasks of a philosopher by employing the text as illustration or proof and leaving it at that. Consequently, the approach (viewed from the standpoint of the later, poetic thinker) looks almost too evidentiary, too dependent on the notion of visibility and explicitness; hence, in contrast to later writings, where the text at issue is often extremely brief and the commentary extended, here the text is extended and the commentary brief. Although a polarity exists, at the same time, between the emphasis on visibility and Heidegger's invitation to "hear" the passage, he does not think it through, and this contrasts again with the later approach, in which the problem is worked and reworked until hearing and seeing are brought toward convergence.

Interestingly, Heidegger takes no explicit account of a characteristic of Malte's encounter that surely affects every reader, and this is the mood of *Angst,* or dread, that pervades the text. Yet the mood figures prominently in *Being and Time* as one of the "existentials" that define what it means to be human, and dread figures as a leading type of disposition *(Befindlichkeit).*[3]

"Disposition" is an ontological way of expressing the ontic manner in

3. Werner Marx, *Heidegger and the Tradition,* trans. Theodore Kisiel and Murray Greene (Evanston: Northwestern University Press, 1971), p. 90n., makes a telling case for translating *Befindlichkeit* as "disposition." Stanley Corngold, *"Sein und Zeit:* Implications, for Poetics," in *Martin Heidegger and the Question of Literature: Toward a Postmodern Literary Hermeneutics,* ed. William V. Spanos (Bloomington: Indiana University Press, 1979), pp. 193 ff., ties *Befindlichkeit* to mood, placing Heidegger against the background of a nineteenth-century *"history"* of mood whose principal figures are Kierkegaard, Dilthey, and Nietzsche.

which we find ourselves, by which Heidegger means the kind of condition that would be reported if I asked you, "How did you find him?" and you replied: "He was in a bad mood." Here the response deals not with the procedure by which you located the person asked about but the manner in which that person found himself during your time with him; in other words, how he "was." Using the term *Stimmung*, or mood, and its variants—but without developing, as he will later do, the musical implications of the term, which frequently refers to the tuning of a musical instrument—Heidegger observes that Being-there is always attuned in one way or another; that is, it always has *some* mood. Moods are another form of

> primordial disclosure . . . in which *Dasein* is brought before its Being as 'there.' Furthermore, a mood of elation can alleviate the manifest burden of Being; that such a mood is possible also discloses the burdensome character of *Dasein*, even while it alleviates the burden. A mood makes manifest 'how one is, and how one is faring' ['wie einem ist und wird']. In this 'how one is,' having a mood brings Being to its 'there.' [SZ, 134/173]

What is disclosed by a mood, Heidegger goes on to explain, is the fact that I am "delivered over" (SZ, 135/173) to the Being I have to be; or as he also says, this entity that I am is thrown into its "there." This term, for its part, is defined by disposition and understanding and discourse (as discussed above), as well as those phenomena, such as idle talk, which exemplify what Heidegger refers to as "falling." There is, in other words, no shortcut to defining the "there": it stands for everything in the list (as well as two other phenomena, which will not be considered here).[4]

By the somewhat misleading term "falling," Heidegger does not have in mind, for example, a decline from some lofty or primal status but merely the tendency that we all have to go muddling along, absorbed in idle talk, meaning gossiping and chatting and "spreading the word." As what is rumored and talked about moves along in its own inertia in the form of what "they" (*das Man*) say, it becomes normative, so that we find ourselves experiencing literature or events in public life as "they" experience them, without really knowing who they are or, better, without recognizing that they are not anyone but instead are everyone and no one. Absorbed in these anonymous others, Being-there is tempted to ignore what is disclosed in disposition and to take the easy way of believing that it is leading a full life in the best of all possible worlds. The result is a "'*downward plunge*' [*Absturz*] . . . into the groundlessness and nullity of inauthentic everydayness" (SZ, 178/223). Instead of

---

4. These are curiosity (SZ, 170–73/214–17) and ambiguity (SZ, 173–75/217–19).

holding Being-there into its authentic possibilities, understanding rushes into the inauthenticity of the "they"; in an effort to catch the spirit of the dynamic, Heidegger says that "the movement of falling is characterized by *turbulence* [Wirbel]" (SZ, 178/223). Falling and thrownness then emerge as intimately related and mutually sustaining:

> Falling is not only existentially determinative for Being-in-the-world. At the same time turbulence makes manifest that the thrownness which can obtrude itself upon *Dasein* in its state-of-mind *(Befindlichkeit)*, has the character of throwing and of movement. . . . *Dasein*'s facticity is such that *as long as* it is what it is, *Dasein* remains in the throw, and is sucked into the turbulence of the "they's" inauthenticity. [SZ, 179/223]

An alternative to falling is resoluteness, meaning a determination to end one's absorption in the "they" and face up to one's authentic possibilities for existence. The authenticity of resoluteness is guaranteed in turn by care, a concept central to understanding Being-there but one that may best be approached (following Heidegger's own lead) by way of the phenomenon of dread.

In contrast to fear, which is a type of emotional distress directed toward some object (whatever it is, in a particular situation, that is fearful), dread has no object. It is the feeling that comes upon us when, of a sudden, a situation becomes strangely skewed, out of kilter, or in some other way unfamiliar. It may manifest itself in the feeling that one is in a dream or in the sense that what one is doing is unreal and theatrical: without warning we experience our human condition, in all its thrownness and fallenness, see it living and bare. Malte's encounter with the awesome life still clinging to the torn-down houses is a paradigmatic case, as is Roquentin's encounter with the unexpected, overwhelming, existing "thereness" of the root of the oak tree in Sartre's novel *Nausea*. Both are experiences of what Heidegger calls the uncanny *(unheimlich)* (SZ, 189/233). In such a state we look for something *in* the world to explain the dread, only to discover that its source is not anything present-at-hand or ready-to-hand but the world itself. The connection with resoluteness becomes immediately evident when we consider that dread exposes us not only to the fact of Being-in-the-world but to the challenge of deciding what to "do" about it: "Anxiety makes manifest in *Dasein* its *Being towards* its ownmost potentiality-for-Being—that is, its *Being-free for* the freedom of choosing itself and taking hold of itself" (SZ, 188/232).

When uncanniness yanks us abruptly out of the comfortable everyday public realm of the "they," we may decide to flee from what we now face—the sense that we are "not-at-home" in the world after all—back to that more familiar, more secure domain. But the very possibility of deciding one way or the other presupposes that I care. Since, as Being-there, I am "an entity for which, in its Being, that Being is an issue" (SZ, 191/236), I *must* care. This is especially clear in the way that Being-there comports itself in the subordinate modes of concern *(Besorgen)* and solicitude *(Fürsorge)*. Concern means taking an interest in something, such as a mortgage, while solicitude means taking a supportive interest, as in helping someone whose mortgage is about to be foreclosed. But again, concern and solicitude presuppose care, *Sorge*, in a basic sense, by which I do not mean caring in the sense of "I care for fudge" but caring in the sense of my necessary commitment to existing in some fundamental way. Because this means deciding for this or that potentiality, I am already directed toward the future and in this sense am already ahead of myself even as I continue to exist alongside the things that I meet within-the-world; and this is another way of describing care.

It is no accident that putting the matter in this way implies the temporality of care, for if one achieves, say, resoluteness, one achieves it always at some time and follows through with it, or fails to follow through, in some time. If resoluteness means "Being-ahead-of-oneself," it follows that we take our direction, as it were, from the future, though less in the sense that it guides us than in the sense that the possibility of our moving toward it is the very condition of our moving: "The 'ahead-of-itself' is grounded in the future" (SZ, 327/375).

The significance of this is further shown by contrast with the kind of time *(zeithafte)* that pertains to beings present-at-hand. Since Heidegger offers no examples for direct comparison, let us consider that a tree has grown up to maturity, whereupon a heavy rainstorm uproots it and it dies. Although we may henceforth speak of a time when it was and of a time when it is no more, we cannot speak—except nonsensically—of its having had a future in the way that *Dasein* has a future. The tree cannot resolve, for example, to go on living as against committing suicide; nor does it become immersed in what "they" are gossiping about—what would "they" mean in such a case: the forest? Nor does such a being experience dread in the facing of having to choose what it is going to be. Assigning *Dasein* this kind of time means nothing less than transforming it into a being that is present-at-hand.

The future is so fundamental for Being-there, on the other hand, that even the "past" and the "present" are explained in relation to it. Heidegger's explanation of this is concise and, if one has the patience to follow it closely, clear: "The character of 'having been' arises from the future, and in such a way that the future which 'has been' (or better, which 'is in the process of having been') releases from itself the Present.

This phenomenon has the unity of a future which makes present in the process of having been; we designate it as 'temporality'" (SZ, 326/374). Approaching from another angle, one might say that, if I am already ahead of myself, then what I am presently can emerge only from a movement wherein I have been on my way toward what I have yet to be. Or: from the process of my having-been even now toward a future, there emerges what I am to be as having-been.

To prevent slipping back into the habit of segmenting time into discrete periods, Heidegger invokes the concept of *ecstasis*, recalling the root sense of standing outside, a sense we register when we speak of existence as a movement or a process, understanding, as we do, that this always transpires in departing from some given "standing." Time in the ordinary sense, Heidegger argues, "consists, among other things, precisely in the fact that it is a pure sequence of 'nows,' without beginning and without end, in which the ecstatical character of primordial temporality has been levelled off" (SZ, 329/377). Such nows appear indefinite and static, a series of vague points strung out between one shadowy period that no longer is and an equally shadowy period that is not yet, whereas "ecstatic" time is by its very nature definite and dynamic—and indeed it is the very possibility of such a primordial temporality that enables us to settle for something less, namely, the idea of time as a sequence of nows.

The problem with a point is that it sounds like something, which is to say something present-at-hand, and the same applies to all schematizations that tend to make time look like space or like something in space. All draw their perspectives from entities that can be measured, but "Temporality 'is' not an *entity* at all. . . . Temporality temporalizes (*Zeitlichkeit zeitigt*), and indeed it temporalizes possible ways of itself. These make possible the multiplicity of *Dasein*'s modes of Being . . ." (SZ, 328/377).

Heidegger alone cannot establish such a history; at best he can rediscover something of the original idiom, now half-heard, if at all, in which it was spoken; a rediscovery that will require the tuning of his own idiom to the fundamental tone of the poetry and thought of others, even when the effort produces dissonant effects. The chapters that follow will listen to the varying, sometimes elusive shadings of that idiom, and they will endeavor to clarify, where its purport seems in doubt, what it is saying or trying to say. Only through such reflection can one help to preserve that new beginning that Heidegger undertakes in the shadow of metaphysics:

> In metaphysics reflection (*Besinnung*) is accomplished concerning the essence of what is and a decision takes place regarding the essence of truth. Metaphysics grounds an age, in that through a

specific comprehension of truth it gives to that age the basis upon which it is essentially formed. This basis holds complete dominion over all the phenomena that distinguish the age. Conversely, in order that there may be an adequate reflection upon these phenomena themselves, the metaphysical basis for them must let itself be apprehended in them. [H, 69/115–16]

Prominent among these phenomena are texts by certain poets whose practices make them paradigmatic, in one respect or another, for our own epoch. The first of these, in rank as well as time, is Friedrich Hölderlin, who therefore figures prominently in these pages. Yet some of Heidegger's best writing concerns a twentieth-century poet much influenced by Hölderlin, namely, the Austrian Expressionist Georg Trakl; it is, for example, through Heidegger's reading of Trakl that we can best understand the relation of poetry to the world as a whole. Heidegger is equally concerned to reopen questions raised by ancient Greek texts, especially those of the pre-Socratics, such as Anaximander and Heraclitus; to explore the meaning of early Greek poets, such as Sophocles and Homer; and to elucidate the relevance of a poet like Angelus Silesius, whose work, falling nearer the modern age, suggests a way to unseat metaphor on the way to unseating the metaphysics on which metaphor depends.

In connection with the latter issue (to be explored more fully in a later chapter), Heidegger refuses to accept the distinction between the literal and the figurative, which, with the subject-object dichotomy, merely replicates the distance that is presumed to separate the sensible and the insensible, or supposes that Being, for example, could have its ground in reason, conceived as something apart from Being. One virtue of great poets and great thinkers is that they glimpse, sometimes actually convey, a different and superior vision that is not "beyond" the everyday but is the everyday simply seen. "There lives the dearest freshness deep down things," says Hopkins; and if Heidegger concurs, he also conveys his sense of that freshness, old and ever new, in a language that, contradicting certain conventions, sometimes strains itself into unimagined possibilities "Where, selfwrung, selfstrung, sheathe- and shelterless, | thóughts agaínst thoughts ín groans grind."

The strain, and hence the pathos of Heidegger's poetic thinking, arises partly from the desire to evoke a sense of the unity of things that has been turned, by metaphysics, into disunity and opposition; hence, by the measure of metaphysics, the resulting discourse must itself appear contradictory. But if the thinking poet Octavio Paz is right, the fault lies with the tradition, which has forgotten what poetry knows:

Now, the poem not only proclaims the dynamic and necessary coexistence of opposites, but also their ultimate identity. And this reconciliation, which does not imply a reduction or transmutation of the singularity of each term, is a wall that Western thought has refused to leap over or to perforate as yet. Since Parmenides our world has been the world of the clear and trenchant distinction between what is and what is not. Being is not nonbeing. This first extirpation . . . constitutes the basis of our thinking. . . . Mysticism and poetry have thus lived a subsidiary, clandestine and diminished life. The split has been inexpressible and constant. The consequences of that banishment of poetry are more evident and frightening each day: man is an exile from the cosmic flux and from himself. Because now no one is unaware that Western metaphysics ends in a solipsism.

Heidegger's discourse may be regarded as an attempt to make the split visible, as it were—an attempt that, following Paz's reckoning, requires it to express the inexpressible. Small wonder that Heidegger, after *Being and Time*, turns increasingly to poetry, for poetry speaks a truth that metaphysics cannot know, and speaks eloquently at that. One could even say that it expresses the inexpressible but for the fact that it is only within metaphysics that certain things cannot be truly and beautifully said.

To destroy the solipsism (Paz continues),

Hegel went back to Heraclitus. His attempt has not given us back our health. The rock-crystal castle of dialectic is revealed to us as a labyrinth of mirrors. Husserl restates all the problems and proclaims the need "to get back to the facts." But Husserl's idealism also seems to lead to a solipsism. Heidegger goes back to the pre-Socratics to ask himself the same question that Parmenides asked and to find an answer that will not immobilize being. We have not yet heard Heidegger's last word, but we know that his attempt to find being in existence ran up against a stone wall. Now, as some of his writings show, he has turned to poetry. Whatever may be the outcome of his adventure, the fact is that, from this angle, Western history can be seen as the history of an error, a going astray, in both senses of the word: in losing our way in the world we have become estranged from ourselves. We have to begin again.[5]

Returning to the Heidegger text cited above, we may note the manner in which the basis of phenomena comes to appearance: namely, by a process of letting-appear. Although this idea is employed in *Being and*

5. Octavio Paz, *The Bow and the Lyre*, trans. Ruth L. C. Simms (Austin: University of Texas Press, 1973), pp. 86–87. Alvin H. Rosenfeld employs insights from different sections of the same book in "'The Being of Language and the Language of Being': Heidegger and Modern Poetics," in *Martin Heidegger and the Question of Literature*, pp. 200 ff.

Time, it becomes extremely prominent in the later writings, as the discussions that follow will attest, because of the turn that Heidegger makes when, instead of completing the 1927 opus, he moves on to other tasks, including, significantly, an extended exploration of the thought of Nietzsche. Paz is right. Heidegger could not find Being in existence, that is, in *Dasein,* because Being proved to be "other" than *Dasein,* as it proved to be other than beings that are present-at-hand or ready-to-hand. With the discovery there occurs a change in mood and manner; no longer does thought pursue the essence of "the human"; the goal is now, by a gradual attunement, to bring thinking to articulation through proximity to Being. Proximity, nearness, the notion of place as an essential realm other than space: all of these related ideas will be taken up in the chapters that follow. Here we need only observe that in *Being and Time* Heidegger is already searching for a more primordial way of uncovering and conveying the "why" of what-is through its "where," a way that, among other things, brings the phenomenon of spatiality out of its status as a phenomenon over against temporality:

> *Dasein* takes space in; this is to be understood literally. It is by no means just present-at-hand in a bit of space which its body fills up. In existing it has already made room for its own leeway. It determines its own location in such a manner that it comes back from the space it has made room for to the 'place' which it has reserved. [SZ, 368/419]

The translator's "leeway," *Spielraum,* is literally a play-space, a space or room for play; that is, not some predetermined fixity given in a spatiality free of time but an area cocreated through its openness for occupancy by *Dasein*—and *by* that occupancy. Similarly, the beings that we encounter within-the-world are not predetermined in their "where" but rather emerge—even as the very basis of phenomena emerges—through the act of letting-be:

> When we let entities within-the-world be encountered in the way which is constitutive for Being-in-the-world, we 'give them space'. This 'giving space', which we also call *'making room' (Einräumen)* for them, consists in freeing the ready-to-hand for its spatiality. As a way of discovering and presenting a possible totality of spaces determined by involvements, this making-room is what makes possible one's factical orientation at the time. [SZ, 111/146]

A more poetic manifestation of such letting-be appears below in chapter 3, where *Einräumen* is related to the evocation of a festal room, while in chapter 8 we shall see Heidegger putting to use an expanded

sense of place. But before leaving the early Heidegger we should note
the treatment of the play of space and time in *A Phenomenological Interpretation of Kant's "Critique of Pure Reason,"* published shortly after
Being and Time. (In the passage Heidegger also touches on the
phenomenon of "dimension," which will appear in connection with
what I call "elemental" thinking.)

Heidegger takes as his point of departure the fact that Kant turns to
play to define the function of time and space: "Thus time is the condition of the play of sensibility; space however is the play of forms." Play,
Heidegger adds, is characteristically free yet has a direction and a
rhythm; more important, it provides a means of dealing with time and
space that does not bind either to what is present-at-hand—whereupon
Heidegger's own discourse becomes playful, though pertinently so:
" . . . we play with time, or better: time plays with itself. Space and time
are the configurations of pre-forming *(Vorbildung)*. . . . they pre-form the
space of play, which is the dimension within which the present-at-
hand can occur, in which and within which it can practice" (KK, 131).
Although *Einspielen* can refer to the training activities of a team, its
other sense—practicing a musical instrument—is apposite for two reasons. First, it accords with the theme of the passage and with the playful
manner in which the theme is carried out. Second, it points forward to
the role that theme and manner will play in the later writings, which, as
we shall see, have, at the very least, quasi-musical qualities.

Such letting-be can appear to run counter to the character of violence
that belongs to Heidegger's existential analysis; but in fact that character presents itself as violence in the same way as the "inexpressible,"
that is, it constitutes a problem only for a point of view other than the
point of view of this thinker. The character of violence arises from the
way in which *Dasein* exists. Immersed in the world, we are constantly
falling, in the sense already discussed, and this falling guides the manner in which, on an everyday basis, we understand ourselves. But such
an ontic understanding is not adequate for an ontological inquiry that
by definition seeks *Dasein's* primordial reality. Therefore, to complete
its task, interpretation, working persistently against this tendency to
cover up, must "wrest" disclosure from *Dasein,* must, finally, "capture"
this Being that seems to withdraw. Because such an effort goes against
everyday understanding, it appears to be excessive and coercive.

> Common sense concerns itself, whether 'theoretically' or 'practi-
> cally', only with entities which can be surveyed at a glance cir-
> cumspectively. What is distinctive in common sense is that it has
> in view only the experiencing of 'factual' entities, in order that it
> may be able to rid itself of an understanding of Being. It fails to
> recognize that entities can be experienced 'factually' only when

Being is already understood, even if it has not been con-
ceptualized. Common sense misunderstands understanding. And
therefore common sense must necessarily pass off as 'violent'
anything that lies beyond the reach of its understanding, or any
attempt to go out so far. [SZ, 315/363]

All modes of letting-be, including the releasement of *Gelassenheit,* do
not therefore involve violence in the usual sense of the term, though
they do require on the part of the interpreter a resolute attitude and a
degree of exertion. There is nonetheless a change in tone, and even to a
degree in stance, from the early Heidegger's uncovering quest in *Being
and Time,* his evocation of the *polemos* of powers in *An Introduction to
Metaphysics,* his concern for dread and death and care and other somber
aspects of existence. What all this passes into, without breaking the
continuity of his fascination with being, is a sense of composure without resignation. It is this that we have in mind when we speak of
releasement. But releasement, it must be said, is no mere state that,
having been once attained, can be perpetuated either by an inertia of
the will or by mystic concentration. It designates a constant comportment, carried out with effort, even with a kind of pathos, but also with a
joy arising from thinking's role in the phenomenon Heidegger calls
"the play of the world," which provides the focus of the concluding
chapter.

2

Art as Origin

It is through the work of art . . . that everything else that appears and is to be found is first confirmed and made accessible, explicable, and understandable as being or not being.
An Introduction to Metaphysics

Any inquiry into the origin of the work of art confronts a circularity, since wherever it begins is where it begins again. If one starts, as Heidegger does, from the relation of the work to the artist, one finds that the role of the artist can be clarified only through the role of the work; the work of art can be clarified in turn, however, only by understanding the nature of art per se: if we are to speak sensibly of a "work of art," we must know what we mean by "art." With this, we turn back toward the work, since the meaning of art can be comprehended only on the basis of art's actual works, whereupon we find ourselves beginning where we began, with the role of the artist.

The process, we may say, is the very embodiment of the hermeneutic circle, as sketched in *Being and Time*, and Heidegger's response to it is, in essence, the response of 1927: "Thus we are compelled to follow the circle. This is neither a makeshift nor a defect. To enter upon this path is the strength of thought, to continue on it is the feast of thought, assuming that thinking is a craft" (H, 8/18). Here, as in the earlier work, the problem is to find the right way to enter the circle. But he does not find the problem difficult: a work of art, whatever else it may be, is always, at a minimum, some sort of thing, or at the very least possesses some thing-like characteristics, such as the weight and texture of stone in architecture, the shapes and shades of color in a painting, the tones of a musical composition. Hence an inquiry into the origin of the work of art may properly begin with an inquiry into the thing.

No matter where one begins, the goal remains the same: "Our aim is to arrive at the immediate and full reality of the work of art, for only in this way shall we discover real art also within it" (H, 10/20). These words by the student of Husserl echo the teacher's famous admonition, "Back to the things themselves," an admonition made credible, in part, by the availability of the practice of that *epochē*, or phenomenological

24

bracketing, developed by Husserl and employed (in the main implicitly) by Heidegger. Husserl needed a way to suspend, put out of action, or neutralize (the terms are synonymous) the self-evident, everyday, "natural" point of view so as to get at the phenomena of experience just as they present themselves.

> If I do this, as I am fully free to do, I do *not* then *deny* this "world," as though I were a sophist, *I do not doubt that it is there* as though I were sceptic; but I use the "phenomenological" *epoché*, which *completely bars me from using any judgment that concerns spatio-temporal existence.*[1]

By the time of *The Origin of the Work of Art*, Heidegger is less inclined to employ phenomenological terminology than he was in *Being and Time*, which bears the subtitle *A Phenomenological Ontology*, and such phenomenological procedures as he employs are everywhere played down. I mention the *epoché*, therefore, by way of acknowledging what is now a general, widely diffused, but still important technique in Heidegger's thinking. Also influential, though in a significantly different way, is the assumption that the thing provides the most convenient point of departure for defining any sort of being other than a thing. In light of the objections Heidegger raises, in *Being and Time*, against just this practice, this may seem an odd position to take. But the difficulty dissolves when we recall that the "destruction" of tradition, undertaken in that earlier work and continued, *mutatis mutandis*, in *The Origin of the Work of Art*, always proceeds from within that tradition. This means that, in the present work, the shortcomings of employing the thing as norm can best be demonstrated by working through the implications that such a perspective entails.

Earth and World: The Being of Equipment

One implication is the notion that the thing amounts to a combination having its origin, on the one hand, in a kind of irreducible stuff and, on the other, in the manner in which that stuff is distributed:

> That which gives things their constancy and pith but is also at the same time the source of their particular mode of sensuous pressure—colored, resonant, hard, massive—is the matter in things. In this analysis of the thing as matter (*hulē*), form (*morphē*) is already coposited. What is constant in a thing, its consistency, lies in the fact that matter stands together with a form. The thing is formed matter. This interpretation appeals to the immediate

1. Edmund Husserl, *Ideas: General Introduction to Pure Phenomenology*, trans. W. R. Boyce Gibson (1931; rpt. New York: Collier, 1962), p. 100.

view with which the thing solicits us by its looks *(eidos)*. In this synthesis of matter and form a thing-concept has finally been found which applies equally to things of nature and to use-objects. [H, 16/26–27]

It is hard to think of a conceptual pairing with more durability than this pairing of matter and form, which appears in the equally familiar, equally dichotomous guise of content and form or content and structure. The pairing is perfectly obvious, one is inclined to say; but if Heidegger learned anything from Husserl, it was the danger of accepting the self-evident, especially when it manifests itself as the received wisdom of tradition: hence the call in *Being and Time* for an approach that penetrates the façades of received wisdom in order to arrive at that which, as a condition for all subsequent handing-down and reception, is primordially given.

As one way of bracketing the dichotomy of matter and form, Heidegger employs a tactic, also used by Wittgenstein, of simply refusing to play the game in question. Wittgenstein, of course, makes the refusal itself into a game, so that the problem being treated (e.g., the problem of "expression" in *The Blue and Brown Books*) is turned into an absurdity through the iteration of unanswerable questions. Heidegger, for his part, does not take the same direction, but he is every bit as playful (as subsequent discussions will show), and he too opposes by questioning. In the present case, he merely replaces the unacceptable dualistic concept with concrete descriptions and the fundamental ontological distinctions that they, when properly followed up, necessitate.

This is conspicuously the case with his analysis of the work of art in relation to the tool or equipment *(Zeug)*, a focus to which the previous quotation, above, begins to shift at the end. In *Being and Time,* we recall, a "natural" thing, such as a rock, is a being of the type called present-at-hand. It is simply there before us as something that has grown into what it is without human mediation. A piece of equipment, by contrast, possesses the kind of Being termed readiness-to-hand. Having come into its own through human mediation, it stands ready to be used, manipulated, and so on, its peculiar instrumentality consisting in part in the fact that equipment always relates to other equipment: every tool we write with, such as a pen, relates to some other writing-oriented tool, such as ink and paper. Another peculiarity is that equipment always relates *toward,* the goal of this relation being the work to be produced through the exercise of the equipment. Precisely that orientation—our preoccupation with the work to be produced—draws our attention away from the *Being* of equipment as such; Heidegger's way of putting it, as I pointed out, is to say that what is ready-to-hand in effect withdraws from us. Finally, the work that is to be produced—

the work envisaged as the "toward-which" of the equipment—itself possesses the same kind of Being as the equipment.

A concern with the peculiar character of equipment is by no means confined, in the early writings, to *Being and Time*. In *The Basic Problems of Phenomenology* Heidegger devotes considerable space to distinguishing between a shoe and the maker of a shoe and to showing that, different as they are, the shoe—a piece of equipment—is nonetheless intelligible only in relation to the shoemaker's Being-in-the-world. The motif of the shoe continues, interestingly, to weave through work after work, evidently because it is one of the main things that suggested to Heidegger the necessity of thinking more rigorously about differences among types of Being. What appears to have happened, over the years, is that, in pondering this issue, Heidegger hit on a crucial, unique phenomenon addressed only indirectly in the earlier work: the phenomenon of the thing as it appears in a work of art. It is more than a coincidence, then, that he is particularly intrigued by a pair of farm shoes in a painting by Van Gogh:

> From the dark opening of the worn insides of the shoes the toilsome tread of the worker stares forth. In the stiffly rugged heaviness of the shoes there is the accumulated tenacity of the slow trudge through the far-spreading and ever-uniform furrows of the field swept by a raw wind. On the leather lie the dampness and richness of the soil. . . . This equipment is pervaded by uncomplaining anxiety as to the certainty of bread, the wordless joy of having once more withstood want, the trembling before the impending childbed and shivering at the surrounding menace of death. This equipment belongs to the *earth*, and it is protected in the *world* of the peasant woman. From out of this protected belonging the equipment itself rises to its resting-within-itself. [H, 22–23/34]

The description imparts what Sartre calls meaning: the participation of a present reality in the Being of other realities, rather than (as in signification) the substitution of a present object for an absent one. Whereas signification posits a transcendent relation between objects and can only prepare a basis for intuiting, meaning is directly intuitive and is a transcendence fallen into immanence: the odor of a handkerchief, the atmosphere of a century emanating, in a museum, from an exhibited wig or sedan chair.[2]

Further, Heidegger's account, notwithstanding its homeliness, gives prominence to three emphases of Sartre's ontology: certainty, plenitude, and the determination of essential Being. The peasant

2. Jean-Paul Sartre, *Saint-Genet: Actor and Martyr*, trans. Bernard Frechtman (1963; rpt. New York: New American Library, 1964), p. 332.

woman is sure of her world; the usefulness of the equipment rests in the fullness of its reliability; and this reliability in turn is the essential Being of equipment. The point is not that Heidegger's peasant woman is a philosopher *manqué*. His suggestion that perhaps she merely *wears* the shoes is a strategy for answering, before it is even asked, the possible objection that the thinker is reading too much into the account. Heidegger wants to show, as simply as possible, how the world and earth truly come to be, for this woman, in and through the reliability of her equipment. As we saw in the previous section, Heidegger's terms for the two main regions of things, at this time, are world and earth. To offer concrete examples, world in the case of the peasant woman would include all the work she performs but also her rest, since rest is rest from work. It would also include any other involvement in her surroundings or "environment," such as the gathering of the family at the morning meal before going into the fields or in the evening after coming back, or in church on the Sabbath, when all pray together for a bountiful harvest. Earth, a topic to which I return below, entails everything (including those same fields, the furrows drawn across them, and the moisture in which seeds germinate) which supports existence but which remains less accessible, hence less interpretable, than the world in which that existence is at all times situated.

This is the sense, then, in which the Being of equipment may be said to gather all things. But that capacity, we should note, is not attributed to Van Gogh's painting, which, in comparison with the temple, works in a somewhat roundabout fashion. While the Being of the equipment gathers, the painting speaks in such a way as to let us experience that Being. One can only guess why Heidegger remains silent on this distinction, which evidently works to the disadvantage of the painting. Perhaps he draws back from recognizing the problem as Kant draws back (in Heidegger's interpretation) from recognizing time as the core problem for the transcendental imagination.

The Being of this equipment, Heidegger says, has been found, and this not through description or explanation but because the painting speaks and is heard: "In the vicinity of the work we were suddenly somewhere else than we usually tend to be" (H, 24/35). The statement acknowledges the power of art and its compelling appeal, in the sense of a call to the freedom of whoever hears; Rilke's "Archaic Torso of Apollo" concludes in a similar spirit with the statement, "You must change your life."

It is by no means the case, however, that the work merely gave better visibility to Being, as seemed to be the case in Heidegger's version of the narrative by Rilke's Malte, who evoked the Being of the houses that were no longer standing. On the contrary, it is first through the work, and only the work, that the Being of equipment comes to appear at all. "Van Gogh's painting is the disclosure of what the equipment, the pair of peasant shoes, *is* in truth. This entity emerges into the unconcealedness of its Being" (H, 24/36).

The relevance of Heidegger's remark, in *Being and Time,* about the withdrawing of equipment now becomes particularly apparent: only so long as the underlying Being of the tool remains undisclosed and disregarded is the tool really usable. That is to say, the peasant woman is too busy *using* her shoes as equipment to experience their *Being* as equipment. Or, to put it in still another way, when I use a tool I am directed *through* but not *to* its usability: a hammer in use is subsumed in hammering, its specific readiness-to-hand consisting in and through the act of using it to hammer. Moving closer to the work of art, we might say that in use the Being of equipment remains transparent, whereas in art it becomes opaque.

What the shoemaker produces in the shoes is just the shoes as equipment, in their usability; obviously, in this sense, the painting does not produce at all. It speaks, and speaking—or more precisely, the speaking that is art's—brings forth the truth: "The art work lets us know what shoes are in truth" (H, 24/35). The statement concerning what happens in the temporal dimension of the experience, the suddenness in which it speaks, echoes the book's epigraph, which evokes those overgrown paths through the woods that suddenly end in areas untrodden. It also resonates with Rilke's line, quoted above, about changing one's life as a consequence of an experience with art.

As for truth, if it is not something produced, neither would it be correct to define it as something that produces. Truth is a happening, and the function of the particular painting, as of art in general, is to make this sort of happening possible. In and through the work of art the truth of the shoes, their Being as equipment, "has set itself into the work. 'To set' means here: to bring to a stand. Some particular entity, a pair of peasant shoes, comes in the work to stand in the light of its being. The being of the being comes into the steadiness of its shining" (H, 25/36).

Truth, as here understood, is, again, unconcealment, *alētheia.* In the language of *Being and Time:* "Truth (uncoveredness) is something that must always first be wrested from entities. Entities get snatched out of their hiddenness. The factical uncoveredness of anything is always, as it were, a kind of *robbery.* Is it accidental that when the Greeks express themselves as to the essence of truth, they use a *privative* expression—*a-lētheia?*" (SZ, 223/265). The implication is that the unconcealment that comes to pass in a work of art is not created, either by the artist or by the work. What comes to pass is what is allowed to come to pass; later in the

essay Heidegger will make much of the idea of letting-be and the related idea of rest, interweaving it with the idea of standing, which we
have just encountered. All of which leaves little room for the artist,
except, it seems to me, in one respect, and that is the tactical parallelism
between the *alētheia* emerging through the work and the "toward-
which" of equipment. I suggest, in other words, that as the craftsman
may be said to shape materials toward the work to be achieved, so also
may the artist be said to "shape toward," the goal of the latter endeavor
being precisely unconcealment, *alētheia*. But note that the activity this
entails is led futurally, as it were, by what is to be achieved. It is the
goal, the "toward-which," of the activity that draws the work to its
fullness, not the mind or talent of the artist. A further consequence is
that the "model" that governs the making of this or that work of art can
be nothing but some other work of art. Again, there is an analogy with
equipment, which, we recall, relates always to some other equipment.
In summary, what fundamentally guides the work of art is always and
necessarily a work of art, not the artist, who is in fact as guided "toward" the goal of the achieved work as is the craftsman.

Heidegger's theory assumes, at the same time, a parallelism between
the role of the artist and the role of the interpreter of art. Consider, for
example, the statement that, in order

> to gain access to the work, it would be necessary to remove it from
> all relations to something other than itself, in order to let it stand
> on its own for itself alone. But the artist's most peculiar intention
> already aims in this direction. The work is to be released by him
> to its pure self-subsistence. It is precisely in great art—and only
> such art is under consideration here—that the artist remains in-
> consequential as compared with the work, almost like a passage-
> way that destroys itself in the creative process for the work to
> emerge. [H, 29/40]

In this description the prevailing orientation is first, implicitly, that
of the spectator or audience and then, explicitly, that of the artist. The
orientation is that of the audience—Heidegger's reader, who has encountered art in the past and will do so again—when the first action is
performed vis-à-vis the work. This is an action that does not change the
work; it merely removes the work from relations: he might as easily
have said that the relations are removed from the work. In either case,
the work *qua* work is not touched. Audience and artist meet, as it were,
in the middle, for we are told that the latter, like the former, simply
leaves the work alone, letting it rest so it can stand. A shift occurs,
however, insofar as the artist's action—while not creative in the usual
sense—is more active than that of the spectator or reader. The office of
the latter is to allow or let, *lassen;* the office of the former is to let go, or

release, *entlassen*. If the artist thereby does more than his counterpart in the description, he does much less than the artist in other theories of art, for he cannot release what has not, in some sense, already come to be.

The Work's Essential Place

The peculiar problem of the work of art as something owned or exhibited raises serious questions concerning what I would like to call the work's essential place. All such works are "torn out of their own native sphere"—literally, their essential place *(Wesensraum)*—and "withdrawn from their own world" (H, 30/40). Heidegger's reference to a printed work (his example is an edition of Sophocles' *Antigone*) implicitly raises the question of the status of an art work when it has been reproduced and has thus lost what Walter Benjamin calls "the authority of the object":

> The authenticity of a thing is the essence of all that is transmissible from its beginning, ranging from its substantive duration to its testimony to the history which it has experienced. Since the historical testimony rests on the authenticity, the former, too, is jeopardized by reproduction when substantive duration ceases to matter. And what is really jeopardized when the historical testimony is affected is the authority of the object.

The equivalent of Heidegger's essential place is Walter Benjamin's "aura": "One might subsume the eliminated element in the term 'aura' and go on to say: that which withers in the age of mechanical reproduction is the aura of the work of art. One might generalize by saying: the technique of reproduction detaches the reproduced object from the domain of tradition."[3] For Benjamin the loss of aura, derived in large measure from Marx's concept of alienation, is thrown into relief by the difference between the mode of Being of a work in its original state and its mode of Being in a transmitted or "alienated" state, the latter providing the point of entry for the aesthetic theorist or historian. But for Heidegger the "substantive tradition" fades away when a work is appropriated to any context other than the one in which it comes into Being. Even if we were able to see a work in an original setting, as in the case of the temple in Paestum or the Bamberg Cathedral, the original world of the work no longer exists. Deracinated, such works are, as it were, bygone to themselves, despite the fact that they can still be encountered as something materially there. In this condition, the works,

---

3. Walter Benjamin, "The Work of Art in the Age of Mechanical Reproduction," in his *Illuminations,* trans. Harry Zohn, ed. Hannah Arendt (1968; rpt. New York: Schocken, 1969), p. 221.

instead of standing in themselves, stand over against us, in a version of the subject-object dualism that Heidegger everywhere and in every way struggles to overcome.

"Where does the work belong? The work belongs, as work, uniquely within the realm that is opened up by itself" (H, 30/41). The meaning of this variation on the theme of essential place is not strictly original with Heidegger, since it arises from his sense of ancient Greek approaches to experience. I add the qualifier "strictly" because there is a good deal of originality—certainly of individuality, and even idiosyncrasy—in Heidegger's reading of the Greek philosophical and poetic tradition. In any case, his observations on the difference between place and space, as he formulated them in his *Introduction to Metaphysics,* provide a useful context for the question he has just posed in *The Origin of the Work of Art:*

> That wherein something becomes refers to what we call "space." The Greeks had no word for "space." This is no accident; for they experienced the spatial on the basis not of extension but of place *(topos)*; they experienced it as *chōra,* which signifies neither place *(Ort)* nor space *(Raum)* but that which is occupied by what stands there. The place belongs to the thing itself. Each of all the various things has its place. [EM, 50/54]

Earlier, Heidegger had described the space surrounding the shoes in Van Gogh's painting as indeterminate until, eventually, world and earth were discovered through the equipmental Being of the shoes as revealed by the painting. World and earth were ultimately seen to be—in and through the shoes—the truth of what happened in the work. The temple, by contrast, shows itself for what it is immediately:

> A building, a Greek temple, portrays nothing. It simply stands there in the middle of the rock-cleft valley. The building encloses the figure of the god, and in this concealment lets it stand out into the holy precinct through the open portico. By means of the temple, the god is present in the temple. This presence of the god is in itself the extension and delimitation of the precinct as a holy precinct. The temple and its precinct, however, do not fade away into the indefinite. It is the temple work that first fits together and at the same time gathers around itself the unity of those paths and relations in which birth and death, disaster and blessing, victory and disgrace, endurance and decline acquire the shape of destiny for human being. The all-governing expanse of this open relational context is the world of this historical people. [H, 31/41–42]

If we went further in reading Heidegger's description, we could infer that its goal is a straightforward chronicle of the manner in which the temple develops. According to such a view, humankind would form a sort of historical background against which the temple, appearing at some discrete time, could perform its peculiar act of unification. Now this view is not wholly mistaken, since it is obviously the case that, prior to the development of the temple and other forms of sacred architecture, cultures already existed, all displaying various paths and relations. The actual aim of the description, however, is not historical in this sense. History for Heidegger, as previously noted, is ontological history. What counts is the Being at issue for *Dasein*—whether that *Dasein* is an individual or a culture (e.g., "Greek *Dasein*")—and not the mere succession of events. Heidegger therefore continues to maintain his rigorous distinction between, on the one hand, authentic, ontological history, *Geschichte*, and, on the other hand, history as the range of phenomena—periods, dates, events, and the like—that are the focus of history in the sense of *Historie*.

What is in principle prior to the unifying that the temple achieves is its capacity to gather. Only because it gathers does it unify. More formally phrased, gathering is an essential determination of its Being.

Aisthēsis versus Mimēsis

> Standing there, the building holds its ground against the storm raging above it and so first makes the storm itself manifest in its violence. The luster and gleam of the stone, though itself apparently glowing only by the grace of the sun, yet first brings to light the light of the day, the breadth of the sky, the darkness of the night. The temple's firm towering makes visible the invisible space of air. . . . Tree and grass, eagle and bull, snake and cricket first enter into their distinctive shapes and thus come to appear as what they are. The Greeks early called this emerging and rising in itself and in all things *phusis*. It clears and illuminates, also, that on which and in which man bases his dwelling. We call this ground the earth. [H, 31/42]

If this has something of the rhapsodic about it, it is nonetheless quite specific in the concepts it puts forward, as the following analysis will attempt to show. First, the decision to stress architecture rather than painting corresponds to Heidegger's belief in the preeminence of *aisthēsis*. In *aisthēsis*, what a being is appears immediately to sensory perception and is therefore, in Heidegger's understanding of *alētheia*, more primordially true than *logos*: "Just as seeing aims at colours, any *aisthēsis* aims at its *idea* (those entities which are genuinely accessible only through it and for it); and to that extent this perception is always true" (SZ, 33/57). The problem with *logos* is that it constitutes "that way of comporting oneself which can *also cover things up*," whereas "the 'truth' of *aisthēsis* and of the seeing of 'ideas' is the primordial kind of uncovering" (SZ, 226/268–69).

Aisthēsis is also more immediately true than *mimēsis*, which becomes the norm for ascertaining the adequacy of art in consequence of the hegemony, established in principle by Plato and carried out in Platonism, of idea as the essential representation of the Being of beings:

> Being as *idea* is exalted, it becomes true being, while being itself, previously dominant, is degraded to what Plato calls *mē on*, what really should not be and really *is* not, because in the realization it always deforms the idea, the pure appearance, by incorporating it in matter. The *idea* now becomes a *paradeigma*, a model. At the same time, the idea necessarily becomes an ideal. The copy actually "is" not; it merely partakes of being, it is a *methexis*. The *chōrismos*, the cleft, has opened between the idea of what really is, the prototype and archetype, and what actually is not, the copy and image. [EM, 140–41/154]

By adhering to *aisthēsis*, Heidegger can steer around the assumption, held by a number of modern aesthetic philosophies, that a painting of shoes (to continue with that example) must derive from shoes as material model. When Heidegger protests against the concept of "agreement" in art, he is really protesting against just this view. The obvious advantage of architecture, then, is that it cannot be held to such accounting.

To be sure, some Christian churches are built in the form of a cross, and other types of buildings are believed, in certain cultures, to be the cosmos in little, and such constructions can be regarded as "imitative" in a very broad sense. But the link between such putative sources and the architectural work per se is by any measure less constraining than the link between a painting and its sources (though an interesting test case might be found in Abstract Expressionism and other nonfigurative painting styles).

Second, the decision to deal not merely with architecture but with sacred architecture makes it possible to explore those dimensions of actual and potential experience that we normally call religious and that Heidegger associates with a variety of phenomena and terms, including the holy, the divine, the gods, god, and the godly. These appear prominently in Heidegger's writings, especially those dealing with the poetry of Hölderlin, and they will be a major focus in the pages that follow.

A corollary of this advantage is that sacred architecture easily inspires, and at the very least permits, the kind of high rhetorical tone that Heidegger—a man of sober mind, if there ever was one—likes to sustain. For Heidegger's poetic thinking, which includes but is not limited to his writings about poetry, is always a call to decision, a call to do something in this life on this planet at this time or in the future. Architecture provides a suitably imposing theme because dwelling is a pervasive, compelling need imposed on us by the very elements. The high seriousness of this art form also comes into view in comparison with, for example, the theater, graphic arts, or the novel, all of which make room for the comic, whereas the comic is all but absent from architecture, at least as we know it in the West.

The third point I want to consider has a bearing on these issues since it also concerns authorial decision-making and other "strategic" considerations. It is the question of just where Heidegger positions himself in thinking about the temple. Given his distaste for representational thinking—which would see the temple as an object over against the subjective mental processes of an observer—we may grant him the benefit of the doubt and say that his view is not merely spectatorial. On the other hand, it is not as fully dimensional as it might have been had he decided, say, to take the reader within the edifice in order to experience the gathering that the temple brings about. Heidegger perhaps deemed such a possibility misleading because it could imply a dichotomy of inside versus inside, whereas the temple offers itself as a total unity.

Because the temple is constantly and in all ways completely itself, it can be seen completely from almost anywhere. The disclaimer is occasioned by the problem we encounter if we imagine seeing the edifice from an airplane at 30,000 feet: in fact we would not be able to single it out at all. My point is that Heidegger assumes, to borrow terms from other works, that an experience of the temple must transpire in its neighborhood, a region that is not just anywhere but a definite somewhere understood as a nearness (*Nahnis*). Clearly, it does not follow that someone high in a plane would be unable to entertain thoughts about a temple. Heidegger's assumption, rather, is that a genuine thinking experience, an experience requiring rigor and intensity, depends on our willingness to maintain a living relationship—living being understood as dwelling—as well as an appropriate sense of proportion or scale.

The sort of Being that Heidegger associates with an experience of a work of art is so thoroughly situated in its abode that it projects itself and its works within that abode. Were we dealing here with *Being and Time*, the world could appear as that within which *Dasein* projects itself and its works; but in *The Origin of the Work of Art* earth has become so strong a presence that world itself must be thought in relation to earth. For Heidegger the earth has an impenetrable opacity.[4] Break open a

4. Cf. the valuable discussion of the same topic by Karsten Harries in *Martin Heidegger and the Question of Literature: Toward a Postmodern Literary Hermeneutics*, ed. William V. Spanos (Bloomington: Indiana University Press, 1979), pp. 160 ff.

rock, and you find nothing inside; nor has anything been opened up; and if you weigh the rock, its heaviness is simply brought into a certain type of calculation. Similarly, analyze a color, break it down into wavelengths, and it disappears. "The earth thus shatters every attempt to penetrate into it. . . . The earth appears openly cleared *(gelichtet)* as itself only when it is perceived as that which is by nature undisclosable, that which shrinks from every disclosure and constantly keeps itself closed up" (H, 36/47). To avoid implying that the earth simply hides out, coolly unavailable, Heidegger invokes anew the criterion of plenitude— earth's way of closing itself up is such that it nonetheless "unfolds itself in an inexhaustible variety of simple modes and shapes" (H, 36/47)— pointing out that the sculptor uses the stone without using it up, just as a painter employs, without consuming, his colors. His use of color is such that colors are first brought to light. Extending the thought, we see that the poet, in his own way, also brings the world to light. He uses it without using it up. To say that other speakers do use it up amounts to saying that they keep it from the light. The issue of whether something can be used up depends on whether it has, as it were, something to lose. Earth has nothing to lose. If it is kept from the light, it remains itself, closed up in itself. Yet it has something to gain, insofar as the artist can bring it for the first time to light. If the sculptor, by failing to achieve his artistic purpose, uses up the earth, nothing has been lost from the point of view of earth. It stays where it was, shrinking back as ever from being opened-up. What has been lost is lost to man. The man who uses up loses earth for himself by failing to bring it to light.

The man who speaks inauthentically—unpoetically—also suffers a loss. Instead of using the word, by bringing it to light, he uses it up. The difference is that, now, something precious is lost. The word, in contrast to the stone, for example, has nothing to fall back on. The stone remains a stone. But what is a word if it is not used? Not to use a word is to lose it.

Setting Up and Setting Forth

While continuing to think about earth, we must bear in mind that the first quotation concerning the temple dealt with the role of the work in setting up *(aufstellen)* the world, the latter being understood as, roughly, all that human beings experience and achieve in their time on earth. So crucial to Heidegger is this "worlding" capacity of art that he can say "To be a work *(Werksein)* means to set up a world" (H, 33/44). Far from being dissociable, the process by which a world comes into its own through the temple is an emerging totality no aspect of which can be overlooked. Instead of saying that world and earth are thus involved through the work of art, we might say, borrowing a term from Poe, that they are *inter*volved. In a crucial passage Heidegger, pursuing the question of what happens to matter (*Stoff*) in the process of making a work, states the following:

> By contrast the temple-work, in setting up a world, does not cause the material to disappear, but rather causes it to come forth for the very first time and to come into the Open (*Offenen*) of the work's world: the rock comes to bear and rest and so first becomes rock; the metals come to glitter and shimmer, colors to glow, tones to sing, the word to speak (*Sagen*). All this comes forth as the work sets itself back into the massiveness and heaviness of stone, in the firmness and pliancy of wood, in the hardness and lustre of metal, in the lighting and darkening of color, into the clang of tone, and in the naming power of the word. [H, 35/46]

Although some readers will find the description acceptable as it stands, others will feel that the notion of intervolving is a murky affair at best. But the murkiness can perhaps be explained by the difficulty of stating in discursive prose an insight, simple in itself, that teases thought in the direction of poetry. For Heidegger is already moving, in this comparatively early work, toward the density of his later and still more evocative poetic thinking. Yet what he is saying—the "statement" he is making, if you will—is not in itself, it seems to me, very hard to understand. He is not denying, in the first place, that a rock in its native state would lack the physical characteristics that come into play when it is incorporated into an edifice. Walking along, one might happen upon a rock positioned beneath another rock so as to provide support for it, and this could be called carrying. As an arrangement of mere matter, never touched by hands, the rock is simply that igneous entity that is mutely there—though even this is misleading, inasmuch as "igneous entity" tries to account linguistically for something that needs no such accounting. The point is that, before being named, rock is not rock; it is merely something about which there is nothing to say. But in setting up a rock, and in doing this, furthermore, through the setting-up of a work of art, we are no longer dealing with a nameless entity but with a named thing: "rock." Such a thing now carries cultural weight in that it holds forth in space and time the meaning imparted to it, which it in turn imparts. To put it another way, one could say that no entity enters an institution without being named and, indeed, that the naming is co-equal and coeval with its being institutionalized.

All of this happens through what Heidegger calls the Open of the world—open because every component of the totality of the temple-work comes literally out into the open, which is equally the process of simply coming into its own. For example, consider the way marble looks in its "natural" state compared with the way it looks when positioned and polished in an edifice, or consider the difference between unrefined gold and the gold that gleams in the frescoes of a Romanesque church. In coming into their own by thus coming into the Open, the components serve to compose the totality of the work, which is in this way set up. Setting-up is at the same time played off against that other coequal and coeval process (or better, that aspect of the same process) by which the work sets itself back (*zurückstellen*) into all the essential qualities of the components, such as the massiveness of the rock. All of this is, I think, Heidegger's way of avoiding the implication that a work of art ever goes beyond the "earthiness" or "worldliness" that inheres in its Being. For it is just because the work reposes in those essential qualities that it is sufficiently grounded to be a work, even as its being a work makes it possible for those qualities to come into their own.

The setting-back belongs, in any case, to the setting-up that is the work of art, and it is setting-up that constitutes the first term in a little lexicon which, in my analysis, will finally contain four terms. The second term, setting forth, is coequal and coeval with setting up a world and designates the manner in which the work regards the earth. The latter concept, however, has taken on a wider meaning, for it now embraces not only such obviously earthy things as rock and wood but the naming power of words. Earth, that is, embraces all that comes into its own in coming into the Open of the work—the sound of music as well as the sound of words—because ultimately the temple as work of art and institution *is* all these. Again we see the value of sacred architecture as an all-encompassing artistic totality.

But if Heidegger is being as careful as I think he is being, he does not suggest that words as such belong to earth, even though the following statement might seem to imply as much: "That into which the work sets itself back and which causes it to come forth in this setting-back of itself we called earth. . . . Upon the earth and in it, historical man grounds his dwelling in the world. In setting up a world, the work sets forth the earth" (H, 35/46). In this context it is important to remember the phrase "the naming power of words." It is just that, the power of naming, and not words as such, that belongs to earth. The phrase assumes a rough parallelism between the realizable essential capacities of material earthly entities and the capacity of language. As the capacity for bending characterizes wood, insofar as it belongs to earth, so the capacity of naming characterizes the word, insofar as it too belongs to earth. But as another phrase reminds us, it takes more than earth to "bring out" this capacity, for it is first through the work that the word comes out in the Open, which means that it reaches saying (*Sagen*). Language, then, belongs both to the setting-up of a world and the setting-forth of earth.

Standing-in-Itself and Resting-on-Itself

The two remaining terms—and a hint of the relation between them and our two preceding terms, setting-up and setting-forth—are announced in the following:

> The setting up (*Aufstellen*) of a world and the setting forth
> (*Herstellen*) of earth are two essential features in the work-being of
> the work. They belong together, however, in the unity of work-
> being. This is the unity we seek when we ponder the self-
> subsistence (*Insichstehen*) of the work and try to express in words
> this closed, unitary repose (*Ruhe*) of self-support (*Aufsichberuhen*).
> [H, 36–37/48]

Because there is an advantage in retaining as much as we can of Hei-degger's distinctive wording, *Insichstehen* will be termed standing-in-itself and *Aufsichberuhen* will be termed resting-on-itself. Both terms refer to crucial aspects of the *quidditas* of the work of art, the "what it is," and this is simply the fact that it consists precisely in itself, enjoy-ing that essential place which is sufficient unto itself by virtue of being occupied. From the standpoint of the preservers of the work—its audience—this means letting the work be itself, a comportment that should not be confused with passivity or indifference. We do not let a work be by becoming inert in its presence but by experiencing its presence as a working, such that we may be changed by the work. The letting-be, in other words, is a significant contribution to the process of preservation that enables the work to persist in its working, such per-sistence being a condition of a genuine origin, which must keep on happening if it is not to lose the momentum that first gave it the pros-pect of happening once and for all. *What* is "left alone" in the work is that self-defining, immediately recognizable quality that distinguishes a work from other beings and so makes it possible to experience its working in the first place. In another theory this might be designated the "autotelic nature" of the work, its "inner core," or something of the kind; most such formulations, however, make the work sound too au-tonomous and too automatic—too much like a machine that runs itself. And while it is true that Heidegger also believes that a work of art is peculiar to itself, he sees it as a more situated phenomenon, a phenomenon requiring a complete epochal context for its realization, and one that makes demands upon the people who preserve it.

But, it may be objected, if the work is like that, how could one do anything *but* let it be? The answer, I think, is that one could easily, and unfortunately, diminish the experience of it. This could be done, for example, by deploying, between oneself and the work, all manner of representations, such as the concept of a dichotomy between form and content or the concept that the work stands over against some other

reality, as a signifier stands over against a signified. The effect would be
to diminish the transformational power of the work, failing to preserve
it, and so failing—in Heidegger's way of thinking—to let it be. To
amplify a point already made, letting-be, releasing, and other "passive"
modes of experience are not dissimilar to the *epochē*, which by exclud-
ing the intrusive permits the otherwise occluded phenomenon to be
seen—in other words, it actively lets it be.

Movement and Repose

Up to now the theory that has been unfolding has seemed dynamic,
consisting as it does of movements through which a work of art relates
in the most essential ways to earth and to world. Yet we have just been
observing certain of the work's essential features shift in what looks like
another direction—from setting-up and setting-forth to sheer
standing-in-itself and the even less dynamic phenomenon of resting-
on-itself. The explanation lies in Heidegger's way of thinking not
merely the intervolvement of movement and repose, or rest, but the
assimilation of the former to the latter. Heidegger's way is to imagine
that repose and movement are not opposites, or, more affirmatively,
that they belong together in the unity of difference:

> Only what is in motion can rest. The mode of rest varies with the
> kind of motion. In motion as the mere displacement of a body,
> rest is, to be sure, only the limiting case of motion. Where rest
> includes motion, there can exist a repose which is an inner con-
> centration *(Sammlung)* of motion, hence a highest state of agita-
> tion, assuming that the mode of motion requires such a rest. Now
> the repose of the work that rests in itself is of this sort. We shall
> therefore come nearer to this repose if we can succeed in grasping
> the state of movement of the happening in work-being in its full
> unity. [H, 37/48]

It is just this definition of rest that Heidegger applies to the essential
characteristic of the Being of the work of art defined as resting-on-itself.
But moving rest or reposeful movement are not easy notions. Examples
may help. The anthropologist Victor Turner has described liminal states
(from the Latin *limen* or threshold) in which an individual passes from
one stage to another, a tribal *rite of passage* being one familiar type.[5]
Equally liminal are certain states in which a threshold movement seems

5. Victor Turner, "Process, System, and Symbol: A New Anthropological Synthesis,"
in "Discoveries and Interpretations: Studies in Contemporary Scholarship," *Daedalus* 1
(Summer 1977), issued as vol. 106, no. 3, of the *Proceedings of the American Academy of Arts
and Sciences*, pp. 61–80.

to transpire of itself, carrying the performer along with it in an intimacy without volition or exertion. Such an experience is reported of race-car drivers who, moving at extremely high speeds, are so "at one" with the process that they feel suspended in, to borrow Robert Musil's phrase, an act without an actor. The equivalent in everyday driving is velocitation, or the gradual unknowing adjustment a driver makes until a rate of travel is experienced as being slower than it is and even, at times, as being scarcely distinguishable from motionlessness. The literature of mysticism too, as we know, bears witness, in the case of ecstasy, to a movement at once dynamic and motionless, temporal and out of time. Finally, architecture abounds in examples of the phenomenon Heidegger seems to have in mind. The flying buttresses of Notre Dame move insofar as their positioned thrust most massively resists all countermovement from the central edifice; and yet it is just this movement that sustains the repose of the work, which is to say its capacity to remain in a standing that rests on itself, and so rests because of the support sustained by the structure's stayed and staying architectural movement-in-repose. Although this description is mine, I believe that it indicates the kind of thing Heidegger is trying to suggest and, more particularly, that it shows, from another angle of vision, the value for Heidegger of approaching such issues as the foundational nature of art from an architectural or quasi-architectural premise.

Striving and Strife

There remains the question of how best to characterize the manner in which world and earth relate to each other through the workings of the work. "World and earth are essentially different from one another and yet are never separated. The world grounds itself on the earth, and the earth juts through the world" (H, 37/48–49). Such a relation may put the reader in mind of D. H. Lawrence, who situates the primary vital tensions in two sexual identities, the one struggling for and at the same time against the other. The relation Heidegger describes, though based on different principles, is closer to this conception—which at first appears to be but finally is not dialectical—than to the conception of difference one finds in the binary-opposition principle of structuralism. Heidegger distinguishes, if implicitly, between two types of opposition. In one type, two parties, fundamentally indifferent to each other, meet in a sterile clash; in the other, the two are concerned with each other in a way that enables each to heighten the other—indeed, to bring the other to fulfillment. The present opposition belongs to this latter type. On the one hand, the world, as though impatient with anything closed, endeavors to surmount the earth. On the other hand, earth,

unwilling to change its ways, draws the world back toward itself. Heidegger names this opposition a *Streit,* literally "strife" or "struggle" but
also, by implication—as Hofstadter's translation attests—"striving."
Such striving strife, if we may call it so, is no mere discord but a mutual
effort through which each lifts the other into the "self-assertion" of its
own nature (H, 38/49). Again Heidegger shifts away from the expected
emphasis, for this self-assertion is not, after all, very assertive; it is "the
surrender to the concealed originality of the source of one's own being.
In the struggle each opponent carries the other beyond itself" (H, 38/49).
By shifting in this way, Heidegger's very presentation embodies the
current and countercurrent of a relationship that is a play of identity
with difference.

If world and earth thus relate through the setting-up of the former
and the setting-forth of the latter, and if both of these developments
come about through the work of art, then we have before us one of the
ways in which the work of art can be said to originate. The work of art
endures in the striving between world and earth, which it is the task of
art to instigate *(Anstiftung).* We shall see, below, other terms about
origins and beginnings. It is equally the task of art to continue this
striving strife, which it can do because the very movement that constitutes rest (as we saw), also, itself, gathers the struggle. This being so,
Heidegger can hold that "The repose of the work that rests in itself thus
has its presencing in the intimacy of striving" (H, 38/50). The essence of
the Being of the work, then, consists in setting up a world and in setting
forth the earth, processes that are themselves part of the work's way of
standing and resting in itself, the latter being understood as gathering
the struggle persisting in the strife that is instigated by the work.
Though Heidegger does not directly connect instigation with the question of a work's essential characteristics, and though the problem of the
work as an origin has to wait a surprisingly long time before being
confronted in the essay, it should be stated here that instigating,
Anstiftung, bears a close resemblance to *Stiftung,* instituting or founding, and that it already points to what is perhaps the most crucial power
of the work, which is the power to originate.

Lichtung

Since instigating and founding come about through the Open sustained
by the work, we may now consider the mode of openness that Heidegger calls the *Lichtung.* This untranslatable neologism draws the light, or
Licht, of the initial syllable into the accepted sense of clearing, so that in
English we might arrive at something like "lightening clearing"; or we
can follow Hofstadter's lead (as I will do) by adopting both "clearing"

and "lighting" (a less formidable word than "lightening"), employing one or the other according to context.

Behind Heidegger's presentation there is an unstated line of thought extending from the idea of *aufstellen* and *herstellen* to the idea of the open *Stelle*, or place, which he refers to as he sidles up to the *Lichtung*: "In the midst of beings as a whole, there an open place occurs (*west*). There is a clearing, a lighting" (H, 41/53). The function of the *Lichtung*, stated in preliminary and general terms, is to provide a way for human beings to experience what they themselves are and can be as well as things that are not themselves, the actuality and the potentiality both answering to the capacitating power that rests in Being.

Far from being all light or all clearing, the *Lichtung* harbors concealment in the same way (though Heidegger does not draw the comparison) as truth. For inasmuch as truth is unconcealment, it can be grasped only in relation to concealment, as we are reminded by the privative *Un-* in the German noun, as by the privative *a* in the Greek *alētheia*, which Heidegger repeatedly employs as a benchmark. His definition of the term *Lichtung* may reflect a desire to replace these negative linguistic formations with a more positive image—positive because the *Lichtung* can be described without reference to a non-*Lichtung*. The disadvantage of such an image is its very suggestive power. Truth is a happening, and art happens too, but the *Lichtung* appears almost too much like something there in space, just waiting to be entered. This is, I think, why Heidegger tears down, almost before he sets up, an analogy with the theater: "the open place in the midst of beings that are—the clearing—is never a rigid stage with a permanently raised curtain on which the play of beings runs its course" (H, 42/54). Rather, the clearing is itself an *event*, and one, furthermore, that reminds us again of Heidegger's concept of truth; for the *Lichtung* happens as *Verbergung*, concealment, the verbal form of which provides the basis of *Unverborgenheit*.

A correct understanding requires elucidation of three other related terms, which at first contact may seem more difficult than they are because Heidegger presents them in a series of remarks built around verbal and nominal forms beginning with *ver-*, a prefix with mainly negative connotations, including loss, reversal, using up, and change for the worse. The chief of these are *Versagen*, refusal, referring to the fact that things sometimes do not appear to us at all, and *Verstellen*, dissembling, which is more complex, since it involves an appearance pointing us one way when we should be going another. Refusal and dissembling are the two modes of concealment, they are how concealment happens, whereas our final term, *Verweigern*, denial, is a companion term for concealment. As such, it does not amount to a major new technical term but represents a desire to heighten the reader's sensitivity to concealment by laying out its many varieties. Thus it is no surprise that the term with final gathering power remains the original one, *Verbergung*, and that when it recurs, in the context of a further discussion of truth, it brings the reader back to the issue of strife. As concealment and unconcealment struggle with each other in *alētheia*, so concealment and the *Lichtung* struggle with each other. Strife, to put it another way, is the struggle between any condition of being closed (*das Verschlossene*) and the Open, belonging both to world and to earth, which comes about through the work of art.

Given that a world and the earth both belong to the Open, Heidegger appears to be making a shift when, in a passage reminiscent of the first passage concerning the temple, he identifies the world as the clearing thanks to which the basic types of decision can be taken up. Such a formulation appears to give the *Lichtung* over to the world when in fact Heidegger is, I believe, trying to suggest just the opposite. There is a danger, he seems to feel, that the reader will associate the world too exclusively with the Open and the earth with what is closed, envisaging a kind of modern combat myth between implacable opponents. In my view, if Heidegger assimilated the clearing to the world, this was only in order, as it were, to set it back, even as the work sets itself back into the earthly. Hence "Every decision . . . bases itself on something not mastered, something concealed, confusing: else it would never be a decision. The earth is not simply the Closed but rather that which rises up is self-closing" (H, 43–44/45). That is to say, all essential decisions—including decisions Heidegger may want the reader to ponder after reading this essay—necessarily work toward realization by struggling not only with the unknown but with forces and facts that human action does not affect. These essential decisions are not the day-by-day choices one regularly makes—in shopping for groceries, say—but basic choices about living in a particular kind of culture with a certain distinctive social order, a distinctive way of thinking, a distinctive type of art. They are not in fact choices made by individuals, for, despite the fact that he only occasionally says so, Heidegger is thinking throughout the essay of the decisions made by a people: "The world is the self-disclosing openness of the broad paths of the simple and essential decisions in the destiny of an historical people" (H, 37/48). Through such openness—which is synonymous with Open—a people achieves truth, which is not to say eternal verity but a struggle between concealment and *Lichtung* that persists in time. If that struggle is conceived of as an even match in which the *Lichtung*, as clearing and illumination, never really clears or illuminates, there would hardly be any reason to speak of truth. But unconcealment *does* occur, the Being of things *is* disclosed, and only because this is so do we carry on any activity, including philosophy, which formulates its questions on the background of an assumed reality.

Truth does not by any means happen solely in works of art. It also happens, *inter alia*, in the founding of countries, in making sacrifices, in thinking; what is peculiar about the work of art, as a way of letting truth happen, is that it brings forth "a being such as never was before and will never come to be again" (H, 50/62). Being and time: there must be a time in which this being has not yet become, but, once it has become, there is no reason for it to become any more. Now a theory of creation based on such thinking differs radically from psychological theories or theories in which a "genius" invents a work *ab ovo*. In Heidegger's thinking there exists, for lack of a better term, a pervasive mutuality in which all aspects pertaining to artistic creation—artist, art work, audience, and art itself—occur in concert, each tuned to the other, so that the happening of art, the happening of truth through art, comes from the fourfold totality or it does not come at all.

Measured directly against the previously discussed works (a task that Heidegger does not attempt), the theory proves to be adequate for one, less so for the other. Each work is conspicuously something that, before it was created, had not yet become and that, having become, never becomes again. But in the case of painting, difficulties arise from the unexplored relation between that which the painting immediately shows and that which it mediately, through that showing, depicts, the latter being the "model" or thing that came into being before the painting. In the case of the Van Gogh, that preexisting thing would be some pair of actual peasant shoes—but these are not what the painting lets emerge. What the painting lets emerge is the *Being* of equipment generally. The issue is not at all something, a being, but Being, *Sein*. The something that originally and exclusively shows forth from the painting is just these configurations of colored strokes. But the real achievement of that showing is not the achievement of the configuration (and in this the painting contrasts with the temple-work, which would be equivalent, in a manner of speaking, to actual shoes and to shoes-as-painted, both at once); the real achievement is the capacity of the work to reveal ontologically, that is, to show Being. Such Being is not of the individual object, shoes, but, because the essential characteristics distinguished in shoes are valid for all equipment, of equipmental Being per se.

Audience

Decisions are made by a people, such as the Greek people in antiquity, or the Germans, whom Heidegger apostrophizes at the close of *The Origin of the Work of Art*, or the more indefinite "we," mentioned from

time to time, who are his readers. All are versions of an issue that other
aesthetic theories address as the issue of audience. Heidegger never, to
my knowledge, employs the term, and certainly he gives the question
less explicit attention than Sartre and much less than Ingarden, all of
which may indicate that he takes the importance of the audience so
much for granted that he feels little need to say much about it. When he
does address the topic, he adds (as suggested above) a fourth constituent to the three previously described constituents—the artist, art as
such, and the work of art—and argues, moreover, that the role of this
further constituent, the audience, is intimately connected with the
ability of the work to originate and—a crucial point—is itself poetic:

> Not only the creation of the work is poetic, but equally poetic,
> though in its own way, is the preserving of the work; for a work is
> in actual effect a work only when we remove ourselves from our
> commonplace routine (*Gewöhnlichkeit*) and move into what is dis-
> closed by the work, so as to bring our own nature itself to take a
> stand in the truth of what is. [H, 61/74–75]

Heidegger does not define what is peculiar about the way in which the
preservers of a work are poetic, but he offered a hint by stating that
through our experience of the Van Gogh painting we suddenly became
different from the way we were. The word for this latter state was
gewöhnlich, to which the *Gewöhnlichkeit* in the passage quoted above
obviously corresponds. For an audience, then, being poetic would
mean deciding not merely to appreciate a work, in the sense of savoring
its formal features, but deciding to let a work transform our way of
living. Equally important, it means persisting in that condition by preserving the work, which means, in turn, continuing the *ecstasis* through
which we move, through the work, out of the ordinary. Far from being
passive, such a process requires (admitting that Heidegger would not
employ either term) action by an audience. The work of art is not responsible, in other words, for the whole of a beginning, but, like the
statue of Apollo in Rilke's poem, it brings the audience to the point of
deciding that it will preserve, in the manner described, what the poem
has instituted. The existence of a work does not in itself change your
life; it says: *you* must change your life. Preserving then means continuing in that change.

Founding

The work of art needs a people if it is to achieve its goal of founding,
Stiften or *Stiftung*, for only through preserving, Heidegger insists, is
founding effective, and only thus can art as origin persist. Founding

proves to be threefold: it is at once a giving or bestowing, a grounding, and a beginning. According to Heidegger's nonmimetic theory, a work of art is "in addition to" or "besides" anything else. This being the case, what it brings may be regarded as a kind of excess, a cup that runneth over, so that the bringing resembles a giving. It could of course be argued, on the "promimetic" side, that this is equally true in a representational relationship, since the work of art "adds" things of its own (shapes and colors and the like) to already existing entities. But even if this is allowed, the imitative work, by virtue of the fact that it derives—that it could not come into Being without specific reference to something prior—can never *be* itself to the same extent as a nonmimetic work. To put it another way, one could say that there is a greater sense of the art work's fullness in a theory, such as Heidegger's, which emphasizes giving, than there is in a mimetic theory, which emphasizes borrowing.

If we went further, it would appear that art is a mysterious and gratuitous occurrence that makes no demands on the people who "receive" it. The second and third aspects, each in its own manner, show what else must happen and in what way. Founding in its second mode relates to that ground on which *Dasein* "is already thrown" (H, 62), and this is both earth and world. In the event, Heidegger's account concentrates so much on the earth that it comes to seem predominant, whereas Heidegger assumes that earth and world are coeval and coequal. This apparent asymmetry may be traced in part to the very ease with which the mind can move between ground as ontological foundation and ground as literally ground, or earth; and given Heidegger's poetic drift, the metaphorical possibilities may simply have been too tempting to resist. Thus he creates a picture in which, through a subtle pun, *Schöpfen*, or drawing—as in drawing water from a well—bears upon *Schöpfung*, or creation in an artistic sense: "All creation, because it is such a drawing-up, is a drawing, as of water from a spring" (H, 63/76). But for all the subtlety and ingenuity in the exposition, the underlying idea seems to me both sound and clear. It consists in part in the belief—never actually stated—that receiving, as the passive behavior conventionally corresponding to a giving, is only one possible form of involvement and in the present case not the best one. For example, the process of coming into an inheritance might require a series of actions on the part of the inheritor, so that the inheritor could be said to come forward to meet the coming-into "halfway." The rest of Heidegger's idea of grounding consists in conceiving what might be demanded of a historical people. The answer is that a condition applies to the peculiar sort of giving that happens through art, and it is that what is given must be collaterally brought forth, much as water is brought forth from a source. We need only a little effort of imagination to see the analogy between this and the view that the preservers of a work (as noted above) must act in their own right.

Thus we arrive at the third mode of founding, which also depends for its force on the nonmimetic theory, though by now my reliance on that negative term, necessary as it has been, may have become burdensome. To put the matter somewhat more affirmatively: if a work of art does not derive from or refer to anything prior, if it sets up and sets forth and thereby founds, if it brings forth something, and so fully that it need never again become—if all this is the case, then it is also the case that a work of art really does constitute an origin, and all that I have just been stating serves to define what the origin of a work of art means.

By way of elaboration, it should be stated that a corollary of preservation, and indeed a *sine qua non* of it, is preparation. Far from originating by spontaneous generation, a work is prepared over a long time and yet it is a leap, a word with cognates permitting a great deal of suggestive wordplay. *Ur* is first or primal, *Sprung* is a leap, so that origin may be defined as a primal leap. But there is more: "A genuine beginning *(Anfang)*, as a leap, is always a head start in which everything to come is already leaped over, even if as something disguised. The beginning already contains the end latent within itself" (H, 63). If it is clear that this theory imposes a time requirement for the originating of a work, the specific nature of that origin as understood in some other theories—that is, the duration in which a work is conceived and executed by an artist—remains a mystery.

Art and History

As we have seen, the artist, in Heidegger's view, is practically subsumed into the process by which a work comes about, so that he or she is quite as anonymous as the individual maker in Joyce's conception, though less aloof and less individual. Since Heidegger says nothing specific, in this phase of his theory, about who does the preparing, we may infer that, at the very least, preparation must involve artists. The notion of an extended time of preparation also implies that the primal leap occurs only when a totality of conditions exists, a notion entailing the view that art cannot happen at just any time. In this, Heidegger is closer to socioeconomic theories of art than to "genius" theories; and though he might not wish to say, with the Marxists, that this totality requires class and related considerations as essential features, the theory does not appear, in principle, to exclude them.[6] In any case, we infer, second, that this totality, too, must undergo preparation, though

6. See Mark Poster, *Existential Marxism in Postwar France: From Sartre to Althusser* (Princeton: Princeton University Press, 1975), pp. 222–24.

not in a manner that permits the process to become conspicuous. We should perhaps infer finally, though tentatively, that preparation is required of art *tout court, die Kunst,* the term to which Heidegger makes an unannounced switch as he nears the conclusion of the essay. What is the reason for the switch, and what does he mean by "art"? The two questions must be taken up together.

The switch occurs when, in returning to the issue of strife (discussed above), he states that the first essentially historical art, in the West, came about in Greece. That art was historical because it opened up for the Greeks the totality of beings, a development thrown into relief by the medieval redefinition of beings as the creations of a deity and by the modern transformation of beings into what is technically manipulable. But note the sentence that just precedes this brief chronological sketch: "What was in the future to be called Being was set into work, setting the standard" (H, 63/77). This should remind us that the work of art is a *sine qua non* of historicity, since art cannot *be* apart from *works* of art. Yet art is not synonymous with the work of art, because (if my reading is correct) art has two basic meanings here. One meaning has to do with the *quidditas* of a work of art as distinguished from the concrete nature of the particular work. Art in this case designates that which makes it possible for the kind of work that a painting is to be experienced in a different way from the kind of work that (for example) plumbing is. The same distinction makes us prefer to speak of an art museum rather than a work-of-art museum, of the history of art rather than the history of works of art. In its second meaning art designates those very works: it is simply the aggregate of them all. Because the concept of art thus has two ways of being general, it is not surprising that Heidegger adopts it when attempting to lay out broad perspectives on great epochs of Western civilization.

According to Heidegger's theory of history, if I am not mistaken, one set of conditions that makes for art will not be quite the same as any other set making for art. To put it another way, it is always the case that the art of any culture is historical in its own way; but, equally important, it is always the case that a culture in which art is prepared and preserved is by definition historical.

It is not far from this to the view, which Heidegger in fact accepts, that art *is* history: "The origin of the work of art—that is, the origin of both the creators and the preservers, which is to say of a people's historical existence, is art. This is so because art is by nature an origin: a distinctive way in which truth comes into being, that is, becomes historical" (H, 64–65/78). A large claim, to be sure, but not much larger than the one put forward in Shelley's "A Defense of Poetry":

> The most unfailing herald, companion, and follower of the awakening of a great people to work a beneficial change in opinion or institution, is poetry. At such periods there is an accumulation of

the power of communicating and receiving intense and im-
passioned conceptions respecting man and nature. . . . Poets are
the hierophants of an unapprehended inspiration; the mirrors of
the gigantic shadows which futurity casts upon the present.

Heidegger, of course, wants to avoid the implication that poets are
privileged in the ways that Shelley suggests. In Heidegger's fourfold
totality of art work, artist, art, and audience, the roles that are played
are different, but they are equal. The same does not apply, however, to
his conception of poetry, which proves to be so powerful that it sub-
sumes art itself: *"All art,* as the letting happen of the advent of the truth
of what is, is, as such, *essentially poetry"* (H, 59/72). To be sure, as art
was said to be only one of the ways that truth can happen, so poetry is
only one way of being poetic in the broad sense. To understand the
peculiarly high place that verbal art nonetheless holds in the present
theory, it is important to understand that Heidegger is continuing to
embrace within poetry the realm of verse *(Poesie)* as well as every manifestation of poetic language *(Dichten)*, including the work that language performs in "nonlinguistic" areas, such as the plastic arts.

Heidegger's elevation of poetry is no more idiosyncratic than
Merleau-Ponty's position regarding the advantage that literature enjoys
over painting with respect to historical time.

To the exact extent that it renounces the hypocrite eternity of art
and, boldly confronting its times, displays them instead of
vaguely evoking them, literature surges forth victorious and gives
significance to an age. Although the statues of Olympia play a
great part in attaching us to Greece, they also foster (in the state in
which they have come down to us—bleached, broken, detached
from the work as a whole) a fraudulent myth about Greece. They
cannot resist time as a manuscript, even incomplete, torn, and
almost illegible, does. Heraclitus' writing casts light for us as no
broken statues can, because its signification is deposited and concentrated in it in another way than theirs is in them, and because
nothing equals the ductility of speech. In short, language speaks,
and the voices of painting are the voices of silence.[7]

The difference between Merleau-Ponty's position and Heidegger's—
similar as they are—is that poetry and painting are discrete and com-
petitive for the French thinker but are connected, the one to the other,
in a foundational way for the German.

Language, as we have seen, "is poetry in the essential sense." Poetry,
thus defined, entails authentic poetry *strictu sensu*—the *Dichtung* pro-

7. Maurice Merleau-Ponty, *Signs*, trans. Richard C. McCleary (Evanston: Northwestern University Press, 1964), pp. 80–81.

duced by major poets like Hölderlin and Goethe, Homer and Sophocles—as well as poesy (Poesie) in the sense of mere verse. If it is accurate to say that both therefore take place in language, it is equally accurate to say that language is that "wherein" the others take place as well.

To approach the matter from a slightly different perspective, language may be said to open up an area, a room for play, within which architecture, painting, and the other arts can come about. For if—as Heidegger asserts—the opening that guides these arts is itself made possible by language, and if language preserves the original essence of poetry, then poetry must be, after all, more original than the other arts. Poetry thus relates to the latter—as unattractive as the idea will be to many aesthetic theorists—as the highest member of a hierarchy (the positioning of the arts, the one to the other, remaining unspecified and perhaps unspecifiable). In this way, without repudiating the sister arts, Heidegger comes to the view, never quite made explicit, that they are less directly involved with truth. These arts, he allows, have nonetheless their "own ways and modes in which truth orders itself into work" (H, 61/74). In contrast to the setting-into-work of truth, previously described, the happening of truth as mere ordering indicates a lesser initiative, as though all that remains to be done is to rearrange what has already been established. In the end, therefore, it is not the work of art as such to which truth is attracted but a particular type of work.

It may be objected that Heidegger is not describing but evaluating. The trouble with such an objection, in a sense, is that it does not go far enough, for the ordering of the hierarchy is given, in principle, with the premise that language as essential poetry first brings what-is-to-be into the open. For if Dichtung is the most original of the arts, it follows, so long as one judges by the standard of originality, that the other arts must be, so to speak, less foundational.

Saying

An issue of far-reaching significance remains to be considered, and that is the role of saying, which Heidegger here employs in two forms, the standard noun Sagen and the coinage die Sage (which later becomes, at least on occasion, a technical term).[8] To obtain a sufficiently wide context for the concept, we will need to analyze, from a different angle than before, Heidegger's vision of the temple-work. In so doing we may

8. See the discussion in David White, Heidegger and the Language of Poetry (Lincoln and London: University of Nebraska Press, 1978), esp. pp. 37 ff., which may be compared with the discussion of originating language in Edward W. Said, Beginnings: Intention and Method (New York: Basic Books, 1975), pp. 341–42.

attain a fuller sense of the relative capacities of the several arts even as
we enhance our understanding of the relation between saying and cognate terms, such as naming.

> The temple, in its standing there, first gives to things their look
> and to men their outlook on themselves. This view remains open
> as long as the work is a work, as long as the god has not fled from
> it. It is the same with the sculpture of the god, votive offering of
> the victor in the athletic games. It is not a portrait whose purpose
> is to make it easier to realize how the god looks; rather, it is a
> work that lets the god himself be present and thus *is* the god him-
> self. The same holds for the linguistic work *(Sprachwerk)*. In the
> tragedy nothing is staged or displayed theatrically, but the battle
> of the new gods against the old is being fought. The linguistic
> work, originating in the speech of the people, does not refer to
> this battle; it transforms the people's saying *(Sagen)* so that now
> every living word fights the battle and puts up for decision what
> is holy and unholy, what great and what small, what brave and
> what cowardly, what lofty and what flight, what master and what
> slave. [H, 32/43]

The Van Gogh painting had revealed earth and world; so does the
temple. But the temple, through the sculpture it shelters and through its
own presence as the sacred, lets the god be present, whereas no such
claim was made for the painting. A difference of another sort separates
the temple and sculpture, on the one hand, from the linguistic work, the
work in words, on the other. Both the temple and the sculpture body
forth the divinity in a palpable way. But the work composed of words
clearly does not do this. It is made up of components that are not there
before us in the same way as the temple or the sculpture. The work in
words, the "literary" work, rests instead on a double premise. The first,
which is invariable, is that the work is rooted in a legitimizing, preserving collectivity, the people. The second, which is variable, is that the
decision be brought about by a certain *type* of word; for not every word
can do this, only every essential *(wesentliche)* word.

On the capacities of painting, Heidegger, by contrast, remains silent.
He neither distinguishes between essential and inessential colors or
lines, nor—more to the point—does he suggest that a painting carries
on a battle between old gods and new or brings mankind to decisions
about crucial matters. From the long description of the temple, and the
likeness drawn between it and the sculpture, it appears at first that
Heidegger prefers the three-dimensional to the two-dimensional. The
inclusion of the work in words would then be hard to explain unless
one argued that tragedy, as the struggle of old gods and new, transpires
in a more inclusive, more cosmic realm than painting and that, as

something performed by living human beings, it has the full dimensionality of real life. I think there is something to the argument; and the idea of full dimensionality, of a kind of Being from which no human actuality is omitted, has validity.

The emphasis on architecture, sculpture, and the verbal work may have more to do, however, with Heidegger's choice of a period than with his choice of genres. Or, more precisely, the choice of genres goes along with the choice of period, however tacitly. Heidegger tends to balance the essentially and the contingently historical by locating essence in the past so that it will be possible to say—as he soon will do—that something older is more essential. Heidegger's temple is conspicuously an ancient temple, his sculpture an ancient sculpture, his tragedy an ancient tragedy. (Typically, his remarks on the latter artistic form are based on Fragment 53 of Heraclitus, one of the pre-Socratics, who are a perpetual source of inspiration for Heidegger.) It follows from this that music will be underemphasized because it has not endured and that painting on canvas will be underemphasized because, as a relatively recent invention of a secular age, it does not bring about the same encounter with the divine that is the province of the ancient arts. But, it may be objected, a painting can be sacred in its own way. To an extent Heidegger might agree, attesting his analysis of the Van Gogh painting as evidence; but he would argue that it is a lesser way because it does not make possible the gods as it makes possible world and earth. The temple, votive sculpture, and ancient tragedy derive a legitimacy from their direct relation to the people. This is not to deny that the people are also "in" the painting, through the presence not only of the peasant woman but of earth and world as well. One had to reach these, however, through the mediation of the equipment in the painting rather than through the painting of a self-sufficient whole. Such mediation is what makes the painting representational, and the representational from Heidegger's point of view posits a distance that three-dimensional and verbal forms of art are able to resist or overcome.

Heidegger tries to overcome this distance in his own way when, as mentioned above, he brings subject and predicate as close together as possible. To be a work, he says, is to set up a world, and a world is more than a sum of things at hand: "World worlds, and is more fully in being than the tangible and perceptible realm in which we believe ourselves to be at home" (H, 33/44). The tautology does not surpass predication any more than it avoids the positing of a subject; it is simply an attempt to bring the relation a little closer to identity. The difficulty of breaking away from distancing patterns of thought is demonstrated again when Heidegger insists that the world is "never an object" and, in the following sentence, that it is "the ever nonobjective," both statements being the negation of a distance that, ideally, he should never have had to acknowledge. And in fact a decade later, in the Rilke essay, he will state that this is an unacceptable way of speaking.

The shift from the example of the temple to that of the sculpture may be less innocent than it looks. Heidegger had already argued that the god was present through the temple in a kind of regional or neighboring way. A sculptured image of the god, however, *shows* how he looks, and on this basis Heidegger can argue that such a work *is* the god. Now, one can view the difference from the nexus of the near and the far that never ceases to fascinate Heidegger. In the case of the temple, the god is near, which is why he can speak of the temple as furnishing a holy region; but in the case of the sculpture of the god, the nearness collapses into the image. In other words, the shift starts from resemblance and moves to identity—but that, for me, is precisely the problem. Heidegger seems to benefit from the fact that, despite his rejection of the image as copy, the sculpture lets the god appear in a form that does not guarantee more presence than the temple, except insofar as the sculpture somehow images the god. If we are to avoid the concept of *re*presentation, it may seem that we have nothing left at this point but a concept of *pre*sentation, such that one type of work, the sculpture, "presents more"—permits more godly presence—than another type of work, the temple. But that cannot be, since sculpture enters the discussion as another example, along with the temple, of the work of art as an abode of a god. The situation is complicated by the fact that Heidegger does not deal with sculpture in general, any more than he deals with architecture in general, but only with a particular piece of sculpture, and one, moreover, that is not only religious but goes further than the temple toward the embodiment of godly presence. Having followed this line of thought, the reader may the more readily envisage gods as also present in tragedy and perhaps overlook the fact that Heidegger is thinking specifically of ancient Greek tragedy. But what of this genre in its modern manifestations, and what of the novel? There can be no answer to such questions as long as the theory tests itself almost exclusively on cultural examples of undoubted religious significance.

The example of tragedy—more broadly, of the work in words—is more valuable for what it reveals of the role of saying, and here there is a parallel with the painting by Van Gogh. For that work, we recall, was deemed to have spoken to us, so that afterwards we were no longer the same: that is, painting speaks and, through speaking, transforms. Similarly, the work in words transforms the people, which means the "us" of an epoch. It transforms them by making it possible for them to decide what we would normally call their values, and it does this through its effect upon saying—a claim that is not made in behalf of the painting. Since Heidegger does not here clarify the difference between saying and speaking, we must draw inferences as best we can. Evidently, speaking is good but saying is better. That is, saying is more foundational, more grounded and grounding, than speaking. In the present environment of literary-critical discourse, some readers may liken such a distinction to the distinction between *langue* and *parole*, but that is not what I have in mind. I have in mind that saying implies the whole scope and possibility of any worldly act, including speaking, naming, and other modes that we shall examine below. I say "implies" because I do not think that the term has yet become precise and technical. It would be better to think of it as exemplifying one stage of poetic thinking, which can be more patient about its own proliferations than the reader, who wants to settle upon determinate meanings with as little delay as possible.

But in the interest of as much clarity as is presently feasible, it does help to note the reciprocity that obtains between the work in words and saying as *Sage* and *Sagen*. The reciprocity consists in the fact that the work rises from a people's saying, which is what I meant by suggesting that saying looked to be both more grounded than speaking and more grounding. Included in any grounding would be all that a people can possibly make an authentic decision about, which is another way of specifying all that they can possibly do. If such is the case, then saying is a good deal more than "linguistic," in the usual sense of that term, being the capacitating power that makes possible any work whatever, not merely works in words. In the absence of saying, not only would tragedy disappear; there would be no painting, no sculpture, no temple, nor, for that matter, any political state or society.

Saying as ground is no timeless substratum. It is, on the contrary, the ground that exists for such and such a historical people, for such and such an epoch; and as a capacitating power that exists in time, it is susceptible to the influence of what it supports: it too can be transformed. The transformation, however, cannot be total, lest the ground cease to be itself. That is why Heidegger toys with something like *a transformational direction:* the work, rising from saying, moves saying toward decision-making. What happens in Greek tragedy is not the representation of a struggle but an actual struggle: it is a people acting both through the capacitation of saying and through the mode of preserving that the work in words enables. The direction is thus both temporal, since all of this happens in time, and ontological, since every essential decision is a decision about how to be.

The same might be averred of the temple, through whose presence, we recall, the word comes to saying even as other components—metals, colors, sound—move into modes of manifestation not open to them in

their prearchitectural state. In this process there is a continuity, similar
to the continuity of a ground, but also a discontinuity or new direction
that transforms the component, though not to the extent that the distance between its state in "nature" and its state in architecture becomes
obliterated; for if it were obliterated, Heidegger would not be able to
discern that the creation of the temple makes any difference to something entering into its creation.

This capacity of the temple, it should be noted, does not contradict
the idea that saying is foundational, since the plastic arts are themselves
made possible by saying. This is because saying, like poetry, embraces
vastly more than we normally allow to fall within its purview; hence, in
a later passage equating poetry with saying, Heidegger surmises that
poetry embraces not only all art but more besides—without being able
to specify what this "more" specifically entails (H, 61/74).

The best place to begin our consideration of those other modes referred to above—all of which bear on the role of saying as well as on a
second issue, to be explored below—is the following passage:

> Language, by naming beings for the first time, first brings be-
> ings to word and to appearance. Only this nominates beings *to*
> their being *from out* of their being. . . . Such a saying is a project-
> ing of the clearing, in which announcement is made of what it is
> that beings come into the Open *as*. Projecting is the release of a
> throw by which unconcealedness submits and infuses itself into
> what is as such. Projective saying is poetry: the saying *(Sage)* of
> world and earth . . . and thus of the place of all nearness and remote-
> ness of the gods. . . . Actual language at any given moment is the
> happening of this saying, in which a people's world historically
> rises for it and the earth is preserved as that which remains
> closed. [H, 60–61/73–74]

After naming is shown to bring beings to word, naming appears as
saying, *Sagen,* which in turn becomes poetry, only to become saying as
die Sage and, finally, language. We have here another and more pronounced case of proliferation, which seemingly darkens any prospect of
distinguishing one term, with any real clarity, from another. The dilemma can, however, be explained, at least in part.

1. The text as given in *Holzwege* combines three separate presentations on, respectively, the thing and the work, the work and truth, and
truth and art, a fact that goes some way toward explaining why a passage can employ the terms employed in another passage in ways that
appear to be now different, now similar; and for my part I am not sure
that all of the attendant difficulties can be resolved.

2. *The Origin of the Work of Art* is an example of a pattern, repeated
not infrequently in the canon, in which the thinking proceeds in a
direction that might be called, roughly, "from different to same." This

is not a narrowing but a broadening aimed at simplicity combined with inclusiveness. The present essay tries to create for the reader an experience of art as origin, which is to say, as history, in Heidegger's sense of the term, and to this end it is important to let art pass through the entire terminology so that it emerges with maximum resonance, particularly with the resonance occasioned by its subsumption into poetry. This makes for a powerful kind of statement (art is history, art is origin) that is daring to the degree that it risks poetic richness at the expense of logical coherence.

3. For these reasons, and one more, it should be recognized that a basic quality of poetic thinking is ambiguity. The additional reason is that Heidegger sees ambiguity as an essential characteristic of *Dasein's* basic relation to others as well as to itself (SZ, 173–75/217–19). In everyday life and in making important decisions there is much that we are unclear about, though we may think we understand all we need to understand, and the same can be said of poetry, which can hardly be free of this characteristic if its scope is as wide as Heidegger believes and as closely connected with the way a people chooses to live.

4. Nonetheless, an examination of Heidegger's statements from a literary and rhetorical (as distinct from a philosophical and logical) point of view may furnish some helpful guidelines. So regarded, the quotation above begins to peak with the sentence beginning "Projective saying," and for several reasons. One is the momentum that has been building, despite the variety of ways in which it has been deployed, behind *Sagen*. Another is that *Sagen* has the capacity to project, this term designating the power to weigh possibilities and to make decisions. If saying can do this, then saying can be identified with poetry, here regarded as the primordial ground of all the arts and, as we have seen, of much more; and all of these considerations would be enough to make this section a crux. But now, for the first time in our passage, and indeed in the section from which it is drawn, there appears a colon (a form of punctuation that often opens up perspectives for Heidegger himself), marking the moment in which the new term, *die Sage*, becomes manifest as that which unites world and earth and the gods, revealing its connection, furthermore, with unconcealedness, the prime term for Heidegger's concept of truth. The result is what Kenneth Burke would call an entitlement, a kind of power given to saying as *Sage*—or better, recognized in it—which raises it to the level of *primus inter pares*. This means that saying really can do all the things that we have inferred it can do, and it also gives a fuller idea of what that entails.

5. It entails, at a minimum, the emergence of what is other than saying, namely the unsayable *(Unsagbare)*, which resembles the closed or concealed aspect of earth, and which is practically synonymous, it

seems to me, with what Heidegger will later call the unsaid *(das Un-gesagte)*:

> the unsaid describes a state of affairs which could not be other-wise and which is independent of human cognition as such. The unsaid is not unsaid because of our ignorance, either of what is in past or future time, but because of the necessarily unspoken re-lations connecting what has and will be said to what is actually being said in present speaking. The unsaid complements and ful-fills the spatio-temporal character of language as saying by pro-viding a necessary condition for the continuation of meaningful sentences spoken in virtue of saying.[9]

In *The Origin of the Work of Art* the unsayable is connected with prepa-ration: "Projective saying is that which, in preparing the sayable, si-multaneously brings the unsayable as such into the world" (H, 61/74); and preparation, as here understood, would presumably be indissoci-able from the preparation required for the work of art. As for the rela-tion of what can be said to what cannot be said, this may be seen, without taking undue liberties, as the emergence of the former upon the background of the latter. Equally important, it is only because the say-able emerges that we come to recognize the unsayable.

6. Saying also entails, finally, the relations obtaining among world, earth, and gods, each of which is specifically named and prepositionally tied to *die Sage*. This give us the greater part of what Heidegger's later writings will describe as "the fourfold," associated with the poetic thinker of the 1950s. But the whole of the fourfold is already effectively present in *The Origin of the Work of Art*, though in a less developed state, given the fact that mortals—the remaining constituent of the fourfold—are included but without being so named. For mortals are necessarily involved if the saying is the saying of the world and of the earth and of the gods, none of which may be thought of without refer-ence to *Dasein*. What is more, mortals in effect *are* named, the only difference being that they are called "a people." By thus connecting saying with the fourfold, the present essay anticipates the specification of that larger capacity of saying at which we have been looking from several points of view and that will provide, with the fourfold, a focus in chapter 7.

9. White, *Heidegger and the Language of Poetry*, p. 40.

3

Learning to Read

> ...we have need of this thinking, not merely and not mainly
> in order to be able to read poems, but, after all, to learn
> once again how to read.
>
> A letter to Emil Staiger

Emil Staiger's 1950 lecture on "The Art of Interpretation," with Eduard Mörike's lyric "On a Lamp" ("Auf eine Lampe") as its central text, provoked discussion in both of the cities—Amsterdam and Freiburg—in which he presented his views. One member of the Freiburg audience—the most eminent Western thinker of his time and a man whose work had influenced Staiger—took exception to some of these views, setting off an exchange of letters. This correspondence between Staiger and Martin Heidegger, quickly reaching print, prompted Leo Spitzer to enter the debate with an article of his own in the same publication, the Swiss journal *Trivium*.[1] The result is a series of interpretations that, beyond their considerable intrinsic interest, shed light on some interesting differences between literary criticism and philosophy; more important from the standpoint of the present book is the fact that they provide additional perspective on, and a further point of entry into, the demanding terrain that is Heidegger's poetic thinking.

In what follows I will trace the path of each interpretation, beginning with Staiger's account of Mörike's poem. But first the text:

> Noch unverrückt, o schöne Lampe, schmückest du,
> An leichten Ketten zierlich aufgehangen hier,
> Die Decke des nun fast vergessnen Lustgemachs.
> Auf deiner weissen Marmorschale, deren Rand
> Der Efeukranz von goldengrünem Erz umflicht,
> Schlingt fröhlich eine Kinderschar den Ringelreihn.
> Wie reizend alles! lachend, und ein sanfter Geist

---

1. Emil Staiger "Zu einem Vers von Mörike: Ein Briefwechsel mit Martin Heidegger," *Trivium* 9 (1951): 1–16; Leo Spitzer, "Wiederum Mörike's Gedicht 'Auf eine Lampe,'" ibid., pp. 133–47. Numbers appearing in parentheses in this chapter refer to the pages in these texts.

Des Ernstes doch ergossen um die ganze Form—
Ein Kunstgebild der echten Art. Wer achtet sein?
Was aber schön ist, selig scheint es in ihm selbst.

Still undisturbed, o beautiful lamp, thou adornest,
Gracefully suspended here on fine chains,
The ceiling of the now nearly forgotten festal room.
On thy white marble bowl, its rim
Entwined by an ivy garland of gold-green ore,
A band of children joyously dances round.
How charming is it all! laughing, and a gentle spirit
Of gravity yet flows around the entire form—
An art work of authentic kind. Who heeds it?
But what is beautiful shines blissfully in itself.

For Staiger, as for Heidegger, the crux is the final pronouncement,
which he contrasts with Goethe's "Beauty remains itself blissful" (Die
Schöne bleibt sich selber selig) from the second part of Faust. Whereas
Goethe speaks decisively and unambiguously, Mörike, according to
Staiger, is more tentative. Staiger reads "seems" for "shines," underlining the uncertainty surrounding the appearance of the beautiful.
Only an epigone, says Staiger, could exercise the ultimate Raffinement
of replacing the expected in sich selbst with the grammatically unlikely in
ihm selbst: "If he had written in sich selbst, he would have gone too far
over into the lamp. The beautiful is put at a distance again when it is
blissfully in ihm selbst" (p. 2). Staiger had learned from Grimm's dictio-
nary that this construction was in general usage around 1800 and was
employed by speakers of Mörike's native Swabia in subsequent years.

In the first of his two letters Heidegger interprets scheint, whose
meaning he tacitly accepts as the principal issue, as an expression of the
Hegelian aesthetic. The lamp is "the symbolon of the work of art as
such—in Hegel's language, 'of the Ideal.' The lamp . . . unites shining-
to-the-senses and the shining-of-the-idea as the essence of the work of
art" (p. 3). Like Staiger, Heidegger sees a close connection between this
crux and Mörike's unusual way of communicating the concept of "in
itself," but the connection he sees is radically different. Pointing out
that Staiger attributes a predicative function to the manner in which the
beautiful appears, Heidegger counters with the argument that "blissfully" should be taken adverbially, as signifying that the beautiful
shows itself in an essentially illuminating way. Moreover,

> the in itself (in ihm selbst) belongs to shines, not to blissfully; the
> blissfully is only the natural consequence of "the shining in itself."
> The articulation and the "rhythm" of the final verse have their
> weight in is. . . . The "being-beautiful" is the pure "shining" (Das
> "Schön-Sein" ist das reine "Scheinen"). [P. 3]

Heidegger, a more scrupulous scholar than he is sometimes taken to be, locates a similarly constructed "in itself" in Hegel's 1835 lectures on aesthetics: "The beautiful object . . . lets its own concept appear, as realized in its existence, and shows in itself *(an ihm selbst)* subjective unity and vivacity" (p. 3). Heidegger shifts attention, however, from the construction as such to the fact that it expresses an essential difference from the standpoint of Hegel's aesthetics. "In itself" signifies that which has no self-consciousness, no "concept" *(Begriff)* in Hegel's sense; Hegel does not employ *sich* (Heidegger infers) because this would indicate excessive self-orientation. The truth of art consists for Hegel not in its mere appearance but in its shining as self-disclosure. In that mode of presentation, says Hegel, "The ideal artistic form *(Kunstgestalt)* stands before us like a blissful God" (p. 4).

Although both of the observations with which Heidegger closes the letter are meant to reinforce his argument, they are not equally effective. Heidegger first seeks to legitimize his reliance upon Hegel by underlining Mörike's youthful friendship with the aesthetician Friedrich Theodor Vischer, the latter being seen as a mediator between the poet and the older philosopher. As will be shown below, that connection provides Staiger with the opportunity for a tactical counterargument; but it also leads into questions of influence, intellectual milieu, and the like, pulling both commentators away from their shared focus on the two cruxes described above. Because such aspects nonetheless constitute an important force in the to-and-fro of the argument, they cannot be overlooked in the present discussion.

More to the point, for the moment, is Heidegger's feeling for the weakened expressive force of *scheinen* as heard by modern ears. Instead of polemicizing against that development, he suggests reading Matthias Claudius' "Lullaby by Moonlight" ("Ein Wiegenlied, bei Mondschein zu singen"), especially stanzas eight, nine, eleven, and twelve. The text that follows includes the tenth stanza for continuity of sense:

> Sie sah mich an für Freude
> ein Tränchen lief,
> der Mond beschien uns beide,
> ich lag und schlief.
>
> Da sprach sie: "Mond, o! scheine,
> ich hab' sie lieb,
> schein Glück für meine Kleine!"
> Ihr Auge blieb
>
> noch lang am Monde kleben
> und flehte mehr.
> Der Mond fing an zu beben,
> als hörte er,

und denkt nun immer wieder
an diesen Blick,
und scheint von hoch hernieder
mir lauter Glück.

Er schien mir unterm Kranze
ins Brautgesicht,
und bei dem Ehrentanze;
du warst noch nicht.

She looked at me, for joy
shed a tear,
the moon shone on us both,
I lay and slept.

Then she said: "Moon, oh shine,
I love her so,
shine happiness for my little one."
Her eye stayed

a long while fastened on the moon
and pleaded for more.
The moon began to tremble,
as if he heard

And now keeps thinking
of that look,
and from on high shines down
to me pure happiness.

He shone beneath my bridal wreath
into my face,
and at my wedding dance;
you were not yet there.

Staiger responds to this attempt to strengthen the case for *lucet* with a familiar ploy of scholarly controversy: he ignores it, choosing to take up—to Heidegger's disadvantage, as it proves—the latter's recruitment of Vischer. Staiger's long quotation from Vischer will not be reproduced here; it is enough to note the distinction it draws between *Schein* as mere appearance and a more substantial *Schein* signifying appearance in the sense of a manifest presence. Noting the duality, Staiger infers that Vischer views appearance as *videri,* only to downplay the evidence on the grounds (supported by a letter from the poet) that Mörike had read little of what Vischer wrote. A second letter indicates that the poet was also unfamiliar with the writings of Hegel, whereupon Staiger charges Heidegger with placing too much emphasis on philosophical concepts and too little on the shifting, oscillating aspects of poetic practice. Staiger allows that the "old fox" Mörike may after all have been thinking about *lucet*, but only in a playful, tentative way; moreover, according to Staiger, it may be that any or all of the lexical options for *scheinen* may be construed as present, if only peripherally: Staiger's untranslatable term is *mitschillern*, to be iridescent-along-with or, if you will, co-opalescent.

Tracing this disagreement with Heidegger to the difference between poetic language and philosophical language, Staiger takes particular issue with Heidegger's insistence on the primacy of "is" in Mörike's final line. In an effort to coopt his opponent, Staiger contrasts this reading with Heidegger's interpretation of two lines from a Hölderlin poem:

> Des gemeinsamen Geistes Gedanken sind,
> Still endend in der Seele des Dichters. . . .
> [E, 67]

> Are thoughts of the common spirit,
> Ending still in the poet's soul. . . .

The interpretation hinges on the comma at the end of the first quoted line, a detail Heidegger likens to the chisel tap with which a sculptor alters a work in progress. Heidegger, who sometimes attributes to the poet editorial emendations that may or may not reflect the poet's own design, stresses Hölderlin's care in furnishing this punctuation, where-upon Staiger assigns credit for the comma to the early editor Norbert von Hellingrath, on whose very text Heidegger was then relying. How-ever, on both rhythmical and substantive grounds Staiger accepts Hei-degger's emphasis on *sind;* the problem is that Heidegger does not advance from that gloss in the same way as he advances from his gloss of the verb in Mörike. The detail in the Hölderlin passage enables Heidegger to develop the significance of the type of presence connoted in the poem, a presence that is at once a preservation and a kind of ongoing advent of the holy. Heidegger says less about "are" than about "still," observing that the term defines the participle that follows it: "The inspiration is let in and sustained, and certainly 'still.' The shock is stilled and preserved in the calming" (E, 67).

In his long final letter Heidegger tries to steer the discussion away from the Hegel-Vischer nexus by explaining that he had merely in-tended to indicate the intellectual atmosphere of Mörike's time. Hegel's philosophy and the Hegelian school were then so dominant, Heidegger insists, that one did not need firsthand knowledge of Hegel's or Vis-cher's books in order to understand that *scheinen* referred to the self-disclosure of presence in an illuminating way, an idea whose antiquity

Heidegger underlines and enlarges upon in a compressed version of his treatment of the same question in *Being and Time:*

> The Greek expression *phainomenon,* to which the term 'phenomenon' goes back, is derived from the verb *phainesthai,* which signifies "to show itself." Thus *phainomenon* means that which shows itself, the manifest. *Phainesthai* itself is a middle-voiced form which comes from *phainō*—to bring to the light of day, to put in the light. *Phainō* comes from the stem *ph*–, like *phōs,* the light, that which is bright—in other words, that wherein something can become manifest, visible in itself. [SZ, 29/51]

Later in the passage Heidegger employs the range of terms—*Schein, scheinen, Erscheinung*—that he will invoke in the commentary on Mörike's poem, but with a different understanding of them. To the philosopher of 1927, *Scheinen* signifies mere seeming or semblance, while the more powerful, more comprehensive concept is appearance, *Erscheinung,* which, as the editors of the English text point out, embraces no less than three senses:

1a. an observable event *y,* such as a symptom which announces a disease *x* by showing itself and in or through which *x* announces itself without showing itself;
1b. *y's* showing itself;
2. *x's* announcing-itself in or through *y;*
3a. the 'mere appearance' *y* which *x* may bring forth when *x* is of such a kind that its real nature can *never* be made manifest;
3b. the 'mere appearance' which is the *bringing-forth* of a 'mere appearance' in sense 3a. [SZ, 29/52 n.1]

The poetic thinker of 1950, increasingly concerned with the essential differences, draws a more elemental and clearer distinction. *Scheinen,* he concedes, can have the sense of "merely appearing as if," but it can have this sense only in relation to the deeper sense of self-manifestation. When he then states that the Greek term *phainesthai* carries both senses, he seems to compound two types of mere appearance (3a and 3b) and to contrast these with the types of genuine appearance of phenomenal self-showing (1a, 1b, and 2), which are similarly compounded. Heidegger might be happier, on the other hand, if we said, more simply if also more ambiguously, that the distinction now lies between mere appearance or semblance, on the one hand, and that which defines the very condition of any appearance whatever; and this is the fact that some presence shows itself as being present. This sense of the term provides what Heidegger calls the foundational realm in which the various senses of *Schein* and related terms, such as mere semblance and appearance, unfold. Thus the Greek sense of phenomenon supports a richer meaning than the Latin *videtur*, which is based on the viewpoint of a mere spectator.

Further recourse to Hegel enables Heidegger to turn Staiger's use of Vischer to the advantage of his own argument: Vischer's distinction between appearance and mere semblance can be found, Heidegger reports, in the same area of Hegel's work from which his previous letter had drawn. More meaningful is Heidegger's use of "area" *(Umkreis)* as one of several concepts suggesting realm, region, range, and the like, the aim being not to spatialize discourse but to hold discourse open to the play of certain considerations. Thus, in *Being and Time*, Heidegger speaks of tools and other types of equipment as each belonging somewhere and of therefore being disposed in a certain direction, a "whither," constituting, finally, an entire region *(Gegend)* (SZ, 103/136). Similarly, in a passage quoted above, Heidegger speaks of the foundational realm of *Scheinen*, a concept obviously related not only to the concept of the place occupied by a poetic canon but to the concept of essential place set forth in my discussion of *The Origin of the Work of Art*.

Although Heidegger finds in Hegel's concept of the beautiful various types of appearance, he insists that a certain mode of manifestation belongs to the work of art by necessity. That a tree in a painting is not a real tree and that it yet reveals the reality of the tree are, he maintains, considerations that touch upon the very essence of the work of art. It is a showing of the real, a manifestation or appearance of a reality in contrast to the mere appearance *(Anschein)*, denoted by *videtur*, which is limited to one or another aspect *(Ansicht)* that the poet sees in his role as epigone. But Heidegger presses the argument further than it will go, it seems to me, when he warns that Staiger's interpretation leads to the view that the authentic appearing of a work of art, its self-showing, can be nothing more than mere semblance. On the contrary, Staiger's historical orientation limits the extent to which the poet's situation can be generalized. It is, in Staiger's words, the situation of a man unable to experience a work of art as immediately and intensely as Goethe would have done. But such a failure would not be very poignant, would not even be very interesting, if we were not expected to believe that the work of art is inherently more than mere semblance: a missed experience is nothing unless there is something worth missing, and what is worth missing in the poem, according to Staiger's reading, is the inherent quality of the beautiful. If the inference Heidegger draws were valid, then a Goethe, restored to life and brought within the presence of the lamp, would also perceive nothing but semblance. But we are surely meant to suppose that the opposite is the case and that the poem depends for its main effect upon the felt difference between the poetic sensibility in the age of German classicism and the age of Biedermeier. If there is any falling-off in the experience of a work of art, it is in the person experiencing and not in the work of art. (Let me add that these remarks are not addressed to the veracity of Staiger's reading, which differs considerably from my own for reasons to be taken up below. I seek merely to distinguish between an assumption Staiger actually makes and an assumption attributed to him by Heidegger.)

With a reminder that the atmosphere of Mörike's time was so full of the ideas associated with Hegel that one did not have to know Hegel to be affected by them, Heidegger appears ready to abandon the approach—a version of the traditional history of ideas—which he himself had introduced into the debate. The shift seems to be confirmed by the statement that the *scheint* crux can be settled only by reference to "the poem itself" (p. 10), but in fact Heidegger is circling around—as is his custom—to a restatement of the relevance of atmosphere; for the poem itself, he says, remains in the ambience of the spirit of language *(Sprachgeistes)* peculiar to its period and "oscillates in a fundamental mood *(schwingt in einer Grundstimmung)*" (p. 10) from which it speaks. Heidegger, alas, is no clearer about what he means by the poem itself than are most literary critics who invoke the concept. From the exegesis that follows, it appears that the poem itself is simply any text that undergoes a close reading, with particular attention to formal structure and to the meanings of certain key words. The majority of readers will have little fault to find with an analysis that then proceeds to look first at the initial three lines, which constitute one sentence, then at the next three, which constitute another, then at lines seven and eight, which has a dash at the end, then at the closing lines. But the same cannot be said for the substance of the commentary, which develops in directions of which neither a Staiger nor a Spitzer could ever approve. Heidegger's strategy is, as it were, to make his own text as full of light as Mörike's poem. But he does not do this, as might be expected, merely by stressing the lamp's production of light; the illumination of the lamp emanates from the totality or world, which is composed in turn of everything set forth in the descriptive or—to move closer to Heidegger's language—original presenting part of the poem, namely, the first six lines. The world thus disclosed is not that of the lamp, although the lamp and its performance are obviously crucial; it is the world of the room.

The first three lines, according to Heidegger, tell the manner in which the lamp is present. In a gambit of neologizing that is one of his most characteristic devices, Heidegger, turning a noun into a verb, states that the lamp *anwest*, "presences," and that its way of presencing is by adorning the room. No sign of light yet, and therefore nothing to disturb Spitzer, who will protest, against the readings of both Heidegger and Staiger, that the poem makes no reference to light. Heidegger, however, understands that the lamp is not burning and, in the passage I am about to quote, includes a sentence to that effect; the point of departure is in any case the one Mörike specifically provides—the performance of adorning:

> Lines 1–3 say that the beautiful lamp presences *still undisturbed*, and how it presences—namely, by "adorning" *the ceiling of the now almost forgotten festal room.* The ceiling thus adorned by the beautiful lamp irradiates the room out of the lustre *(Glanz)* of this adornment. The lamp, without burning, lights the room. It furnishes this room with its (verbal) nature, which "now is nearly forgotten." This says: what is illumined appears as having already been in the light of the beautiful lamp. [P. 10]

If the first three lines emphasize, in a fairly general way, the "how" of the lamp, the next three emphasize the particular way in which its "what," its embodied, modeled configuration, is brought to appearance.

> On thy white marble bowl, its rim
> Entwined by an ivy garland of gold-green ore,
> A band of children joyously dances round.

Heidegger connects the golden-green coloration, without explaining his reason for doing so, to "what is glowingly, growingly Dionysian" *(das glühend-wachstüm-liche Dionysische,* p. 11). But a clue to the association is contained in the next sentence: "The round dance of the band of children irradiates the splendor of the festal room." The movement of the children, in other words, exemplifies Heidegger's conception, voiced in several works of the early 1950s, of a fourfold world of sky, earth, mortals, and divinities who move together in a round dance, their very participation constituting the way in which they mirror one another, play into one another, ring one another together, and thus sustain one another within their differentiated unity. This matter will be treated at greater length in the last two chapters.

If I may anticipate a point that I will make in the concluding chapter, Heidegger is able to increase the resonance of the round dance by tracing it to the bacchic dance, in celebration of the gods, such as we observe in ancient Greek drama. Hence, though Heidegger does not explicitly consider that golden green is the color the ore of the lamp might acquire with age, this possibility is included in the temporal continuity that links the lamp's present manifestation, through its long lingering in time, to the epoch in which it first came to be.

On the other hand, it must be admitted that Heidegger misses an opportunity to enhance his reading of this phase of the poem, and indeed of the whole. I refer to the implications, for the constitution of the world of that room, of the beautifully enclosed roundness of the shape doubly encircled, once by the ivy garland and once by the dancers. This seems to me a fascinating case of a performing presencing that is complete both in itself and in its self-disclosing. This characteristic of the lamp invites comparison, at the same time, with the attributes of the jug in "The Thing," where Heidegger shows in impressive depth and detail how an artifact can gather, to the place it holds open, each and every region of the fourfold world. By not moving in this direction, Heidegger leaves the reader to infer the significance of the Dionysian reference and its relevance to his conception of the world, which, by the time of the debate over the Mörike poem, has already been worked out in all its essentials.

The thinker is on more familiar ground when, after dissociating the children from the poet's supposed recollection of his own past, he remarks that "Ivy garland and ring of children belong to the artistic structure of the beautiful insofar as this furnishes with light (*lichtend einräumt*) the world of the festal room" (p. 11). The value of the tautological statement is that it makes explicit Heidegger's desire to trace whatever is given in the poem to the totality that is at once limit and ultimate possibility—namely, the world *of* the room, *in* the poem.

Heidegger sees lines 7 and 8 as bringing to language everything that has gone before, a view supported by Mörike's use of *alles* and his allusion to the wholeness of the lamp's form. The concept of bringing to language does not mean that the poem only now begins to speak. If language is fundamentally poetic, as Heidegger argues in *The Origin of the Work of Art*, and if everything that has been spoken up to now in the poem is spoken poetically, then it is not immediately obvious that the words in lines 7 and 8 function in an essentially different way from the words in lines 1 through 6. Heidegger may mean something like: in these lines there emerges a fuller sense of the whole set forth in the preceding lines. Or: what has been spoken so far gathers force as it becomes more present and is therefore more "said." This would correspond to the concept of saying advanced in other works of the same period:

> "To bring to language"—we ordinarily use this expression to express that something is set out in discussion and treated. But when we think the expression thoughtfully according to the weight of its words, it attains a deeper meaning. Then "bring to language" means: to raise into words first of all what has previously never been spoken, and to let appear through saying (*Sagen*) what has so far been hidden. [HH, 25]

In any event, the heart of the matter, for Heidegger, lies in the polarity between charm and earnestness or, perhaps better, gravity: "charm and gravity of what is present play gently into one another and play around *the entire form*" (p. 11). Why this polarity? To a philologist, Spitzer will say, the laughing refers to the children, the gravity to the garland, while charm refers to everything. For Heidegger, too, the adjective "charming" applies to everything: given Mörike's wording it is hard to imagine anyone construing the phrase in any other way. But the wording that follows invites the adjective "laughing" to be associated with everything as well, the second modifier reinforcing the first: everything is charming and everything is laughing. The reinforcement is further supported by contiguity and parallelism: the words occur close together in the same line, they are both modifiers, they both have two syllables, they rhyme, and they are nearer each other in meaning than either is to gravity. Heidegger's interpretation, however, gives priority to the first word, possibly because it comes first and because the expostulatory character of the phrase makes it stand out, whereas the second word is a kind of back-up. Heidegger in effect allows the second to be subsumed into the first, so that the laughing might be regarded as being of the same affective quality as charm. He then nominalizes, converting "charming" to "charm" to accentuate its opposition to gravity, which is nominal in the original text. But this is a friendly opposition, as indicated by the poet's choice of "and" over "but" or "yet"; for either of those latter conjunctions would reflect a common-sense point of view (charm and the laughter stand in marked contrast to gravity), so that, after referring to charm and laughter, one would expect to hear something like: "and yet the whole is earnest." Despite the fact that Heidegger overlooked the possibilities in the details I have been examining, we shall see many occasions on which he starts from a similar point of reference, although the direction he takes and the distance he goes are often very different.

Heidegger is more successful when, immediately following his remarks on lines 7 and 8, he looks back again at all of the preceding lines, concluding that they have brought the lamp's presence to light, though it takes a play on words to suggest the type of illumination at work: "The poem, to be sure, does not ignite *(anzündet)* the lamp, but kindles *(entzündet)* the beautiful lamp" (p. 11). Such play—such verbal excess, Spitzer would say—is not so much an attempt to specify the nature of the light as an attempt to reinforce, through sustained poetic thinking, the theme of poetry's founding power as delineated in *The Origin of the Work of Art*.

Asking rhetorically why the poem does not end at this point, Heidegger, reverting to his standpoint on the role of language in lines 7 and 8, replies that "what is to be spoken poetically has not yet been brought to language" (p. 11). Coming to language means in this case naming. It is not enough that the lamp gets into words; it must be given its unique name, with the aura that surrounds the act of establishing onomastically the identity of a being. That name is the entire phrase "a work of art of authentic kind," Heidegger says; but the naming does not prove, after all, to be what is to be spoken poetically: "The authentic kind of beautiful lamp, beauty itself, remains unspoken" (p. 11).

Heidegger sees, with Staiger, a shift in thought at the end of line 8. The shift, says Heidegger, names a difference, but difference in Heidegger's usage, as noted in the preceding chapter, is neither oppositional nor dialectical. It is a type of relation that cannot be stated in the language of either traditional philosophical discourse or scientific discourse. Heidegger's alternative is suggestiveness, often oxymoronic in its drift, as here; for the difference both divides and unites, setting lines 1–8 apart from lines 9–10 yet gathering back what it sunders, so that lines 9–10 are brought to bear in general on lines 1–8 and, in particular, on lines 7–8.

The question following the phrase "a work of art of authentic kind" implies a negative answer. Who notices? the poet asks, answering: no one. For that reason Heidegger agrees with Staiger that the mood of the poem is melancholy (a reading to which I will take exception below), but the conclusion to which this leads differs markedly from the conclusion drawn by Staiger:

> The poet can only be characterized by this melancholy mood because he belongs among those who still preserve the sense of the essence of the work of art. Therefore the melancholy cannot weigh him down. He steadies himself in it. For he knows: the true kind of a work of art, the beauty of the beautiful, does not hold sway by the grace of human beings—according to whether or not they pay attention to the work of art. [P. 12]

The work of art remains independent in this sense because, in a paraphrase of Mörike's last line: "The beauty of the beautiful is the pure letting-appear of the *entire form* in its essence" (p. 12). The clue to the relation between the question and its answer lies in the interpretation of a detail very similar to my interpretation of "and" above. Again the crux is a conjunction: "Was aber schön ist, selig scheint es in ihm selbst." *Aber*, "but," undercuts the importance of human attention, initiating Mörike's iteration of the self-sufficiency of the beautiful. But for Heidegger the conjunction does more than throw into relief the word "beautiful," which immediately follows; it also accents the verb. "The *is* names 'being beautiful in itself' in contrast to 'merely becoming represented' through attention to the beautiful" (p. 13). Heidegger distinguishes such a function from the function of the *sind* in the Hölderlin poem, seeing the latter as signifying existence "in the metaphysical sense of existentia" (p. 13) rather than "being," which Heidegger refers to as *wesen*, a verbal neologism formed from the noun *Wesen*, essence or nature, and often connected by Heidegger (most strikingly, perhaps, in "Anaximander's Maxim") with *Anwesen*, presence, which also becomes, as above, a verb. To say that something *an-west* is, roughly, to say that it presences. Similarly with Heidegger's conversion of the noun *Welt* into a verb: the world worlds. *Wesen* presents a stickier problem because there are no adequate English analogues. "It essences," for example, suggests the kind of dichotomy Sartre draws between existence and essence; and, though Heidegger happens here to draw on a similar dichotomy, it still smacks too much of the traditional philosophical terminology, which Heidegger yearns to replace. The most advisable course, it would seem, is to get along with "presences," while furnishing, for the sake of accuracy, the German term.

Such linguistic formations can produce, by way of partial summary, the concentrated richness of the following: "But what presences as something beautiful *(Was aber als ein Schönes west)*, what else can it do but, as adorning-illuminating, let a world in its (verbal) essence appear? This the beautiful may do only insofar as it illuminingly lightens, which means: shines" (p. 13). Heidegger adds that what rounds itself out, as the poem speaks its final words, is less the total form of the lamp than the totality of the poem "On a Lamp." But what he wants finally to drive home, and what he seems to think he has not sufficiently clarified, is the superiority of *lucet* over *videtur*, with all that this signifies for the other questions we have considered, such as the degree to which the lamp appears as self-sufficient manifestation of the beautiful: "The meaning of shining in *shines* does not point in the direction of phantom but in that of epiphany. The artistic structure of authentic kind is itself the epiphany of the world it lights up and preserves" (p. 13). By the time of this exchange with Staiger, and indeed by the time of *The Origin of the Work of Art*, Heidegger has moved so far from his early concern for spiritual, especially Christian, experience, undertaken prior to the writing of *Being and Time*, that the reader is ill advised to listen for more than residual religious overtones. And as tempting as it may be for an Anglo-American reader to hear Joycean overtones, there is no evidence whatever in support of such an interpretation. On the other hand, given Heidegger's fondness for Greek antiquity and in particular for the Greek etymon, one can probably hear echoes of *epiphaneia*, manifestation, which is related to the concept of phenomenon discussed above in connection with the same family of Greek root words. Lexically speaking, Heidegger's use of the term cannot be literal, since he does not point to a divine manifestation, let alone a Christian one. But the figurative-literal dichotomy is itself inadequate, as a discussion of metaphor, in a later chapter, will attempt to show. For the epiphany of the poem is as genuine an event from the poetic point of view as the manifestation of a divine being is from a religious point of view, and, insofar as this is the case, the term should be taken as meaning just what it says: the poem, as that which brings the lamp to light, is the supreme manifestation of the very world it provides and preserves.

As paradoxical as the idea may seem, Heidegger's exploitation of the many senses of "shining" and related words is a corollary of the essential simplicity set forth in the poem. Staiger, we recall, had attributed Mörike's substitution of *ihm* for *sich* to the poet's "ultimate refinement." At the same time, he had tied the substitution to the notion that Mörike did not want to imply a closer identification between poet and lamp than his "epigonish situation" permitted. But for Heidegger, putting so much stress on subjectivity complicates unduly the plain thrust of the poem. There is a parallel here with the process noted above, wherein Heidegger compressed the wide range of meanings for phenomenon into a much simpler, more poetic contrast—a kind of friendly opposition, as we saw. Recapitulating the process by which the lamp brings the world of the festal room to its shining, Heidegger proceeds as if Staiger's remark about refinement had been applied to the whole of the poem and rejects it outright. What comes about through the poem is, rather, "a gift from the plainly simple"[2] to the poet, whom he acknowledges to be an epigone. But, given his reading of the poem, he cannot stop there, for the idea that the poet is "too late"—too far, that is, from Goethe and the classical age of German humanism—comes too close to Staiger's emphasis. Moreover, he concurs in Staiger's view that the mood of the poem is melancholy—a concession that need not have been made, as I shall shortly argue. The problem is how to show that the poem redeems, as it were, the mood:

> But the question remains: what is determined by the melancholy? Not the authentic kind of artistic structure, insofar as its essential shining is tuned down to a mere appearance. The mood of melancholy bears upon the artistic structure insofar as it no longer has around it the kind of human attention suited to its nature. [P. 14]

2. Cf. H, 12; E, 102–3; *Zur Sache des Denkens* (Tübingen: Niemeyer, 1969), pp. 54–55.

Such neglect comes about because of the peculiar incapacity of the work of art, which can neither save itself from fading as time goes by nor compel human beings to notice it. Heidegger terms that incapacity a "woe" (*Wehe*), allowing its sound and sense to overlap that of melancholy, *Wehmut*, which is the poem's mood in response to that woe. It is this vision, and not any failure of the beautiful to disclose itself, that causes the poet to feel as he does: "As epigone he has evidently seen more than the predecessors and borne more than they" (p. 14).

The considerations thus brought to the poem, concludes Heidegger, should not result merely in our being able to read the thought in the poem; the point is "to learn once again how to read" (p. 14).

Although Leo Spitzer faults both Staiger and Heidegger, and though it is clear from his tone and manner that he finds some features of Heidegger's approach downright irritating, his conclusions are not as far from Heidegger's as one might have expected. Spitzer, too, draws Hegel into the discussion, and, more importantly, he accepts Heidegger's choice of *lucet* over *videtur* as a gloss of *scheinen*. He considers, however, that Heidegger goes too far in his etymologies and accomplishes little by playing on words.

Spitzer takes his main exegetic cue, as suggested above, from the physical nature of the lamp. The poem, he points out, never explicitly states that the lamp is lighted. One can of course reply that the illumination is to be taken for granted; and there is always that key word *scheinen*. But Spitzer's proposal is supported by Mörike's emphasis on the rounded, intertwining details of its material structure. Viewed in this way, the poem assimilates itself not only to the German tradition of the *Dinggedichte* or thing-poems, such as C. F. Meyer's "The Roman Fountain" ("Der römische Brunnen"), but also to an international tradition exemplified in Mörike's own century by Keats' "Ode on a Grecian Urn" (it is worth remembering that Mörike translated poems from the Greek Anthology) and, in the twentieth, by Wallace Stevens' "Anecdote of the Jar."

Spitzer's philological research brings out a further possible meaning of the crux in the final line, for the key word (*Deutsches Wörterbuch: scheinen*, II.2.d) carries the sense in Mörike's native dialect, Swabian, of "being beautiful or splendid." What is more, the *in ihm* construction discussed above is also Swabian. Any philologist, says Spitzer, would conclude from this lexical information that the poem's concluding line means: "The beautiful is resplendent blissfully in itself" (p. 138). If that comes out sounding no less "odd" than some of Heidegger's paraphrases, it is at least in part because Spitzer deliberately chooses a verb, *prangen*, that is related etymologically to the adjective *prächtig*, "splendid." Some other relevant senses of *prangen* are: "make a show; glitter, sparkle, shine, be exhibited"; hence Spitzer concedes:

> Naturally I cannot deny that in this Swabian construction a fundamental etymological concept of illumination may resonate
> . . . and that as a consequence this accompanying concept of
> resplendence *("Prangens")* is actually brought into relation to
> "lamp," suggesting an inner illumination of the lamp—of the
> lamp which will never again be ignited, but which sustains an
> inner light in itself, illuminates in itself. But the principal concept
> of *"scheint"* is that of "being beautiful." [P. 138]

Obviously, such a reading is persuasive if one agrees that Mörike is here drawing on dialect. In this connection a few questions suggest themselves. Why does Mörike employ dialect only here, in this one crucial line? If readers are not prepared for the shift, are they not likely to miss the "tautology" in the dialectal verb and thus miss a significant meaning? And wouldn't Mörike have foreseen this? Furthermore, why is dialect a more appropriate mode of expression for what is evidently a very general, even universal, statement?

On the other hand, is it not the case that the main sense of the final line is about the same whether we read its cruxes as standard German or as dialect? I have posed this question last in order that we may turn around a bit toward a more Heideggerean direction. Spitzer notwithstanding, Heidegger never states that the lamp is lighted. On the contrary, he stipulates, as noted above, that it is not burning. An unlit lamp, indeed, heightens Heidegger's main thesis, which is that the lamp illuminates by the sheer virtue of being beautiful. The plausibility of Heidegger's gloss survives if *scheinen* is standard, but insofar as Spitzer allows for this concurrent though secondary meaning, it survives the dialectal reading, too. The issue is, in part, one of emphasis: Heidegger may make too much of one possible sense; but the sense is there. The irony is that Spitzer's gloss can be made to serve the very type of argument that Heidegger will make in his commemorative essay on Hebel as well as in *What Is Called Thinking?*: "Dialect is the secret source of every developed language. From it pours out to us all that the spirit of language conceals in itself" (HH, 7). Accepting a dialectal reading of the two cruxes in Mörike's line, one finds a beautifully tautological rendering of the circularity of the lamp as well as of the poem, which, as both Heidegger and Spitzer point out, turns round on itself as the concluding utterance brings to a totality the world initiated in its beginning. When Spitzer duly attempts to restate the utterance in a Heideggerean manner, he is being polemical, but the result resembles a statement one can imagine Heidegger making:

... if Mörike had been Heidegger, he would not have contented himself with the alliteration "schön-scheint," but would have expressed the thoughts in antiquated adnominatio: "But what is beautiful, blissfully *beautifies* in itself" (or perhaps: "what beautifyingly beautifies, blissfully-blissifying selves itself in itself") *("was schönend schönt, selig-seligend selbstet es in sich selbst").* [P. 138]

This is to out-Heidegger Heidegger, yet what comes through the parody is a more compressed rendition of the circularity that Heidegger recognizes and that he distributes—now in one play of words, not in another—throughout his interpretation.

Neither Heidegger nor Spitzer turns for insight to the Mörike canon, but it is worth noting that the poet was much taken by light—the light of the sun, for example, in "Concealment" ("Verborgenheit"), or the shining of joy in "New Love" ("Neue Liebe"), or of flames in "The Forsaken Maid" ("Das verlassene Mägdlein"), where the shining is specifically called beautiful. While these patterns do not indicate that Spitzer's dialectal reading is untenable—it strikes me as tenable indeed—it may indicate that the sense of illumination figures more significantly than Spitzer allows. Such merging of senses, while sometimes worrisome to the "logical" aspects of the philological temperament, is of the essence of poetry. As for the mood of the poem, I agree with Spitzer's insistence that, *contra* Staiger, it is by no means melancholy. Mörike, according to Spitzer, says just what Goethe said: "The beautiful remains blissfully itself," and that very pronouncement may even have been in Mörike's mind when he wrote. Mörike, says Spitzer, stresses the age-old concept of the autonomy of the work of art, overcoming any sense of alienation through "the idyllic calmness of his final verse" (p. 139). Ironically, Spitzer's *Gelassenheit*, "releasement, calmness, or detachment,"[3] was to become a favored Heideggerean term, even the title of a book, and the notion of transcendence developed here closely resembles Heidegger's interpretation of the poet's experience. It should be added that Mörike's poetry is full of sudden illuminations, moments of breakthrough that counterbalance the undeniable darkness of some of this poet's moods.[4] They occur, indeed, in each of the poems listed above.

In her 1977 Presidential Address to the Modern Language Association, Edith Kern summarized the debate as follows:

3. John D. Caputo, *The Mystical Element in Heidegger's Thought* (Athens: Ohio University Press, 1978), pp. 140–217, offers the most extended discussion to date of Heidegger's *Gelassenheit* in relation to Meister Eckhardt.

4. Walter Höllerer, *Zwischen Klassik und Moderne: Lachen und Weinen in der Dichtung einer Übergangszeit* (Stuttgart: Klett, 1958), p. 328. For Höllerer's views on the Staiger-Heidegger-Spitzer debate, see pp. 467–68, n. 9.

Many of you are familiar with the fascinating battle of wits that
was unleashed in the forties and fifties when Heidegger applied
his method to the line of a poem by Mörike, "Auf eine Lampe,"
that had just been given a new interpretation by Staiger in the
Swiss publication *Trivium*. Spitzer, writing in the same periodical,
accused the philosopher of a disregard for philological laws. Yet
Heidegger's faulty etymology (Derrida would call it today a "de-
construction of language") managed to withstand the onslaught of
Spitzer's decidedly superior knowledge of philology and linguis-
tics.[5]

Heidegger could withstand the onslaught, I believe, partly because his
interpretation of the *lucet/videtur* crux is simply more persuasive—as
Spitzer's reading confirms—than the gloss offered by Staiger. Another
prominent scholar, J. P. Stern, remarks: "I have accepted Heidegger's
reading because I know of no poem of Mörike's containing the antith-
esis 'art-reality' which Staiger's reading would imply, but above all
because Heidegger's 'lucet' is relevant to the central image of the lamp
and thus to the integrity of the poem, whereas Staiger's 'videtur' is
not."[6] There is a second reason why Heidegger can stand the philological pressure applied by Spitzer, and that is: he is finally not engaged in
literary scholarship or criticism in the traditional sense. To explore what
he *is* engaged in is the mission of this book; here it must suffice to say
that Heidegger is working in his own distinctive mode of poetic thinking, a thinking that is sometimes logical and philological but is often
neither; a thinking less oriented to outcomes than to an experience of
the *process* of thinking in this particular way. For those who have engaged in that experience the word "way" has, inevitably, a special
value. It suggests a movement, a direction, a track, a drift—but also
adventure, quest and search. Heidegger calls one of his later collections
Holzwege, or *Wood Ways*, and another *Unterwegs zur Sprache*, or *On the
Way to Language*. Such thinking leads to startling discoveries, to strange
new angles of vision; it can also double back on itself, baffle itself, find
itself stopped before an abyss.

There is nothing quite like it in the realm of modern thought.

5. Edith Kern, "Resolved: That the Proper Study of Mankind Is Man," *PMLA* 73 (1978):
364.

6. J. P. Stern, *Idylls and Realities: Studies in Nineteenth-Century Literature* (New York:
Ungar, 1971), p. 93n. Compare Alexander Gelley's valuable essay "Staiger, Heidegger,
and the Task of Criticism," *Modern Language Quarterly* 23 (September 1962): 195–216.

4

The Essence of Poetry:
Hölderlin

The thinker says Being. The poet names the holy.
Afterword to *What is Metaphysics?*

The poetic works of Friedrich Hölderlin provide, in Heidegger's view, an insight into the very essence of poetry. In examining the lectures and essays in which Heidegger presses this case, we need, first, to consider what is meant by the concept of essence; we may then consider what follows from the decision to select this German author, as Heidegger has very consciously done, as the paradigmatic poet of the modern world.

The Meaning of Essence

When we speak of the essence of something, we communicate our sense of what it fundamentally is. About such a goal there is, despite appearances, nothing mysterious; but since the ways of getting there can be roundabout, and since the goal is not one the literary mind typically sets for itself, the feasibility of the enterprise requires a word of explanation.

Husserl suggests that if we want to know the essence of something, if we want to grasp just what it is, we can try some experimental variations on it. That is, our imaginations can apply to it a series of predications, accepting those that fit and rejecting those that do not fit until something is left; and that something will show what it is—its essence.

> Now it is the essence of the independent object which determines the limits within which the contents of the object can vary. A variation which exceeds this limit imposed by the essence would strip the object from its concrete character, its independence, that is to say its possibility to exist. In this way the essence of the object seems to express the conditions which must be realized for the existence of the object to be possible. The predicates of the object may vary without jeopardizing the possibility of the object;

77

> it is only the *essential* predicates which do not tolerate a variation.
> And what is more, it is precisely their constancy which allows the
> variation of the other predicates; each variation, indeed, pre-
> supposes something constant which makes it possible.[1]

Now this process may well lead toward a knowledge of what is merely
possible, with respect to the object at issue; but even our knowledge of
what is possible will be based, circularly, on our sense of what the
object essentially is. It is just this presupposition of constancy—that
such and such a thing really is always itself—that disallows inessential
predicates and permits us to recognize essential predicates when we
encounter them.

We could, if we liked, attribute to a rock all the properties usually
attributed to a tree, and vice versa. We could say that a rock grows out
of the ground from a root system and that a tree is an igneous object
not requiring sunlight or water for growth, and so on. But such statements immediately appear absurd because of a fact that is already assumed as a matter of course in daily life: the fact that we grasp the
essence of things perfectly well (so long as we understand this grasping
as a practical process that is not the less ubiquitous for being only
occasionally, as in this passage, made conspicuous) and that it is just
this constant sense of an essence that makes it possible to distinguish
between variations that work and variations that do not work.

Having read these remarks, readers unfamiliar with Heidegger's
writings may feel misled as soon as they encounter presentations that
at first sight may appear vague, even murky, and that are in any case
rarely exact in a scientific sense.

> If we try to express the inexact data of perception in an exact
> manner, then we cause them to lose their concrete and living as-
> pects. Notions such as "great" and "small," "roundish" and
> "oblique," "warm" and "cold," "heavy" and "light" taken in their
> approximative and vague nature—these are the characteristics of
> the concrete world of our perception, and not the exact notions of
> geometry and science such as "straight line" and "circle," "tem-
> perature" and "gravitation." It is by these concepts first of all that
> the essence of the world is determined; the world of exact scien-
> tific concepts is . . . a derivative.[2]

This being the case, how much greater must be the difficulty of speaking intelligibly about subjects, such as art in general or poetry in particular, that fall only partly within the purview of the realm we call

---

1. Emmanuel Levinas, "Essences and Eidetic Reduction," in *Phenomenology: The
Philosophy of Edmund Husserl*, ed. Joseph J. Kockelmans (Garden City, N.Y.: Doubleday/
Anchor, 1967), pp. 95–96.
2. Ibid., pp. 101–2.

perceptual. That is precisely what Heidegger will attempt to do, both in the earlier and the later writings on Hölderlin.

The result is not, and is never intended to be, a set of formal definitions or conclusions. The result is, rather, an experience of the essentially poetic, occasioned by the interplay between the texts of Hölderlin and the thinking of Heidegger. The point is important enough to warrant emphasis. The texts of the poet are not to be approached as objects, because that places them at too great a distance. Nor are they to be taken, as it were, at face value, for poetic thinking, as practiced by Heidegger, brings forth from a text meanings that the poet may have left unspoken or unthought. It is an extreme case, if you will, of reading between the lines. Far from being a source of embarrassment, the presence of the unspoken or the unthought is practically a cause for celebration. In *Being and Time,* as we saw, Heidegger specifically defends the use of interpretative "violence," and the case is advanced even more assertively in *An Introduction to Metaphysics.* The point is to learn thinking, and such learning cannot be undertaken without contesting accepted frameworks. It can be learned only as swimming is learned (Heidegger argues in *What Is Called Thinking?*), and swimming is learned, not by being contemplated as an object of study, but by plunging into the water. It is not surprising, therefore, that the experience occasioned by the interplay, described above, resembles an immersion.

The Example of Hölderlin

Why does Heidegger choose to examine Hölderlin rather than, say, Goethe or Schiller? There is, to begin with, a parallel between the poet and Being-there, as described in *Being and Time.* Just as *Dasein* is that being for which its Being is at issue, Hölderlin is the poet for whom poetry is at issue. This means that Hölderlin, more than most other poets, delivers himself to the challenge of discovering, living through, and speaking forth the mission of poetry in the modern world. That commitment, in a period less eager than the period of high German classicism to hear the poetic voice, sets Hölderlin, in Heidegger's view, apart from the main line of Western humanism. The exemplars of that tradition, among whom Goethe, Schiller, and Winckelmann are to be numbered, define themselves in relation to a Greek antiquity that had become, for lack of a better term, romanized. Humanism, closely linked to the Renaissance translation of Greek thought and language into Latin, carries out a *studium humanitatis* that revives ancient texts in narrowed, translated form. By contrast, Hölderlin, in Heidegger's view, experiences more fully, because more immediately, the history of Being

that the Greeks inaugurated. Heidegger's argument, in brief, is that this
essential history—essential because it is the fundamental story of
Being—can be disclosed in poetry even though Being itself remains
concealed; that Hölderlin achieves such disclosure in his greatest lyrics,
hymns, and odes; and that Hölderlin, by beginning anew from an authentic experience of Greek art and thought, makes possible a new
beginning for that epoch in which we continue to live. That is why, in
his "Letter on Humanism," Heidegger can acclaim Hölderlin's world-
historical thinking (W, 339) while associating Goethe with the world
bourgeoisie (Weltbürgertum). If I am not mistaken, the comparison does
not overlook the magnitude of Goethe's achievement or the achievement of humanism. On the contrary, the achievement is presupposed
as a phenomenon with its own historical completeness. But it *is* complete, and it stands in tradition rather as an object of veneration than as
an opening toward the future through a fundamental *re*opening of what
is genuinely original in the experience of the Greeks. It is this last that
Hölderlin achieves, and it is this that makes him an appropriate choice
as paradigmatic poet.

A further clue to Hölderlin's appropriateness is suggested by the
second of five guiding statements, drawn from various places in Hölderlin's canon, around which Heidegger constructs a 1936 lecture:
"Therefore the most dangerous of possessions, language, was given to
man . . . so that he may testify to what he is" (E, 33). Man has no nature
unless he makes it; he must declare what he is before he can testify to
what he is. That declaration reveals that man is the one who inherits the
earth but who also inherits a chaos in that he is surrounded by things in
conflict. Conflict is here understood, however, in much the same way as
Heraclitus' *polemos* (a subject of the chapter "Learning to Think"), according to which conflicting powers belong together precisely insofar as
they oppose each other, their "antagonism" being the very definition of
their essential oneness. Hence we are not surprised to learn that Hölderlin calls this relation "intimacy" (Innigkeit), denoting that which
holds things together by holding them apart.

It is left to man, as a being belonging to the earth and caught up in
conflict, to make the most of his freedom, a position that clearly recalls
the outline of *Dasein* in *Being and Time*; indeed, Heidegger here employs
the term *Dasein* as a synonym for man. Further, in order for man to
declare himself, a world must be created, which is not the same as
requiring that man create the world himself. World comes about
through intimacy and free decision, in which human being is fully
involved but which involves more than human being. The working-out
of world, not yet explained in detail, begins to look, in other words, like

a process that comes about in several ways, only one of which is the human way, and is thus an early sign of Heidegger's movement, through his experience of art and poetry, from a preoccupation with *Dasein* to a preoccupation with Being itself, both in itself and in its manifestations. The movement may be observed in *The Origin of the Work of Art*, where Heidegger takes up the same three features examined here—earth, world, and decision—from a different point of view.

What makes language dangerous is the fact that it makes danger possible—a gratuitous statement, it would seem; but the unstated premise is the same as the thesis advanced, in *Being and Time*, regarding our basic relation to unconcealment through language. *Logos* means letting something be seen or letting something become manifest. *Logos*, however, is less primordial than *aisthēsis*, the sheer sensory showing-forth as something, because showing-forth overwhelms us with its immediacy. Language, by contrast, can let something be seen either truly or falsely: through language we are able to lie, distract, deceive. Furthermore, although language enables beings to come into their own through a work of art, so that they emerge for the first time as what they genuinely are, it can also, in other settings, make manifest sheer muddle or the merely commonplace.

> The word as work therefore never directly offers a guarantee as to whether it is an essential word or a delusion. On the contrary—an essential word often looks in its simplicity like an inessential one. And what on the other hand gives itself, in its finery, the look of the essential is only said by rote or repeated. Thus is language ever obliged to place itself in a self-made seeming and thereby threaten what is most uniquely its own—true saying (*Sagen*). [E, 37]

The scope of the threat posed by language becomes clear. For, given the essential relation Heidegger sees between human beings and truth as unconcealment, language's ability to lie can threaten us with the loss of our very nature, and this is the risk he has in mind when he speaks of "the danger." Hölderlin recognized the danger; indeed he was quite explicit about it; it therefore supplies one further justification for selecting Hölderlin as the paradigmatic poet.

The Role of Poetry

Two further guiding statements furnish additional insight into the essence of poetry as exemplified by Hölderlin. Here, from an unfinished poem, is the first:

Viel hat erfahren der Mensch.
Der Himmlischen viele genannt,
Seit ein Gespräch wir sind
Und hören können voneinander.

Much has man experienced,
Many of the heavenly ones has he named,
Since we have been a conversation
And can listen to one another.

The significance of the lines becomes apparent only when Heidegger
goes on to assert that "the Being of man is grounded in language; but
this really happens only in conversation" (E, 38). Most of us would
probably approach the issue the other way round, speaking first of
conversation, then of the grounding of conversation in language. Heidegger proceeds as he does, not because he attributes primacy to
speaking, but rather because, in view of the fact that we speak precisely
to be heard, speaking and hearing are equally original (in the more
technical language that he still sometimes employs, they are "equipri-
mordial"). Being original here means, roughly, participating in a
beginning and preserving that beginning, a continuity of performance
that points both to the power that speaking and hearing possess (an
indication of their Being) and to the duration in which they are carried on
(an indication of their temporality).

The simultaneous emphasis on Being and time also stands behind
Heidegger's attempt to seek out the implications of the opening word
"since," an attempt that goes some way toward clarifying what he
means when he speaks of history and the historical. The path of his
thought starts from the juncture in which what is spoken is one and the
same as what is heard; the juncture, in other words, is the coming-
together in time and Being—the historical unity—of conversation itself,
which sustains our Being-there (E, 39).

One and the same can be disclosed, however, only in the context of
what persists and endures, which in turn comes to appearance only
when illumined by the present. Such an oscillating interdependence
appears paradoxical to our conceptual grammar, which cannot easily
accommodate the idea of a beginning that has no cause but rather issues
forth, tautologically, from itself; but it is no more paradoxical, in a
fundamental sense, than the relation between constancy and change:

From the time man places himself in the present (Gegenwart) of
something enduring, only from then can he expose himself to the
changeable, the coming and the going; for only the perpetual is
changeable. . . . We have been a conversation since the time that
"time is." Since time has arisen and been brought to standing,

since then we have been historical. Both—Being-a-conversation and Being-historical—are equally old, belong together, and are the same. [E, 39–40]

Heidegger never deals with the theme of reconciliation central to the poem, nor does he take advantage of the temporal structure which, as Else Buddeberg has shown, the dialectically inclined Hölderlin has carefully worked out.[3] In Hölderlin's visionary plan of history, the first coming of Christ brings to a close the epoch of the ancient gods, an event recreated by the poet in his own present in expectation of the future moment in which the savior will return. The structure evidently invites comparison with the three ecstases of temporality worked out in *Being and Time*, and yet Heidegger forbears. The reason, I believe, is that the circularity of Hölderlin's structure takes precedence in Heidegger's thinking over its division into parts. In other words, without denying that Hölderlin sees time unfolding in phases, Heidegger infers from the very circularity of the structure that time is ultimately a synchronous phenomenon and that the time it takes for Christ to return, and for the poet to project that return, is, as it were, all the same time. In Heidegger's commentary, "the present of the gods and the appearing of the world are not merely a series of speech events, they are therewith synchronous" (E, 40). The crucial premise—unacknowledged and perhaps unrecognized—is that, when the poet projects, he moves toward the future. Indeed, it is the *future* coming of Christ that makes that other coming a *first* coming, and it is in the light of that future that Hölderlin has a present. Like the *Dasein* described in *Being and Time*, Hölderlin is in this sense always ahead of himself, and by definition "the 'ahead-of-itself' is grounded in the future" (SZ, 327/374).

Equally crucial, and in this case explicit, is the assumption that history is coeval with language. With the naming of the gods the world is constituted so that Being-a-conversation and Being-historical are the same. But the relation of the gods to those who name them is itself circular, for naming responds to an appeal from the gods, who lay upon us their claim to be at the same time that, by letting themselves be named, they bring to language the very beings who name them. This is one way in which Heidegger attempts to erase both cause-effect relationships—and, with them, the notion of time as necessarily consecutive and developmental—and the idea that an origin is something in the past. In the origin that Heidegger depicts, based as it is on the poet's projection from his present of a past already shaped by the future, it is as if the gods, in their being named, already are. But that is

3. Else Buddeberg, "Heidegger und die Dichtung: Hölderlin," *Deutschevierteljahrsschrift für Literaturwissenschaft und Geistesgeschichte* 26 (1952): 312–18.

not very different from holding, as Heidegger does in *Being and Time*, that "*Dasein*'s totality of Being" means, in part, "ahead-of-itself-already-being-in (a world)." In its own way the world, like *Dasein*, is thrown, and, as in the case of *Dasein*, there is no thrower, which is to say no prime mover, but only something like an element in which the throwing occurs; and that element is language. (The question of the element and the elemental will be treated at length in chapter 5.)

If language is understood as naming, as seems to be the case in the present text, then it is in order to ask who does the naming. The answer lies in Heidegger's exploration of the guiding statement that reads: "But what endures, is founded by the poets" ("Was bleibet aber, stiften die Dichter") (E, 40). "What endures" could designate anything that already is or, in the vocabulary of *Being and Time*, anything that is present-at-hand, but Heidegger rejects such an approach as smacking of metaphysics. I refer again to the convention, within metaphysics, of concentrating on beings to the neglect of inquiring into what it is that "accounts" for them; and that is Being. Similarly, things that are named cannot be some mere beings that we happen upon and to which we then attach a word:

> The poet names the gods and names all things as what they are. This naming does not consist in supplying with a name something already known, but, in that the poet speaks the essential word, the being is first named to what it is through this naming. Thus it becomes known as a being. Poetry is the founding of Being through words. [E, 41]

Poetic founding, as suggested in *The Origin of the Work of Art*, occurs in a time that, open toward what is yet to come, is not cut off from what is and has been; for, as a leap, every leap is a fore-leap, every start a head start in a race that is already being run. Thus, if poetic founding initiates, it initiates (as it were) what Being has already begun.

Just as important as the reciprocity of gods and men, noted above, is the founding that occurs through naming:

> But because the gods were originally named and the essence of things comes to words, so that the things first shine forth, because such happens, the Being-there of man is brought into a solid relation and placed on a ground. The saying *(Sagen)* of the poet is founding, not only in the sense of a free gift, but at the same time in the sense of a solid grounding of human Being-there on its ground. [E, 41]

This gift, which comes not from a creator but from Being itself, may be thought of as a requirement, because poets could not name if there were nothing to name and also because (a more surprising thought, first articulated, as far as I am aware, in *An Introduction to Metaphysics*) Being needs beings (specifically, human beings) as the scene of its disclosure. To put it another way, language comes into the world through Being that comes into the world through language.

The final guiding statement at which we must look, "Full of merit, yet poetically / Man dwells on this earth" (E, 42), points directly to the grounding of human being, but, even more than that, it implies that poetry itself constitutes the ground. Heidegger expands on the idea in a passage that echoes *The Origin of the Work of Art*:

> Poetry is the founding naming of Being and of the essence of all things—no arbitrary saying *(Sagen)*, but that through which there first comes into the open all that which we then, in everyday language, talk about and handle. Therefore poetry never takes up language as a material that is present-at-hand, but poetry itself first makes language possible. Poetry is the primal language *(Ursprache)* of an historical people. [E, 43]

But for poets great risks are involved in caring for the gift of Being. In a letter to a friend, Hölderlin expresses the fear that he will receive from the gods more than he can bear; in the feast-day hymn, to which Heidegger will later devote an essay, the poet is called upon to heed the divine and to pass on to the people the heavenly gift; and finally, on returning, insane, to his mother's home, Hölderlin declares that, like a hero of old, he has been struck by Apollo. The summary Heidegger offers is itself poetic: "The too great light has plunged the poet into the dark" (E, 44). From Hölderlin's remark that Oedipus perhaps had one eye too many, Heidegger infers that Hölderlin, far from missing the plenitude of existence, suffered from an excess of it. The thinker can then ask rhetorically: "Or do we recognize that this poet in the ground and in the middle of Being thinks poetically from an excess of pressure?" (E, 47). Whereas Sartre moves from the desire for plenitude to an anatomy of scarcity,[4] Heidegger explores what might be called the territory between much and too much. There is in Heidegger a good deal of that classical temper that favors balance and restraint. Even the oppositions in Heidegger—as acute as they are—have a kind of discretion, as though out of respect for the others' "difference."

But in recognizing the excess that forces Hölderlin to break as a man, Heidegger must avoid making the crisis too subjective, for fear of falling into psychologism or committing some form of that biographical

---

4. Jean-Paul Sartre, *Theory of Practical Ensembles*, vol. 1 of *Critique of Dialectical Reason*, trans. Alan Sheridan Smith (London: NLB, 1976), pp. 122 ff.

fallacy that Sigurd Burckhardt exposes in his theory of intrinsic interpretation.[5] Heidegger tries to solve the problem by relating the poet to
his time: "Destitute is the time, and therefore the poet is too rich—so
rich that he could sink from weariness in thinking of past ones and in
waiting for those to come, and sleep in this apparent emptiness" (E, 47).
In contrast to the previous excess, this one has an aura of futurity
arising not only from the fact that the time needs him but also from the
fact that he is rich and the fact that poetic founding of Being is at once a
giving and an origin.

The Identity of the Poet

Heidegger does not think through, with equal rigor, the problem of
who the poet finally is. The essay offers, according to my count, no less
than four identities responsible for the poems, and it is the discussion
of the danger of poetry that brings this into focus. Suddenly Hölderlin
emerges as a historical person in a more or less conventional sense. To
be sure, Heidegger had earlier mentioned a few dates and had also, for
example, identified the source of a passage as a letter from the poet to a
friend. But in the present context Hölderlin is much more vividly present. He is that man who went mad at a certain time and returned to his
mother's house; the emergence is all the more vivid for furnishing the
basis on which Heidegger proves that poetry is a dangerous occupa-
tion: for the first time, and at the crucial point of an important argument, Heidegger goes outside the texts. If nothing else, this departure
makes it easier to see that "Hölderlin himself" has two counterparts,
one called "Hölderlin," the other "the poet." "Hölderlin" resembles the
incarnate author depicted by Georges Poulet. He is the being who composed the texts under discussion, a being whose existence in a certain
period is presupposed but not exploited. Since this being is the sole
source of the unity of the canon, all that is said in a given work is said
by the author, without the mediation of characters or *personae*. And,
just as Poulet tends to ignore possible differences between the viewpoint of an author and a character created by an author, so Heidegger
tends to ignore possible differences between "Hölderlin" and the
speaker in a given poem.

A third type is simply "the poet," who is not quite Hölderlin *tout
court* and who may or may not be "the poet himself" (E, 56). In these
fluid conceptions are intermingled a view of the poet *in esse*; a view of
poets, in the plural, as all those beings who name all things, as well as

5. Sigurd Burckhardt, "Notes on the Theory of Intrinsic Interpretation," appears as an
appendix to his *Shakespearean Meanings*, ed. R. C. Elliott and R. H. Pearce (Princeton:
Princeton University Press, 1968), pp. 285–313.

the holy, and a view of Friedrich Hölderlin as poet. The poet per se has the same generalized quality as "poetry" and is not to be identified with a particular German who went insane and lived in his mother's house from a particular date—any more than "poetry" is to be identified with this or that particular piece of verse.

I do not suggest that the failure to think through these differences ruins the essay. These issues, it might be said, are ontic rather than ontological and should be left to literary history. Heidegger has a more important difference—the ontological difference—on his mind. From this point of view, the justification for letting Hölderlin become "the poet himself" is the desire to show that the issues being worked out in the essay are to be resolved in everyday life. What is most essential, Heidegger had suggested in the beginning of this essay and at the end of *The Origin of the Work of Art,* is that which forces us to decide whether we are to take poetry seriously in the future. That future, in the light of subsequent passages, is already the needful, the destitute time; and the proof that the issue is essential is that a great poet of this time was driven mad by the pressure to fill that need.

Heidegger's way of letting "Hölderlin himself" shade into "the poet" can be seen in the passage—following the section we have just discussed—in which he circles round to the problem of reconciling the idea of poetry as both innocent and dangerous:

> poetry is the "most innocent of all occupations." Hölderlin writes thus in a letter, not only to shield his mother, but because he knows that this harmless exterior belongs to the essence of poetry as the valley to the mountain; for how would this most dangerous work be performed and preserved if the poet were not "thrown out" (*Empedokles* III, 191) of everyday life and protected from this by the semblance of the harmlessness of his occupation? [E, 44–45]

More fundamental is the poet's role (and here poet is meant in a generic sense) as a mediator situated between the gods, who give signs to be passed on to a people, and that people. As befits the sometimes dangerous nature of the poet's work, the situation is a precarious one, looking back to the condition of thrownness described in *Being and Time* and forward to the process of being "thrown out between" (more of this later), which is the fate of Oedipus:

> Thus is the essence of poetry joined together with the laws—
> striving apart and together—of the godly signs and of the voice of the people. The poet himself stands between those—the gods, and these—the people. He is one who is thrown out—out into that "between," between gods and men. But only and for the first time is decided, in this between, who man is and where his *Dasein* is settled. [E, 46–47]

Nothing Heidegger says here is incompatible with the position articulated in *The Origin of the Work of Art*, but neither is the perspective
quite the same. In that other essay, art, artist, work of art, and audience
were considered equally primordial. Focusing, as promised, on origin,
Heidegger concluded that each of these was the origin of the others; and
in this context none necessarily took precedence. That essay, concluding with the argument that all art is in essence poetry, furnishes a point
of departure for the present one, which attempts to determine, in turn,
the essence of poetry. Because it does this through the work of a particular writer, the role of the artist—who had tended in the previous
essay to fade into "art" and the work of art—acquires a new prominence. If man as such lives *Geworfenheit*, the poet lives a kind of
Hinausgeworfenheit; he can be thrown out, however, only because there
is now something to be thrown out into or, better, thrown *between*. This
realm, limited at each of two extremes by a different type of presence,
appears at this point, I think, because Heidegger is turning to a particular text and must attend to the phenomena that there present themselves. Hölderlin deals with gods and men, the heavenly ones and the
people; so must Heidegger. For that matter, the positioning of the poet
between two differentiated limits of a realm conforms to the sense of
those late lines of the feast-day hymn in which the poet seizes the beam
from heaven in order to hand it on, wrapped in song, to the people.

In Hölderlin's "Remembrance" Heidegger finds a grammatical first person, in both the nominative and the dative case. A problem of identity
thus arises. Heidegger has rejected the biographical approach for fear
that the poem would be bound back to its historical source. From what
is given, he knows that the first-person speaker is, as usual, the poet.
But he also knows that the poem names other poets, as symbolized by
the ships to which the northeast wind promises fiery spirit and a good
voyage. The concluding strophe seems to equate another plural—the
men who went to India—with the ships and in turn with the poets, who
are now named for the first time. Heidegger therefore decides—
explicitly on the basis of the relation of this text to two other texts and
implicitly on the basis of what he has demonstrated about Hölderlin's
poetry elsewhere—that the ships are the German poets of the future
who say the holy and to whom the wind promises "the experience of
fire from heaven in the strange land" (E, 86). Thanks to this wind the
poets find themselves, not as discrete individuals, but in the common

> destiny of their historical essence. Because the northeast [wind]
> gives the guarantee of this destiny, it is the truth of the concealed
> essential will of this poet. Every time in the poem that Hölderlin

says *I* and *me*, he speaks as this poet. This holds good not only insofar as these "personal pronouns" occur in a poem composed by Hölderlin, but because this *remembrance* thinks back to the essential destiny of this poet and not to his "personal adventures." [E, 86]

While Heidegger talks overtly about the essential destiny, the movement of his words carries out an essentializing of their own. The turning point is the sentence ending with the words "of this poet." With this sentence the poets, plural, give way to the poet, singular, the grammatical difference testifying to an underlying sameness: all these poets are essentially this poet. The use of the genitive in the singular is understandable. It would have been difficult to show that numerous poets had the same essential will; the job is easier if all these poets are truly one. Heidegger goes a step further by focusing a double genitive—the truth *of* the concealed essential will *of* this poet—in a way that makes the truth seem indissociable from this poet and his way of willing. It develops that this particular will belongs less to the poet than to what is coming. It is the will *of* what is coming, says Heidegger, employing the genitive yet again in a movement of thought that brings us, in effect, through the poet to the point where "Will is the knowing readiness for participation in destiny" (E, 87).

This is not to say that the poetic speaker remains a nameless, faceless mediation. In clarifying the role of Bellarmin in relation to the journeying men and the theme of reversal in Hölderlin's novel *Hyperion*, Heidegger identifies Bellarmin as the recipient of the letters sent by Hyperion and quotes a passage in which Hyperion remarks that an admirable people is said to be concealed, hinting at the paradox, much probed by Heidegger, of something far which is yet near. Heidegger's attitude toward the identity of the speaker in *Hyperion* is more complex than it appears, however. He tacitly accepts Hyperion and Bellarmin as the speakers so named in *Hyperion*. That is, he accepts what an F. R. Leavis might call their "local" identity. But what Hyperion says is exactly apposite to what is said in "Remembrance." Indeed, Heidegger holds that in Hölderlin's *Hyperion* period the poet's voyage into the farthest remoteness spoken of in "Remembrance" is already under way. Hyperion's statement to Bellarmin is as essentially anonymous, if you will, as the utterances of all those other speakers who appear throughout the discussion without being named and who, for that matter, are not thought of as speakers. In other words, Heidegger regards Hyperion as a name for the poet *in esse*, as defined in the ever-developing context of his interpretation, more than as a character in a novel. This is the second identity of Hyperion, rooted in Heidegger's assumption of the essential unity of the world of Hölderlin, who, as the poet pre-occupied with poetry, brings out everywhere—to borrow from the title of the first Hölderlin essay examined here—the essence of poetry.

In his discussion of the dative *to me* in the opening strophe, Heidegger makes an advance on his previous suggestion that the speaker in the poems is sometimes Hölderlin himself.

> Who is it to whom this wind is the best loved? Who speaks here? Hölderlin himself. But who is Hölderlin here and now in his self? He who finds the fulfillment of his essence in "willing" that this wind be, and as what it is. What is thus admitted in the essential will of a self is the best loved. [E, 85]

Here Heidegger takes note of the biographical author without, as before, appealing to his existence in an evidently contradictory way. To say that the "me" in the poem is Hölderlin himself is to take for granted that Hölderlin, as author of the poem, somehow speaks in it. The basis for this assumption is twofold. On the one hand, it is certain that the work was composed by Friedrich Hölderlin. On the other hand, the assumption is supported by what might be called the contextual certainty that this poet—more than others—identifies himself as present because of his preoccupation with the role of the poet and with the poetic in its totality. But this "himself" is not the same "himself" presented in the previous essay. This "himself" is Hölderlin as "me." The other "himself" is genuinely other: he is that historical being whose personal sufferings as a man bear witness to the danger of poetry, and, as such, he stands apart from Heidegger's attempt to discover the happening of truth set in the work. The poet as "me" is the me *of* "Remembrance" in the genitive sense. He partakes of the poem as that in which he finds himself. When Heidegger comes to define his understanding of self, Hölderlin is no longer named; he has become "the one who," that is, he is essentialized in a manner specifically determined in the poem. His self is not something apart from the realization of his essence but is that realization itself; his willing is not a push but, like Coleridge's suspension, a kind of yielding cooperation. As Heidegger had explained in *Being and Time,* willing occurs only when something is willed, either as something to be cared about or to be brought with care or solicitude into itself. There is no gap or time-lag between the willing and what is willed, as in the case of my deciding to go to the theater this evening. The poet wills what is, *as* it is. Heidegger places quotation marks around the noun to show that he is borrowing the word from ordinary discourse until he can redefine it. This happens soon; indeed, in the clause immediately following, we can already see where Heideg-

ger is going, and our sense of the direction is reinforced by his emphasis, in the following sentence, on the essentiality of this will. It is reinforced further by the statement, already noted above, that "Will is the
knowing readiness for participation in destiny" and by Hölderlin's remark that he wills what is coming (E, 87).

Heidegger later identifies the knowing will with *Geist*, or spirit, despite the fact that he must introduce the term from another poem:
"Spirit loves colony, and valiant forgetting." So runs one line from a
late draft of the concluding strophe of the elegy "Bread and Wine."
Heidegger remarks: "The spirit is the knowing will, which thereupon
thinks that everything that may become and can be something real,
comes into the truth of its essence" (E, 90). We cannot here go into the
ramifications of Heidegger's introduction of *Geist* or the reintroduction,
by way of the feast-day hymn ("Wie wenn am Feiertage...") of the
concept of nature. But we may note Allemann's suggestion that Heidegger ironically accepts the leading presupposition of that literary
scholarship with whose procedures, in the present volume, he so vigor-
ously disagrees. This is the presupposition that Hölderlin's famous
"turning" *(Wendung)* takes place "in the realm of home and the foreign,
of Hesperia and Greece," whereas, for Beda Allemann, it occurs
"primarily between the realm of the mortals and that of the departed
gods, this and the other world."[6] What Hölderlin turns from is the
Empodeclean yearning for mystic unity with the All; what he turns to is
the "royal" *(königliche)*, the earthly, the human. Given Heidegger's belief in the fundamental unity of the Hölderlin canon, it is not surprising
that he brings other texts to bear. What is revealing is that he brings in
so many of them; that he brings them in early; and the extent to which
they help to focus the entire interpretation. This seems to suggest an
analogy with his handling of the biographical Hölderlin, whose appearance at a crucial juncture also coincided with an interruption of the
text at hand. The analogy, however, is deceptive. By showing that Hölderlin actually suffered the kind of fate that poetry was said to have in
store, Heidegger underlined sameness: Hölderlin said what he lived
and lived what he said. But the introduction of various texts in Heidegger's discussion of "Remembrance" serves another purpose. To be sure,
Heidegger presupposes the underlying unity, and in this sense the
sameness, of all utterances. But he brings them in, at this point, to
establish difference. Eager to stress what is new in Hölderlin, he exag-
gerates what is old, not merely by introducing the concept of *Geist*, but
by interpreting it implicitly in the context of traditional Idealism. The
same desire stands behind the introduction of will, which readers of

6. Beda Allemann, *Hölderlin und Heidegger* (Zurich: Atlantis, 1956), p. 175.

Heidegger's voluminous writings on Nietzsche will be understandably inclined to associate with the latter and thus with the Western metaphysics from which Heidegger is trying to break away. And perhaps it is only through this need to clarify a difference he has magnified that Heidegger took up the issue of "self," left unclarified in the previous essay. Accordingly, Allemann concludes that Heidegger has brought Hölderlin back into a tradition from which he had departed in order to have a basis to start from: *reculer pour mieux sauter*. Having enlarged the idealistic in Hölderlin, Heidegger can go on to consider what it is that the poetry of Hölderlin begins.

The Holy

Near the end of his lecture on the feast-day hymn Heidegger, having erased the lines dividing the future from present and past, warns the reader against inferring that the essence of poetry is to be determined through timelessness:

> This essence of poetry belongs to a definite time. But not in such a way that it matches itself to this time as a time that already exists. On the contrary, in founding anew the essence of poetry, Hölderlin defines a new time. It is the time of the god who has fled and the god who is coming. [E, 47]

Heidegger terms this a destitute time because, with respect to deities, it languishes between a "no longer" and a "not yet." Though not identical with Hölderlin's time structure, which comes to a climax with the return of a deity, this position in time is not unlike that of the poet, who finds himself in a present, relating what has-been to a future. What is more, the decisive issues are the same: the importance of the presence of a god and the crisis precipitated by the god's absence. In this way Heidegger does, after all, acknowledge Hölderlin's vision of time; more important, by stressing futurity, which has figured so prominently since *Being and Time*, Heidegger underlines the prophetic strain in many of the poet's characteristic works, which become an appeal to readers for the better realization of their own possibilities.

One of the characteristic works is the stately feast-day hymn, which addresses anew the closely related phenomena of the holy and the gods. Heidegger's interpretation goes directly to the meaning of the word "nature" in the phrase "nature, the mighty, beautiful as a god" ("Die mächtige, die göttlichschöne Natur") (E, 49). This concentration on a single word—one of Heidegger's chief hermeneutic strategies—has drawn attention to itself, and it warrants further attention here. Allemann singles out, as characteristic of Heidegger's practice, the statement: "The inner movement of these three lines strives for and vibrates out from the word 'nature'" (E. 52). But to suggest, as Allemann does, that the whole of Heidegger's interpretation centers on this or that single word is misleading. Faced with a poem that compares the situation of poets with that of a man of the country and deals at length with weather and the earth, any interpreter must focus on the meaning of nature. Heidegger does this; but the meaning of nature is a point of departure for determining the meaning of the holy. It is as important to see where Heidegger goes as it is to see where he starts, and to this end it is well to remember that he discusses the poem in its entirety, even down to details of punctuation, and that this discussion emerges from the context of "Hölderlin and the Essence of Poetry." Furthermore, Heidegger does not speak idly when he refers to the inner movement of the lines he quotes. One arrives at the word "nature" in the second strophe by way of the twelve lines preceding as well as the thirteenth line, of which "nature" is the concluding word. The complex, suspensive hypotaxis brings us by way of the analogy with the man of the country to those (not yet identified as poets) who are brought up by "powerful, godly-beautiful nature." Heidegger, moreover, had drawn attention to the colon, which keeps the flow of the lines going on into the second strophe, and to the syntax, which, foreshadowing a comparison—"When, as . . . so"—unites the opening strophe with the following one or possibly, as Heidegger suggests, with all the following strophes. Although the phrase is admittedly imprecise, I therefore think it fair to say that we know reasonably well what Heidegger means when he speaks of an inner movement.

Heidegger's later focus on the conjunction "and" (in the passage on aether and abyss, cited above) is a wider focus than may at first appear: "This 'and' that follows the 'awakes' does not lead onward to an other which happens outside the awakening, even perchance as a result of it. The 'and' ushers in the disclosure of the essence of that which nature, as the awakening one, is" (E, 59–60; cf. H, 211). Heidegger does not bear down on the function of the word: it is plainly enough a copulative, signifying connection. Heidegger questions, rather, the *authenticity* of connection, which connotes the same objectionable yoking as the conventional subject-predicate structure. Heidegger interprets phenomenologically: encountering a poetic movement in which a word does what it does and not what it is supposed to do, he puts brackets around the lexical definition, the better to hear what he is hearing. It may be objected that he cannot derive so much from a single word. I agree, for the point I am leading to is that Heidegger follows through an entire movement to which the single word provides an access. The isolated word, once it has emerged, slips back into the movement and

ceases to be isolated. Indeed, one may doubt whether it was ever as
isolated as it may have appeared and as Allemann seems to imply. The
problem, I think, is simply that a movement cannot be interpreted *ab
ovo* as a whole without starting somewhere. Here, as in the hermeneutic circle, it is a question of entering at the right place; and the right
place for Heidegger is often the individual word, which is less a point,
in the sense of a discrete locus, as it is, again, a point of departure and
hence another form of beginning.

In Heidegger's view Hölderlin's "nature" does not mean what it
seems to mean; that is, it does not denote the nonhuman world of the
present-at-hand (in the terminology of *Being and Time*). The feast-day
hymn is precisely an attempt to overcome nature in this sense, and it is
a successful attempt inasmuch as Hölderlin achieves another, better
meaning. Hölderlin showed his dissatisfaction with the standard concept of nature by writing some lines on the subject—in the hymn "At
the Source of the Danube,"composed shortly after the feast-day
hymn—then canceling them; or such at least is the inference drawn by
the editor on whom Heidegger relied for many years. Heidegger concurs but argues that in the feast-day hymn the poet had already overcome the standard concept.

The demonstration requires two interpretative moves, the first of
which—not surprisingly, in the light of Heidegger's pre-Socratic
preferences—compares Hölderlin's nature with the early Greek *physis*.
Heidegger sees the poet as somehow guided by the hidden truth of that
word, even though Hölderlin was no more equal to its full power than
his successors and readers, presumably including Heidegger himself.
Therefore the relation between *physis* and Hölderlin's nature remains,
by Heidegger's own admission, obscure. What Heidegger does bring
out is that the poet has in mind something that is "other" than *physis*,
fully understood, and yet linked to it. That "other" becomes, in a second interpretative move, the holy. The reading finds support in the
third stanza, when the poet, at break of day, beholds the engendering
of nature from "the holy chaos." When the poet also declares nature to
be older than time and superior to the gods, Heidegger infers that the
holy that nature names must be prior in two senses of precedence: first
in time and first in rank. The holy begins to remind us of the Heraclitean vision of primordial conflict (Hölderlin's nature, aroused by the
noise of weapons, is pointedly militant), a resemblance that, though
unacknowledged by Heidegger, hardly seems accidental in light of the
attention he pays to that vision in *An Introduction to Metaphysics*. "Hölderlin calls nature the holy, because she is 'older than the times and
over the gods.' ... The holy is the essence of nature" (E, 59). As noted
above, Heidegger speaks in *An Introduction to Metaphysics* of the need

Being has of a scene for its own disclosure, a scene furnished by *Dasein* or, perhaps better, by its involvement with *Dasein*. The equivalent in the present discussion is the clearing the holy provides so that there can be an openness through which everything real can emerge.

The holy becomes practically synonymous with Being, which means that Hölderlin has overcome the standard concept, and which suggests a parallel with the thinker who seeks to overcome metaphysics and thereby inaugurate a saying with a greater capacity for beginning *(eines anfänglicher anhebenden Sagens)* (E, 58) and a thinking with a comparable power. Buddeberg, who has drawn attention to the parallel, also wonders why Heidegger does not make a connection between the time scheme he sees in the poem and his own analysis of temporality in *Being and Time*. The crucial passage treats the problem of time:

> Before and over everything else, nature is in the manner of "some day" *(wie einst)*. It is some day in a double sense. It is older than everything previous and younger than everything later. In that nature awakes, its coming comes, as what is most future-laden, out of what has been for the longest time *(aus dem ältesten Gewesenen)*, and that never ages because it is ever the youngest. [E, 63]

The ambiguous phrase *wie einst*, which can refer to some day in the past or to some future day, is what Heidegger elsewhere calls the basic expression *(Grundwort)* of the passage, which, in its deliberate blurring of times, recalls Heidegger's treatment of time in "Hölderlin and the Essence of Poetry." It echoes, again, the passage from *Being and Time*: "Temporalizing does not signify that ecstases comes in a 'succession.' The future is *not later* than having been, and having been is *not earlier* than the Present. Temporality temporalizes itself as a future which makes present in the process of having been" (SZ, 350/401). The previously cited passage demonstrates just this, it would seem, in a manner that, if not entirely clear, is at least vivid and forceful. With his ambiguous phrase Hölderlin has provided a poetic response to the question with which *Being and Time* closes: "Does *time* itself manifest itself as the horizon of *Being*?" (SZ, 437/488).

There may be at least two considerations that led Heidegger to avoid making explicit the relation between the earlier account and his evocation of time as rendered poetically by Hölderlin. One is that the relation is so thoroughly presupposed that it need not be stated. A second reason, of a more strategic character, is that drawing the interpretation of Hölderlin into the sphere of *Being and Time* could diminish the effect, which Heidegger is trying so hard to achieve, of a beginning saying to which his own beginning thinking is parallel. Making the connection would have aided clarity, which is rarely a main goal in Heidegger, at the expense of the tension and concentration that are a kind of qualitative evidence that the thinker is genuinely on his way.

In *The Origin of the Work of Art* poetry was examined within a fourfold of art, artist, work of art, and audience. In the present lecture we have, by contrast, the poet, the god, and the holy. Now the poet, thrown out in between, with the gods on one side and mortals on the other, has the most direct contact with the holy: in Hölderlin's words, he is struck by the holy beam. This contact is not enough, however: the poet must do something on his own, despite the fact that—given the remoteness of the holy—there seems little enough that he is capable of doing. Wordsworth, we may recall, felt the influence of a hallowed nature not only as something coming from outside but as a correspondent breeze arising spontaneously from within. This spontaneity is perhaps the feature that most distinguishes Wordsworth's attitude from Hölderlin's. In Wordsworth the inner action just happens: of a sudden, and on its own, the breeze occurs. But in Hölderlin the reciprocity brings the poet more directly into the process by which the togetherness of gods and men comes to appearance:

> When now the holy beam strikes the poet, he is not transported into the glow of the beam, but is completely turned back toward the holy. The soul of the poet "trembles," to be sure, and thus allows the stilled in itself to waken; but it trembles from recollection, which means from the expectation of what happened before; which is the self-opening of the holy. The shock breaks the calm of silence. The word becomes. The word-work thus emerging lets the belonging-together of gods and of men appear. [E, 69]

There is a Longinian flavor in this, a grandeur and a certain loftiness—in short, an aura of the sublime. The presence of dread, so evident in *Being and Time* and in Rilke's Malte, gives way to the presence of an awe recalling the *mysterium tremendum* of Rudolf Otto's investigation of the holy, which also focuses, as Heidegger had done, on the phenomenon of the uncanny.[7] Equally important, the holy is an *a priori* category, as Otto demonstrates by arguing from the same Kantian principles that helped Heidegger to find structures of transcendence in the relation of Being to time.

> Heidegger is much less preoccupied than Kant with discovering and tabulating the various *a priori* [e.g., formal, material, con-

7. Rudolf Otto, *The Idea of the Holy: An Inquiry into the Non-Rational Factor in the Idea of the Divine and Its Relation to the Rational,* trans. John W. Harvey, 2d ed. (1923; rpt. New York: Oxford University Press, 1950). On *mysterium tremendum* see pp. 12 ff.; on the holy as *a priori,* pp. 122 ff.; on the uncanny, which Otto also discusses in relation to *deinon* and *Antigone* (two points of focus in *An Introduction to Metaphysics*), see pp. 39–40.

stitutive]. . . . Thus, though he has shown that man's commerce with beings [*l'étant*] requires a pre-conception of Being, instead of elucidating this pre-conception or showing its historical modalities, he prefers to define it as the truth that is the ground of all truth and to identify it with Being. The *a priori* becomes the manifestation in man of the movement by which Being is revealed and, in being revealed, is constituted as time. It therefore expresses the finitude of man, the central theme of Heidegger's existential analytic. This theme possesses undeniable theological echoes—not because the finitude of the creature is measured by the infinity of the creator, but because a) this finitude is the fact of Being in man, b) Being as transcendence achieves in man the act of transcending, and c) man with his future is only the instrument or the witness of an adventure of Being.[8]

The role of instrument and witness makes man more passive than I believe Heidegger wants him to be, though the human role becomes more problematic with the thinker's later development, partly under the influence of Meister Eckhart, of a disposition toward a releasement that carries the idea of letting-be about as far as it would seem plausibly to go. In the passage from Heidegger quoted above, in any case, the apparent passivity of the start gives away toward a more active attitude in the second sentence, where he allows what is already present to return to itself, the implication being that this instance of letting-be is a necessary condition of such a return.

Mediation in any form presents a danger just because it is mediation. Here, the danger is that the holy, by going through something other than itself, may cease to be itself. Turning again to *An Introduction to Metaphysics*, we see a parallel with Being, which needs a scene comprising all entities that can emerge as a world. Being must go through something other than itself in a struggle to remain itself, a struggle carried out against the violence wrought by human beings, who, for their part, struggle to bring Being forth through themselves and all things.

The power that Being has is, of course, overpowering, so that Being remains itself; and the holy does the same. The effect of the threat to the holy is, finally, to dramatize its perdurance in the form of "the everlasting heart *(ewige Herz)*" (E, 73), which is deeply shaken by the holy beam but not consumed by it. A phrase such as this, occurring only one time in the entire Hölderlin canon, is an advantage to the interpreter in the same way as an isolated word or fragment. It provides the opportunity to discover not certainties or probabilities but possibilities, in short, the

8. Mikel Dufrenne, *The Notion of the "A Priori,"* trans. Edward S. Casey (Evanston: Northwestern University Press, 1966), p. 28.

opportunity to make of it an occasion for a new beginning. In Heidegger's conception, we remember, a beginning keeps on starting, as it were; that is, preserving what begins belongs to its beginning. In the present case Heidegger has begun by uncovering the idea of the holy in Hölderlin's nature, whereupon the unique phrase yet again uncovers the same, permitting him to "keep on starting" so as to preserve the movement of his thought.

Hölderlin does make one restriction when he states that the everlasting heart shares a god's suffering; hence the heart should not be construed as the heart of a god. Heidegger goes a step further and infers (silently) that it is not a human heart, either—a bigger step in light of the fact that in the preceding stanza the poets seize the holy beam in order to pass the heavenly gift to the people. This would point to the likelihood, all other things being equal, that the heart is human. But, far from being equal, things are now pretty well balanced in favor of the holy, which Heidegger sees not merely as the predominant theme of the poem but as a kind of presence suffusing the text with its uniqueness. The uniqueness of the phrase "the everlasting heart" becomes a testimony to the fact that this presence is there to be experienced until the end.

I am not sure that Heidegger strengthens his case, however, when he turns to the poet's marginalia. "In crude, excited handwriting the following note is set on the inner margin of the concluding verse:

> Die / Sphäre / die höher / ist, als /
> die des Menschen / diese ist der Gott."

> [The sphere which is higher than the sphere of men,
> this is the god.]

Heidegger interprets the remark to say:

> The higher sphere, the holy beam, threatens even the holy still more deeply with the loss of its essence. But this sphere too is only "the higher," not "the highest." Thus what arises from origin can do nothing against origin. And therefore "the eternal heart," although "deeply shaken," remains "yet firm." [E, 74]

Clearly, the marginal note has some bearing on the poem; whether it has quite the bearing Heidegger gives it is less clear. The difficulty, for me, is not that Heidegger goes "outside" the poem to another text. For one thing, it is always difficult to know exactly what is meant by "outside." But even if we take the word in its common acceptance, we have not got very far, since Heidegger fully accounts for the provenience of his expanded text, and since he is happy to admit that he understands differently—though not necessarily better—than the author.[9] One problem is that Heidegger does not develop his argument to the extent that one would have expected, given the fact he has arrived at a crucial point in his interpretation. A second problem is that, at precisely this point, he slips, in effect, from *Geschichte* to *Historie*. In "Hölderlin and the Essence of Poetry" he turned at a sensitive moment to the biographical figure of conventional literary scholarship, with which he is usually little concerned. The present description of Hölderlin's handwriting is an appeal to the same type of support. This does not mean that Heidegger errs fatally by commenting on the appearance of the script or that its appearance is without relevance. The problem is that he asks for more support from the biographical, "historical" quarter than his own hermeneutic principles give him a right to expect and that this quarter is appealed to at a time when the reader is expecting Heidegger to be fully Heideggerian. It would have been more helpful if he had delved into the relation of the higher to the highest, tying this presentation of the latter into an earlier passage on "the highest" by Hölderlin, and if, in lieu of the merely negative assertion that the higher sphere can do nothing against origin, he had stated more affirmatively and more fully why this is the case. The situation is made the more vexing by the notorious difficulty of deciphering Hölderlin manuscripts. Distinguishing the mere jottings and afterthoughts from passages that could furnish major variants is hard enough; to single out an entry as having been emotionally written—rather than having been written in haste or by a hand shaking from physical fatigue—is harder still. Such stretching is prompted, I believe, by the perception of an unspoken parallel between Hölderlin's suffering and the suffering of the everlasting heart—a parallel that, if made explicit, would have had to be reconciled with the assignment of the heart to the holy. But Heidegger is intent, we must remember, upon bringing forth what is unsaid, even unthought, in the poet's words, and this, he believes, is nothing less than the unique suffusing presence of the holy. Because the holy is prior, in the senses noted above, the suffering it undergoes must be of the most fundamental kind, connected in the most binding way with the process of beginning:

> In that the holy bestows itself through the beam's decisiveness, which is suffering, the holy remains in the truth of its essence and

9. Cf. Kurt Mueller-Vollmer, "To Understand an Author Better Than the Author Himself: The Hermeneutics of the Unspoken," *Language and Style* 5 (Winter 1971): 43–52; David Halliburton, "The Hermeneutics of Suspicion and the Hermeneutics of Belief," *Diacritics* 6 (Winter 1976): 2–9.

thus suffers in a beginning way. . . . Suffering is remaining stead-
fast in beginning. [E, 75]

Such suffering, *Leid*, is an essential pathos like the passion,
Leidenschaft, attributed in *An Introduction to Metaphysics* to Oedipus,
who embodies the passion for the disclosure of Being. The difference is
that, in the present account, the passion belongs to what is being disclosed: it is the passion of the holy itself. The passion reflects the experience of preparing for the coming of a deity, which the holy
mediates by holding itself open as the realm of possibility within which
such a coming could occur.

> The holy names the dispositional capacity in all that is other than
> the deity to receive the appearances of the divine presence. . . . The
> divine is what it is because it is holy in that all the attributes of
> the deity's presence capable of being perceived must appear
> *through* a medium which is receptive and disposed to such ap-
> pearances. This medium is the holy.[10]

The poetry of Hölderlin orients the reader to a future in which the
current epoch, in the manner appropriate to it, may discover the presence of a deity as, in Heidegger's view, all epochs have done in their
own way. The poet reveals the way in which the holy grounds that
beginning of which Heidegger offered a glimpse in "Hölderlin and the
Essence of Poetry": "The holy . . . grounds in its coming another beginning of another history. The holy decides in a beginning way, regarding men and gods, as to whether they are and who they are and how
they are and when they are" (E, 76). Heidegger now brings in the
literary notion of genre only to surpass it. Hölderlin's feast-day hymn is
a hymn in a new sense. It is not a hymn "to" poets or to nature; it is the
hymn "of" the holy. To say that Hölderlin's hymn is "to" someone or
something is to distance it from that to which it belongs. Such a poem
can only "relate to," as subject relates to object. By employing the genitive, Heidegger hints at a subtler type of relationship, a kind of hidden,
essential bonding between, on the one hand, the word and the holy
and, on the other, between Being and being. "The holy bestows the
word and comes itself in this word. The word is the occurrence of the
holy" (E, 76).

The poem accomplishes all this despite the fact that it is incomplete.
One cannot be sure, for example, about the proper shape of the conclusion, which had not been decided upon by Hölderlin. Indeterminacy,
with which Heidegger is rarely comfortable, and decision, which he

---

10. David White, *Heidegger and the Language of Poetry*, p. 127. Cf. Jacques Derrida,
L'Ecriture et la différence (Paris: Seuil, 1967), p. 215 (English translation by Alan Bass,
Writing and Difference [Chicago: University of Chicago Press, 1978], pp. 145–46).

sees as requiring the resoluteness of a *Dasein* relating properly to its own possibilities, come together here in a significant way. The problem Heidegger indirectly sets himself is how to overcome this indeterminacy without the help of the poet's own decision. He makes a first step toward a solution by separating indeterminacy from insufficiency. Far from suffering from any lack, the poem is a plenitude, its incompleteness being "the result of the overflow that wells up from the innermost beginning of the poem and claims the conclusive summary" (E, 75). Such overflow is the corollary of the theory of excess in *The Origin of the Work of Art,* as it is the corollary also of the too-bright light and sheer pressure suffered by the poet in "Hölderlin and the Essence of Poetry."[11] The smiling aspect of the latter excess, we recall, was the overripe condition that makes the poet indispensable in a destitute time. But when the issue of excess arises in the context of the present hymn, it is less in relation to the poet's condition or qualitative state than to what the poet—or, in this context, the poets—perform: "The abundance of what begins gives to their word the excess of meaning which can scarcely be said" (E, 66). If the type of plenitude emphasized in "Hölderlin and the Essence of Poetry" characterizes the poet himself, the type just presented characterizes not so much the poem itself as the relation of its saying to all that remains to be said. The poem readies a beginning. But when Heidegger makes this the beginning *of* the poem, through the use of the genitive, he does not refer to the initial portion of the text; he indicates rather that the poem in its entirety is indissociable from the beginning in the same way as the genre of the hymn is indissociable from the holy.

What particular decisions the poet made about this or that phase of the poem matter less than the fact that the poem is itself a decision in behalf of beginning; in the same way, Heidegger will assert, in the section that follows, that the poem "Homecoming" *is* the homecoming which it is apparently "about." "Hölderlin's word says the holy and thus names the space of time, happening only once, of the beginning decision for the essential structure of the future history of the gods and of mankind" (E, 77).

Homecoming

Such decisions are necessary because, as the introduction to *Being and Time* declares, the question of the meaning of Being has been forgotten.

11. In *Truth and Method,* trans. Garrett Barden and John Cumming (New York: Seabury, 1975), Hans-Georg Gadamer argues (p. 124) that a painted picture, as a representation of some original entity, possesses its own reality, such that the original experiences "an increase in being. The particular import of the picture is determined ontologically as an emanation of the original."

In a broad sense, the discussion that follows this pronouncement is devoted to the theme of remembrance that persists throughout Heidegger's career and that provides the main interest in his interpretation of Hölderlin's poem of the same name. Remembrance and forgetting are not conceived of, however, as mere opposites, nor is the former deemed positive and the latter negative. On the contrary, forgetting is "a 'positive ecstatical mode of one's having been' which permits *Dasein* to back away in order to recover what it was. Just as expecting is possible only on the basis of awaiting, *remembering* is possible only on that of forgetting, *and not vice versa*" (SZ, 339/389).

Forgetting, in turn, is directly related to homecoming, as the "Letter on Humanism" points out: "The nearness 'of' Being, as that which the 'there' of Being-there is, is thought of, in the commemorative address on Hölderlin's elegy 'Homecoming' (1943), from the standpoint of *Being and Time* . . . and is named, from the experience of the forgetting of Being, 'home'" (W, 337–38). This orientation disposes Heidegger, at first, toward the darker aspects of the poem's basic mood, notwithstanding that it has much of the celebratory and prophetic aura we find in other works classified as odes or hymns. I have in mind, in particular, "Celebration of Peace" ("Friedensfeier"), which was probably completed in the same year, 1801, as "Homecoming" and was inspired, even more than "Homecoming," by the Treaty of Lunéville, which Hölderlin believed would initiate an epoch of peace and harmony for his homeland and for all of Europe. A similar spirit pervades "Homecoming," which is prompted by the poet's return from Switzerland to his residence in Swabia. Yet the poem contains an unmistakable elegiac strain, not least when the author laments the absence of names for the holy, wonders how he can offer thanks for the blessings bestowed upon him and his countrymen, and acknowledges that the care that burdens him as poet separates him from them.

Given the prominence of care in *Being and Time*, it is not surprising that Heidegger begins with the last stanza of the poem:

> Schweigen müssen wir oft; es fehlen heilige Nahmen,
> Herzen schlagen und doch bleibet die Rede zurük?
> Aber ein Saitenspiel leiht jeder Stunde die Töne,
> Und erfreuet vieleicht Himmlische, welche sich nahn.
> Das bereitet und so ist auch beinahe die Sorge
> Schon befriediget, die unter das Freudige kam.
> Sorgen, wie diese, muss, gern oder nicht, in der Seele
> Tragen ein Sänger und oft, aber die anderen nicht.

> Often we must be silent; sacred names are lacking,
>   Hearts beat and yet speech fails?
> But poetic song lends its tones to every hour,

And brings joy perhaps to the heavenly who approach.
Let that be made ready, and so this care also will almost be
Removed, which arose in the midst of our joy.
Such cares as these, whether gladly or not, a singer must
Bear in his soul, and often, but not the others.[12]

Although the poem deals with homecoming, "the final strophe, being in the mood of 'care,' betrays nothing of the happiness of one who returns home carefree (sorglos). The final word of the poem is a sudden 'no.' But the first strophe, which names the alpine mountains, stands there—itself a mountain of verses—unmediated" (E, 13). The passage invites close study. Allemann would emphasize that Heidegger focuses once more on the individual word. But I would add, enlarging on a point made above, that Heidegger singles out the words for their singularity and that this singularity emerges in the context of the entire poem in which the above-noted "negative" features are unexpected. This poem, and other poems in varying degrees, has a certain quality of negativity: the poem celebrates the joyful event of coming home, but . . . Heidegger attempts to alert the reader to this quality not only by explicit argumentation but by a kind of tonal evocation of mood. The opening word of the first sentence quoted above is "yet," and the conjunction in the opening phrase of the third sentence quoted is "but" (aber). What is more, the concluding strophe is gestimmte, that is, literally, "tuned," around care, the parent word being Stimmung, or mood, so that the translators of Being and Time turn gestimmt, in most cases, into "have a mood." But here, at any rate, the resonance of the stem word and its permutations is such that a variety of overtones is potentially present. One hears not only Stimme or voice when Heidegger speaks of the poet's relation to his people (E, 46) but all these words— bestimmen, bestimmt, Unbestimmtheit—that cover the range of the determinate and indeterminate. This is permissible because he is thinking poetically, and the extent to which one ought to hear certain echoes is often simply unclear. Here we might mention the case of stehen, "to stand," which at one time functions in a conventional denotative manner and at another is richly evocative. In "Hölderlin and the Essence of Language," language stands good for (guarantees) man's historicity. In the feast-day hymn the word "field" stands for all whereon and wherein man lives; while in his discussion of that poem the second type of usage occurs: "Now must [the poets] stand there, where the holy itself . . . opens itself" (E, 71), whereas earlier in the essay poets are those who "stand" in favorable weather (E, 58). At the same time, Heidegger seems hesitant about borrowing too freely from his own

12. The translation, by Cyrus Hamlin, appears in *Friedrich Hölderlin: An Early Modern*, ed. Emery E. George (Ann Arbor: University of Michigan Press, 1972), p. 231.

philosophical treatise. One reason is that he is not directly concerned, here, with that type of discourse; and he has challenges enough without implying that he is fighting his battle with metaphysics in exactly the same terms as the ones employed in *Being and Time*. He *is* fighting the battle, but the terms have altered, which leads me to my second point: namely, that Heidegger is still developing a language particularly suited to the interweaving of poetry and thinking and that he recognizes that he can do this by stretching the language he has inherited and has already in some sort modified, not by abandoning or merely extending it.

Equally deserving of close examination is Heidegger's interpretation of the poem's opening lines:

> Drinn in den Alpen ists noch helle Nacht und die Wolke,
> Freudiges dichtend, sie dekt drinnen das gähnende Thal.

> There in the Alps it is still bright night, and the cloud,
> Poetically uttering the joyous, covers the night within the gaping
>   valley.

Heidegger comments:

> The cloud lets itself be seen by the open brightness. The cloud speaks poetically *(dichtet)*. Since it looks at that by which it is itself looked at, what it speaks poetically is not vainly conceived and found out *(erfunden)*. Poetic speaking *(Dichten)* is a finding *(Fund)*. And thereby must the cloud freely go out beyond itself to what is not itself. What is spoken poetically emerges only from the cloud. What is spoken poetically does not come out of the cloud. It comes over it as that which the cloud lingers against. [E, 15–16]

Poetic speaking, like the painting in *The Origin of the Work of Art*, does not create in the usual sense but *finds*, a concept that underlines the gratuitous aspect of art; for it is the cloud, rather than the poet, that makes the poetry here. The implication, I take it, is that poetry transpires less as an utterance than as a kind of ordering relation made possible by an inherent reciprocity between its speaking and what it speaks. The movement of the cloud, as depicted here, is a movement of transcendence, but transcendence is shown to require a field in which to realize itself, a something "other" whose presence forms a horizon against which the poetry can emerge. And—difficult point—it is somehow here, in the "against which," that what is spoken poetically occurs, and not in anything that comes forth from the cloud itself or from the sky, which serves at once as horizon and field.

In contrast to the moods of *Being and Time* and Rilke's *Notebooks*, the mood evoked by Hölderlin's conception of the poetry-making cloud is one of joy.

The open clearness in which the cloud lingers makes this lingering serene. The cloud is made serene in the serene. We name this
also "what is spatially ordered" (Aufgeräumte). We think this word
now and subsequently in a strict sense. That which is spatially
ordered is, in its spatiality, made free, illuminated, and joined
together. . . . The joyous has its essence in the serene that makes
serene. [E, 16]

Here, in contrast with *Being and Time*, mood pertains to much more than
a condition of *Dasein*. It is a world condition, to be understood against
the historical background of *Stimmung* as world harmony, in which all
realms of Being act in harmony. Given Heidegger's preoccupation with
ancient poetry and thought, the harmony in question is not that of the
Christian, specifically Ambrosian, tradition, in which everything melts
in a pervasive atmosphere of piety; it more closely approximates that of
the early Greek conception in which "clear-cut forms still continue to
exist individually, not fused into an all-embracing atmosphere."[13] The
source of the harmony depicted by Heidegger is the serene, imagined,
it seems to me, as the equivalent of an ontological foundation. If such is
indeed the case, Heidegger has shifted, or is at least in the process of
shifting, from the position taken in *The Origin of the Work of Art*. There,
we recall, poetry accomplished the founding through which Being
emerges as beings—through which, in other words, all that is comes
into its own. In the "Homecoming" address, on the other hand, the part
of Being is evidently taken by the serene, in its manifestation as the sky,
and the part of beings is taken by speaking, in its manifestation as the
cloud. The statement that the joyous has its essence in the serene,
together with the statement that the serene makes the joyous serene,
would then explain the relation of the cloud to the sky as the relation of
being to Being. But in this recast presentation of the ontological difference, the difference *is* the relation, is the "over against" described
above, wherein that which is poetically spoken comes over the speaking as that which it lingers against. If this is the case, Heidegger may be
suggesting, in his own poetic way, that he did not go far enough in
The Origin of the Work of Art and that he must now consider the
possibility that, as poetry founds the emergence of Being as beings,
poetry is itself founded by that Being. The passage quoted above is that
consideration, inexplicit, playful, tenuous—unless, of course, my
interpretation is a case of my doing to Heidegger what he does to
others, namely, endeavoring to bring forth what remains unspoken or
unthought.[14]

13. Leo Spitzer, *Essays on English and American Literature*, ed. Anna Hatcher (Princeton:
Princeton University Press, 1962), p. 15.
14. This analysis should be complemented by White's discussion (*Heidegger and the
Language of Poetry*, pp. 106 ff.) of clouds and sky as entities in a spatiotemporal setting.

This last example of Heidegger's thinking may be compared with a passionate section that comes about midway in the address:

> When we represent the Bodensee, which is also called "the Schwabian ocean," from the standpoint of geography or travel or local history, then we mean the lake lying between the Alps and the upper Danube, through which the young Rhine also streams away. Thus we still think this water unpoetically. How long? How long shall we will to mean that there is, to begin with, a nature-in-itself and a landscape-in-itself which then with the help of "poetic incidents" (poetischen Erlebnissen) is mythically colored? [E, 21]

Heidegger does not warn against seeing the poetic landscape as merely the geographical one, but he implies their essential difference. The basis of differentiation does not reside in the categories of the poetic, the geographical, and so on. Nor does it reside essentially in the opposition of *Erfahrung* as authentic experience and *Erlebnis* as mere happening or incident.[15] It resides in the relation on which all these differentiations depend: the relation between Being and beings. Heidegger is obviously talking about the conventional thinking one finds, for example, in literary pastoralism; but he has overloaded the convention. One does not have to conceive of a nature-in-itself or a landscape-in-itself in order to regard the Bodensee as somehow figuring in the poem. Nor is such a notion necessary to a common-sense interpretation that considers the poem to concern that particular body of water, in the most literal sense, and nothing else. While striving to avoid an approach that would be narrowly literary or aesthetic, Heidegger slides toward a history-of-ideas approach that, if not narrow, may be misapplied. He might more plausibly have questioned the validity of, say, the concept of *genius loci*, which relates directly to the attitudes Heidegger opposes and which figures prominently in literary convention. Furthermore, such a concept tends to mystify, and Heidegger's effort here is one of demystification. As the passage stands, Heidegger is trying to remove a mystification he has himself introduced. He has made the opponent too much a bad Kantian, the use of the term *vorstellen* being the first phase of a strategy leading toward his repeated reference to the *an sich*. In short, he has trouble articulating precisely what it is that his own approach differs from.

Returning to the problem that had concerned him in the first of the *Holzwege* pieces, Heidegger states: "Homecoming is the return into the

15. On *Erlebnis* see Wilhelm Dilthey, *Das Erlebnis und die Dichtung*, 13th ed. (Stuttgart: Teubner, 1957).

nearness of origin" (E, 23).[16] This gnomic observation sounds more spatial than it is. Origin is not a geographical place, nor is nearness, but each, in its own way, is an essential place. *Nähe*, or nearness, can also be translated as proximity or neighborhood. Neighborhood is "near-to"; and in this sense it does carry the association of a place with which one is familiar. But it is equally an "about-to" in the sense that the seeker nears origin by preparing a beginning, not by recapturing one. In this it is temporal, and so Heidegger points out that the only one who can go back is one who has carried the burden of wandering for a long time. Such seeking is a temporal circle wherein the seeker, approaching origin, experiences what he is looking for so as to come back as a more experienced seeker.

The quality of nearness that fascinates Heidegger may be compared, again, with Walter Benjamin's concept of "aura." Aura inheres in the work of art in whose presence it is manifest, but only when that work preserves its unique presence in its unique setting. Remove it from its setting or reproduce it, and its aura diminishes. Aura is overcome whenever human beings try to bring the object too near. The same applies to nature: in gazing at a mountain range we experience a phenomenon of distance; for aura is a relation of presence to absence permitting experience without possession. It is emphatically, then, a characteristic of art and nature, not of science or technology (against which Benjamin inveighs in an almost Heideggerian manner). A similar relation obtains in Heidegger's sense of neighborhood. The latter term, however, has a greater oxymoronic potential than Benjamin's, and Heidegger makes the most of it. Neighborhood, he says, "lets nearness be near and yet lets it be the sought-after, thus not near" (E, 24). A criterion of approachability is invoked: if what is sought were too far away, it would be unapproachable; if it were too near, there would be no need to approach it. Heidegger had earlier attempted to avoid excessive spatializing by stressing the temporal nature of the enterprise. Now, more directly, he dissociates it from notions of place or spatial measurement. Neighborhood is in no wise "the smallest possible measurement of distance between two places" (E, 24). Rather, it is of the essence of neighborhood that it "brings nearness near in that it keeps it away. The neighborhood of origin is a mystery" (E, 24). The point, then is not to solve the mystery but to experience it *as* a mystery, as what remains concealed, unthought, unsaid.

Although an aura of mystery continues to hover about Heidegger's

16. See Erasmus Schöfer, "Heidegger's Language: Metalogical Forms of Thought and Grammatic Specialties," in *Heidegger and Language*, ed. and trans. Joseph J. Kockelmans (Evanston: Northwestern University Press, 1972), pp. 286–87, 297.

conception of poetic speaking, he makes an effort to clarify what it
accomplishes when he states: "The elegy 'Heimkunft' is not a poem
about *Heimkunft;* rather the elegy is, as the poem it is, the *Heimkommen*
itself, that still self-appropriatingly transpires *(sich noch ereignet)* as long
as its word message peals as the bell in the language of the Germans"
(E, 25).[17] The two terms, *Heimkunft* and *Heimkommen,* are not synonymous, nor are they employed for variety. How they relate is hinted in the
opening paragraph, where, as Mukařovsky would say, the *-kunft* is
foregrounded.[18] Heidegger states simply, in the first sentence, that the
poem speaks of *Heimkunft,* which we think of (he goes on to say) as
arrival, *Ankunft.* Soon he speaks of the one who comes *(ankommt),* then
reverts to *Ankunft* in the last two sentences before the first quotation. A
little after the quotation, home speaks immediately after the *Ankunft* to
the *Ankommenden.* Coming or *kommen,* in other words, is associated
with the advent of the one who arrives and who becomes, as the chief
point of reference, the poet. In the later passage, to which we now
return, *Heimkommen* is foregrounded in line with Heidegger's concentration on that point of reference in the poet. The joy experienced is the
poet's. Because Hölderlin speaks, however, of "our joy," Heidegger
prepares the way for the inclusion of "the others" spoken of in the final
line of the elegy. He also prepares the way, more subtly, by differ-
entiating between the two modes of coming home. We have already
seen one basis of difference. We now note that, whereas *Heimkunft*
stays free of temporary localization, Heidegger calls *Heimkommen* "the
first" coming. *Heimkommen* is the inaugural event; *Heimkunft* is what is
inaugurated.

For the completion of the task of homecoming the poet needs those
others of whom Hölderlin had seemed to speak negatively: "Such cares
as these, whether gladly or not, a singer must / Bear in his soul, and
often, but the others not." Negative traces do indeed cling to Heidegger's gloss as he states that the people of the country should not attempt
to overcome the lack of god but should endure the appearance of god-
lessness until, from the nearness to god's "failure," the beginning
word—the word that names the most high—shall be vouchsafed. They
should endure the absence, for, despite appearances, it is no lack. The
absence or failure of god resembles mystery in that it, too, must be
endured, though the failure is temporally fuller than mystery, since one
misses what was once present. At the same time, failure preserves—like
mystery—a sense of futurity, since that which is no longer present is

17. Cf. Cyrus Hamlin, "Hölderlin's Elegy 'Homecoming': Comments," in *Friedrich
Hölderlin: An Early Modern,* pp. 236, 239, 241.
18. Jan Mukařovsky, "Standard Language and Poetic Language," in *Critical Theory
since Plato,* ed. Hazard Adams (New York: Harcourt Brace, 1971), pp. 1051 ff.

that which is still to come or, rather, that whose abiding continuity will be made manifest through homecoming. The poet's care is to insure that the people stay in proximity to the absence of the gods—which is to say, in the presence of the holy—without reaching after premature solutions.

Negativity dissolves when Heidegger considers the true meaning of the "not" that Hölderlin applies to the people of the country. Hölderlin's word releases the others from the care of poetic saying (des dichtenden Sagens) as such but not from the care of hearing. In fact, the "not" is a secret call to the others, that they may become hearers and learn the essence of home. Heidegger here follows the statement of purpose put forward some three years later in "What Are Poets For?" (1946): "But the only necessity would be and is, by soberly thinking within what is said in his poetry, to experience what is not said" (H, 252). In coming to care, the others become caring. They learn to consider the mystery of the reserving nearness (sparende Nähe), becoming the deliberating ones; from these arise the slow ones of long patience, who learn to endure the absence of gods; and these, the deliberating ones and the slow ones, are for the first time the caring ones. Caring, they are turned with the care of the poet toward the mystery. The relation is in no wise perspectival. What they turn toward is neither object nor representation. The turning is a giving-up to what Heidegger calls—anticipating "What Are Poets For?" and the language of such later works as "The Principle of Identity"—the same. Indeed, it is only because they yield to the same that they become the kindred of the poem to whom the full title of the poem refers.

Without thinkers the poetic word cannot be apprehensible (vernehmbar); and such thinking can be thought by the caring ones, who thereby furnish true remembrance of the poet. For Heidegger no less than for Ingarden or Sartre, others—hearers, people of the country, kindred ones, readers, in short, an audience—are essential to a full poetic experience. They help the poet:

> This helping corresponds to the essence of the reserving nearness in which the most joyous nears. For just as the greeting emissaries must help the serene reach men in the serenefication, so must there be a first one who poetically rejoices, over against the greeting emissaries, in order first to conceal, alone and in advance, the greeting. [E, 30]

All this stress on slowness and patience, along with this peculiar merger of giving and withholding, seems far removed from the Sartrean aesthetic, at least as far as What Is Literature? is concerned. Literature for Sartre is an appeal for engagement and action, and the gift of art is unalloyed by Heideggerian constraints. But we must also remember that Sartre draws sharp distinctions between poetry and prose and that his analyses generally apply to the latter, and particularly to prose fiction. What Sartre would say about a poetry as "pure" as Hölderlin's is by no means clear, especially when we recall his passing observation that history presents forms of poetry different from those contemporary types with which he is concerned. A useful comparison may nonetheless be drawn between the limitations Sartre sets on the writer and those set by Heidegger. The writer needs his audience according to both theories; indeed, Sartre and Heidegger rarely if ever consider the two in isolation. But something more—or rather, something less—than reciprocity is involved, for in both theories the author suffers from a serious shortcoming. Although in both cases he helps to initiate, he does not finish. Sartre's author needs a freedom that is prepared to act, Heidegger's needs people prepared to listen: the author depends on other persons and future time.

A particular limitation of Sartre's author is his inability to experience his own work. Reading, as perception and creation, presupposes that subject and object are both essential: the latter because it imposes itself transcendentally, the former because it is necessary not only to reveal the object but, through the intentionality of consciousness, to produce it in the sense of letting it come to be. The reader, as one who experiences wholly an object that he nonetheless creates, has it both ways. But the author is handicapped. In reading his own work, he forever meets himself, his ideas, his words, his fossilized subjectivity. The work escapes him by not allowing him to escape himself. Heidegger too emphasizes the author's limitation. The poem does not belong to the poet; on the contrary, despite his care, it continually escapes him:

> But because the word, once it is spoken, slips away from the guardianship of the caring poet, he cannot easily hold fast in its truth the spoken knowledge of the reserved discovery (*Fund*) and of the reserving nearness. Therefore does the poet turn to the others, so that their remembrance can help the poetic word be understood, with the result that the homecoming self-appropriatingly transpires for each in his destined way. [E, 30–31]

If Heidegger says nothing about the author's inability to experience his own work, it is because the work was never his own. The poet is not a subjectivity, as Sartre would understand the term. What Heidegger offers is at least a parallelism with the structural relation of inter-subjectivity: there remains, in his account, a "one" in need of "others" and "others" in need of this "one." The need, however, is not the need of subject for another subject, any more than the relation of the poet or the kindred ones to the poem is a relation of subject to object. The need remains that of a component in a fourfold: poem needs poetry needs poet needs people; the statement, we note, could begin at any point, the interrelation being at once a tautology and a totality.

Though future-oriented, Heidegger's vision is not utopian. Freedom involves the freedom to fail; there is nothing automatic about caring, any more than there is anything automatic about the future behavior of Sartre's theoretical reader. Far from being capable of safeguarding his message, the caring poet watches it slip away. The author ventures the loss of what he authorizes and therefore needs the others, whose powers and limitations are complementary: whereas the specific capacity of "creation" may not belong to them, they are endowed with the safeguarding capacity the poet lacks. As for the poem, it could not be without the poet, poetry, or the people; and because the poem is itself *Heimkommen* in anticipation of *Heimkunft*, the future of the poet and his people depends upon the poem.

Remembering the care with which *Being and Time* erases the lines dividing past, present, and future, we can avoid the mistake of approaching the future Heidegger describes as something apart from other times. One is not open toward the future by being closed to the past; as in Kierkegaard, futurity entails a kind of remembrance.[19] In the essay on "Remembrance" this takes the form, as in the feast-day hymn, of a day of celebration that gathers a people together, literally recollecting them by allowing them to rest in the repetition of a time that is the unity of all times. Even more than this, *"Remembrance* is the poetic remaining in the essence of the destined order of poets who in the firm destiny of the future history of the Germans show their foundational ground (*Stiftungsgrund*) in the manner of a feast day" (E, 150). The reference to the Germans can be misleading in the same way as references to the fatherland, the homeland, or home because, although each may refer to specific peoples or places, they can all apply to the human situation generally; and even when the application is more particular, what is at issue is the fundamental historical orientation from an ontological point of view. In the "Letter on Humanism" Heidegger therefore excludes as inappropriate any patriotic or nationalist interpretation of the phenomenon of home as it appears in Hölderlin. Home is rather to be thought of in connection with the metaphysical condition of homelessness—of being thrown into the void—which characterizes the modern dilemma.

19. William V. Spanos, "Heidegger, Kierkegaard, and the Hermeneutic Circle: Towards a Postmodern Theory of Interpretation as Dis-closure," in *Martin Heidegger and the Question of Literature*, pp. 123 ff.

Agonizing as it may be, this particular "thrown" condition provides the means by which home becomes recognized as such: "For the poet, the assault of *techne* against *dikē* is the happening whereby man ceases to be at home. In his exile from home, the home is first disclosed as such" (EM, 127/140). What is not so readily disclosed, and what Heidegger wishes to impart, is the essential relation between home, in this very broad sense, and the holy. Again the "Letter on Humanism" states the matter cogently:

> It is in this nearness [to Being] that the decision is made, if it is made at all, as to whether and how the god or the gods deny themselves . . . whether and how the day of the holy begins to dawn, whether and how, in the beginning of the holy, an appearance of the god and the gods can commence anew. But the holy—that is only at first the essential space for divinity, which itself, again, only vouchsafes the dimension for the gods and the god—comes to appearance only when previously, and during a long time of preparation, Being itself has clarified itself and has been experienced in its truth. [W, 338–39]

The poetry of Hölderlin embodies the essence of poetry because, along with Heidegger's own poetic thinking, it is part of that preparation.

5

Learning to Think

> We achieve what is called thinking when we ourselves think. For such an effort to succeed, we must be ready to learn thinking.
>
> *What Is Called Thinking?*

The purpose of this chapter is to bring out certain aspects of the movement of Heidegger's thinking during a time when it was becoming increasingly poetic; to elucidate some recurring themes and concerns; to clarify, as best I can, a few difficult passages; to make explicit connections or ideas left implicit in Heidegger's presentations; and, where appropriate, to render judgments, especially concerning his vision of poetry per se as it applies to thinking and to the constitution of the world. In that effort one text will be the 1943 lecture "*Aletheia*," dealing with Heraclitus' concept of truth as unconcealment and with a central issue bearing on our experience of any sort of being, namely, the manner in which that being *is*, which is to say, above all, the manner in which it is present. A second text, *An Introduction to Metaphysics* (a series of 1935 lectures reworked for publication in 1953), explores *alētheia* in relation both to *physis*—the process by which all that is emerges or comes into appearance—and to what does not emerge because it *is* not, namely, nothingness. The same text offers the fullest description to date of the ways in which thinking relates to Being and, in Heidegger's interpretation of two plays by Sophocles, the most extended demonstration of the things that thinking can do when it encounters great poetic works. Through additional texts, including *What Is Called Thinking?* (a lecture series in 1951–52) and *The Principle of Reason* (lectures in 1955–56), I will inquire into the medium or element in which thinking takes place and, finally, into the phenomenon of saying, for which the two previously treated texts are a preparation and of which the works to be taken up in chapter 6 are, in part, a culmination.

Alētheia: Truth as Unconcealment

For the thinker of 1943, as for the thinker of 1927, Heraclitus provides an access to the forgotten view that truth consists in simple unconcealment.

The text Heidegger has chosen may be translated "How can one conceal oneself from that which never sets?" What begins to evolve, however, is not an exposition of these words but the elaboration of an experience (the word occurs five times in as many paragraphs) inspired by a scene from *The Odyssey*, an experience whose peculiar qualities may be more easily appreciated if, in the manner of chapter 3, we approach it from a more familiar perspective. Such a perspective is provided by the celebrated passage, from Book XIX, in which the housekeeper Eurycleia washes the feet of the stranger she is soon to recognize as her returned master. At first Odysseus conceals himself:

> Odysseus
> Was sitting by the hearth, and suddenly turned toward the
>   darkness
> For at once he was apprehensive in heart lest when she
>   touched him
> She notice his scar and the facts became apparent.
>   [XIX. 388–91][1]

After describing the servant's reaction, Homer depicts Odysseus' attempt to restrain her:

> Odysseus groped for her
> With his hands and took her by the throat with his right hand,
> And with the other he drew her closer to himself and spoke:
> .   .   .   .
> Since you have recognized me, and a god put it in your heart,
> Be quiet, lest someone else in the halls find out.
>   [XIX. 479–85]

Erich Auerbach comments: "Clearly outlined, brightly and uniformly illuminated, men and things stand out in a realm where everything is visible; and not less clear—wholly expressed, orderly even in their ardor—are the feelings and thoughts of the persons involved."[2] Homer thus creates what Auerbach calls a foreground, "a uniformly illuminated, uniformly objective present,"[3] in contrast with the perspectivistic, historically deep background of the biblical style as represented by the Old Testament. Heidegger, for his part, brooks no such comparison, especially one that, like Auerbach's, is advantageous to the latter style, nor could he feel favorably disposed toward Auerbach's strongly visual orientation. But, above all, the difference between a "thinking" ap-

1. Homer, *The Odyssey*, trans. and ed. Albert Cook (New York: Norton, 1967, 1976). Citations to *The Odyssey* are to this translation.
2. Erich Auerbach, *Mimesis: The Representation of Reality in Western Literature*, trans. Willard R.Trask (Princeton: Princeton University Press, 1953), p. 5.
3. Ibid., p. 6.

proach and philological approach lies in what appears to be an area of agreement, namely, the view that Homer's world is one of illumination. The illumination Auerbach sees is opposed to obscurity as foreground is opposed to background or the objective to the subjective. Indeed, the purpose of his analysis of the scene from the *Odyssey* is to build up the sharpest possible contrast between the Homeric and the biblical way of representing reality. The illumination that interests Heidegger, by contrast, consists, on the one hand, in the light that Homer brings to Odysseus' way of being present in a particular scene and, on the other hand, in the fact that Homer's experience of presence brings us closer to an understanding of the Heraclitean world fire. Heidegger believes that the poet provides an access to the question of Being that is different from but just as valid as the access provided by the thinker, and he believes that it is legitimate to "use" the poet in this way, the dominant consideration being always the question of Being. Auerbach, in any case—or so it seems to me—"uses" Homer quite as much as Heidegger does; and it must remain for the reader to decide whether, on returning to the Homeric text, there is more value in the contrast Auerbach draws between the Greek epic and the Bible or in the interplay between Homer and Heraclitus that is brought about through Heidegger's poetic thinking.

Heidegger chooses as his main Homeric text the scene from Book VIII in which Odysseus weeps unobserved on hearing Demodocus sing in the palace of the Phaeacians. The crucial phase of the scene, only one aspect of which draws Heidegger's explicit notice, proceeds as follows:

> But Odysseus
> Took his great purple mantle in his stout hands,
> Pulled it over his head, and concealed his handsome face;
> He was ashamed before the Phaeacians for shedding tears
>   under his eyebrows.
> And whenever the godlike singer paused in his singing,
> He lifted the mantle over his head and wiped the tears,
> Took a two-handed cup, and poured libation to the gods.
> But whenever he started again and the Phaeacian nobles
> Urged him on to sing, since they were pleased with his stories,
> Odysseus again covered his head over and moaned.
> Now, as he shed tears, he escaped the notice of all the others.
> But Alcinoos alone took note of him and perceived him,
> While seated near him, and heard him as he deeply groaned.
> [VIII. 83–95]

To Heidegger's way of thinking it is proper to treat the crucial term *elanthane* according to the needs of the language into which it is being transferred; and in both English and German it is accurate enough, for most purposes, to say that Odysseus escapes notice. A translation reading "He concealed his tears from all of the other guests," though closer in Heidegger's view to the original, overlooks the fact that the crucial verb lacks transitive force, so that we are better off with something like "he remained concealed." This is considerably different from saying that he concealed his tears or that he concealed himself in the act of crying, for now we are dealing less with an act than with an essential condition. The notion of mood, as developed in *Being and Time*, will not serve either, because Heidegger is thinking of a condition so all-encompassing as to be characteristic of Being itself, and a condition that Heraclitus, in the light of Homer, can help us experience. The nature of the condition is suggested by the fact that concealment "holds sway round the weeper, drawing him away from the others" (VA, III, 59). The conception, if properly understood, discloses, first, the poet's way of experiencing the basic mode of human presence, then the nature of presence itself. Concerning the first, Heidegger observes that "Un-concealment here defines the manner in which the man is present among men. Through its manner of saying, the Greek language makes it known that concealing, and this means at the same time staying-unconcealed, has a commanding priority over all other ways in which what is present presences" (VA, III, 58).

A desire to do justice to the second thing the poet experiences—the nature of presence per se—sends Heidegger back to Homer for an encounter with a word left untranslated in the German text Heidegger employs as a point of departure. *Aideto* reveals that Odysseus is shy before the Phaeacians, as though afraid to reveal his weeping; but for Heidegger this matters less than what remains unthought in the poetic experience, namely, the meaning that Being itself takes on: "Presence is lightened self-concealment (*gelichtete Sichverbergen*) to which the shy-ness corresponds. The shyness is the restraint of remaining concealed from the nearness of present beings. . . . Thus the shyness, and all the high matters related to it, are to be thought in the light of remaining concealed" (VA, III, 59–60). What makes this movement of thought possible is the parallel between Odysseus' relation to others and the relation, in the Heraclitus fragment, between the unnamed "who" and "that which never sets." Although Heidegger does not direct the reader's attention to the process, his presentation unfolds through a three-stage interpretation of the bridging word *vor*, which suggests "in front of" as well as the broader "in the presence of." It is this interpretation that makes it possible to advance from the idea that conceal-ment applies mainly to Odysseus' immediate relations with others to the more powerful idea that Odysseus, and through him Homer, is experiencing what it means to be present. First and most obviously,

Odysseus is "shy"—he remains concealed—before the Phaeacians. But the very obviousness is a problem for Heidegger, who doubts that such an interpretation gets us very close to a Greek experience of concealment. Better is the stage, indicated in the passage quoted above, in which the second sense, "in the presence of," applies; for now the issue is not concealment, which is but one mode of presence; the issue is rather the much larger phenomenon of presence itself. The focus is widened further by a shift of attention from what holds sway around the character to what holds sway *tout court*. What holds sway around Odysseus is the manner of concealment that draws him away from the others, as that manner is experienced by the Greeks. But what holds sway after the shift is presence itself, as experienced by the poet. That is, Homer, like Rilke and other poets, enables us to experience, and hence opens up to our thinking, possibilities that may remain "unthought" (VA, III, 59) by the poets themselves. It is not that Homer has an experience superior to "the Greek experience." On the contrary, Heidegger believes the scene to be poetic in precisely the Greek way as such (*griechisch gedichteten*, VA, III, 59). What Heidegger implies is that the poet experiences "more" by occupying a position between his people and their gods; hence the poet can experience the meaning of Being that has become decisive for that people, which is what Heidegger has in mind when he speaks, as he does here and in many other places, of a people's historical destiny (*Geschick*) (cf. SG, 187).

Since this second stage of interpretation is the last having directly to do with the *Odyssey* (in the third stage Heidegger returns to the Heraclitus text), we may pause for a perspective on what Heidegger has done and has not done in his approach to Homer. He has focused, not atypically, on a linguistic detail, building a context for the concealment that Heraclitus' interrogative maxim takes up for reflection. His approach has been at once particular and general: particular because his scrutiny bears upon an aspect of one scene, general because he also considers Homer's experience of presence—here, as elsewhere, synonymous with Being—and its meaning for our experience. To judge the merit of the procedure, however, we probably should ask what might have resulted if he had looked at Odysseus in the context furnished by Book VIII instead of or in addition to working out a context of his own. He would then have had to reckon with the fact that Odysseus weeps in two episodes within the book, the one clearly balanced against the other. Because he deals only with the first, Heidegger can emphasize the role of unconcealment, which is a demonstrably significant feature of the episode; but if he had dealt also with the second, he would have had to explain why it occurs at all and why it differs from the preceding episode.

It occurs because Homer is showing us a rather different hero from the one presented up to this point in the story. Among the Phaeacians, Odysseus, the wily master of concealment, suddenly finds himself, in a sense, close to home, Alcinous being as hospitable toward his guest as the Phaeacians' old enemies, the Cyclopes, had been hostile; Alcinous even describes himself as Odysseus' brother. The Phaeacian king thus deserves something better than Odyssean deception, and, indeed, the Ithacan finds himself faced with an opportunity to tell, for once, the truth.[4] And although this is just what he does, the moment does not come until the beginning of the succeeding book, after the second of the two counterbalanced episodes. The story of that episode closely matches the story of the first, but with a crucial difference: Demodocus now sings of Odysseus' world at Odysseus' request despite, or rather because of, the fact that Odysseus wept on the first occasion. Odysseus—and this is the crucial point—is setting the stage to weep again, which really means setting the stage for Alcinous to see him again, with the likelihood that Alcinous will once more ask him to reveal who he is and the equally likely prospect that Odysseus will at last tell the truth; and he does.

From the standpoint of this larger context, then, Homer presents a more complex, more interwoven relation between concealment and unconcealment than the one investigated by Heidegger. We may even be inclined to say that, so far as Book VIII is concerned, Homer shows more concern for the latter than for the former. But Heidegger in fact moves in the same direction in his own discourse, the issue of unconcealment being the pivot on which everything ultimately turns. In other words, as so often happens when one takes a broader look at the text than Heidegger does, one finds overlooked possibilities that, far from weakening the thinker's argument, bring to it additional strength and richness. The one respect in which these possibilities offer a corrective, on the other hand, consists in the issue of what I referred to above as a balance. It might also be called a harmony.[5] The point is that, looked at from a broader perspective, Homer has much to say to us, in the phase of his epic, about the *polemos* of concealment and unconcealment, which pulls the story now one way, now another, creating a paradigmatic example of the intimacy between conflict and unity that Heidegger finds at the heart of the Heraclitean sense of struggle (to be considered further, below). This is also what creates the mounting suspense in the book, a suspense relieved by a moment of unconcealment—"I am

4. My argument follows the thesis advanced by Edwin Dolin in *Gräzer Beiträge* 1 (1973); reprinted as "Odysseus in Phaeacia" in Albert Cook, *The Odyssey*, pp. 495–505.

5. Leo Spitzer, "Classical and Christian Ideas of World Harmony (Prolegomena to an Interpretation of the Word 'Stimmung')," *Traditio* 2 (1944): 409–96.

Odysseus, son of Laertes, who for my wiles / Am of note among all men, and my fame reaches heaven" (XIX. 19–20)—which, properly examined, could have provided productive matter for poetic thinking.

In its third stage, Heidegger's interpretation—returning, as noted above, to Heraclitus—directs our attention toward that before which, or in the presence of which, no one can hide. In other words, the emphasis has shifted from the issue of concealment to the issue of what it is that concealment relates to; and if this is "that which never sets," then the fragment really has less to do with a certain way of behaving than with all the things anyone could behave toward, which means all the things that are—the stars and the earth, other persons, "nature," the gods, in sum, everything implied by the idea of the world in the broadest sense. Recast in affirmative form, Heraclitus' "that which never sets" means "that which always unfolds" (das ständig Aufgehende, VA, III, 63), in short, physis.

Elemental Thinking

In Heraclitus' elemental thinking, it is fire that, remaining itself and hence never-setting, makes it possible for anything to unfold. Fire thus becomes synonymous with physis, with cosmos, with world. And just because fire is elemental, its meaning cannot be limited to any single phenomenon, such as flames; rather:

> Fire names the sacrificial fire, the fire of the night watch, but also the shining of torches, the glimmer of the stars. In "fire" the lighting (Lichten), the glow, the glaze, the gentle gleam hold sway. . . . But there also holds sway in "fire" injury, clashing, hiding, dying out. When Heraclitus speaks of fire, he is thinking above all of the illuminating power that holds sway (lichtende Walten), the showing that gives and withdraws. [VA, III, 71]

The illuminating to which Heraclitus gives voice by no means excludes the presence of characteristics we often think of as opposite, in this case that of concealment and unconcealment; as implied by the statement above, concerning the fact that concealing entails staying-unconcealed, the world may be seen as both a lighting and a concealing phenomenon (lichtend-bergende, entbergend-verbergender—VA, III, 72, 75). Taking advantage of the hermeneutic latitude that Heraclitus' fragment allows, Heidegger hazards the suggestion that the "anyone" in the text may be as inconclusive in its own way as the world-fire, in other words, that anyone need not be thought of as some person but may rather be thought of as either a mortal or a god: "the preserving lighting lets gods and mortals be present in unconcealment, so that no one of them can ever remain concealed—and this, not because he is merely being noticed by someone, but wholly because everyone is present *(anwest)"* (VA, III, 73).

This illumination thus does what the world-fire does, is what the world-fire is; in Heidegger's terminology they are "the same," which is not to say, however, that they are identical. To posit identity is to think technically, in the manner of formal philosophy (A = A), whereas "the same" means, less "correctly" and more concretely, that what Heraclitus thinks of as the world-fire is essentially what Heidegger thinks of as the lighting. Far from being interchangeable, like the signs in the tautological proposition A = A, the two versions of the same are different enough to require respective elucidations, yet these very elucidations revolve around the recognition that each thinker is dealing with an issue dealt with by the other. Based as it is on movement, the verb "revolve" befits a thinking that, instead of being bound by a narrow notation, can entertain several meanings as equally valid. That is the virtue of what I have been calling elemental—which is another way of saying poetic—thinking. As Heidegger puts the matter in *What Is Called Thinking?*:

> This ambiguity is never merely the remnant of a single meaning . . . which has not yet been reached. . . . This ambiguity is rather the element in which thinking must move in order to be rigorous. Expressed in an image: the depths and expanse of the water, its currents and realms of quiet, its warm and cold levels are for the fish the element of its own manifold mobility *(Beweglichkeit)*. If the fish is deprived of the fullness of its element, if it is dragged onto dry sand, it can only wriggle, twitch, and die. So thinking and what it thinks must be sought after in the element of its ambiguity, or else it remains closed to us. [WHD, 68]

The elemental, it would appear, no longer plays the role assigned to it, for example, in the introduction to *What Is Metaphysics?* (1949). There, although the tree of philosophy is said to grow from the soil of metaphysics, that soil "is never assimilated into the tree." Instead, the roots lose themselves in the soil, or, as Heidegger also says, the root "does not . . . turn back to the soil" (W, 367), in which case the very element in which philosophy is grounded remains, paradoxically, inaccessible. All of which is a way of restating, in an image, the thesis, advanced earlier in the same discussion, that when metaphysics represents beings, Being itself is thereby in some sort illuminated: "Being has arrived at unconcealment *(alētheia)"* (W, 366); and yet the truth of Being per se—Being in its essential unconcealing capacity—remains unthought. Hence thinking remains both rooted and rootless.

Heidegger's element remains many-faceted, like Heraclitus' world-fire and also like the element of which Hölderlin speaks in a letter quoted in "Hölderlin's Earth and Heaven" (1959): "The powerful element, the fire of heaven and the quiet of men, their life in nature and their limitation and contentment—all of this has constantly moved me, and I can well say that Apollo has struck me" (E, 157). In his notes on Sophocles' Oedipus, the poet speaks, similarly, of "the influence of the element" in which, according to a kind of law of equilibrium, "the whole man" develops. If the passage on the soil of metaphysics gives us one meaning of the element—namely, that of a ground—the latter passages together give a second meaning, that of influence.

Another term conveys a closely related meaning. In *Being and Time* Heidegger refers to a speaker as a medium (SZ, 32), while in *An Introduction to Metaphysics* medium denotes the Platonic "*to en hōi gignetai*, that *wherein* it becomes, the medium in which a thing in process of becoming forms itself and out of which, once become, it emerges" (EM, 50/54). If "medium" is indeed a cognate term, this suggests that Heidegger's element is not only that in which thinking lives but that through and from which—thanks to which—it emerges. Expressed this way, the conception is seen to move toward the temporal, for an elemental thinking sustains a horizon of possibilities and prospects, which belong primarily to the future. It is not surprising, therefore, that Heidegger, believing, as he does, that poetry genuinely originates, holds that poetry itself provides a ground, an influence, a medium—in sum, an element—for saying: "But the answer, wherein man truly listens to the exhortation of language, is the saying *(Sagen)* that speaks in the poetic element. The more poetic a poet is, the freer—that is, the more open and ready—is his saying for the unexpected" (VA, II, 64). Believing that Hölderlin is by these standards paradigmatic, for the reasons already stated, Heidegger can unexpectedly find that the German poet, no less than the early Greek philosopher, concerned himself with elemental thinking. The clue is contained in the lines "But they [the poets] are, you say, like the wine-god's holy priests, / Who fared from land to land in holy night," a clue that leads Heidegger to expand on the notion of the holy discussed in chapter 4:

> Poets are mortals who, singing earnestly of the wine-god, sense the trace of the fugitive gods, stay on the gods' tracks. . . . The ether, however, in which alone the gods are gods, is their godhead. The element of this ether, that within which even the godhead itself is still present, is the holy. The element of the ether for the coming of the fugitive gods, the holy, is the track of the fugitive gods. [H, 250/94]

If Heidegger's element is that from which, through which, and thanks to which thinking emerges, it is also what sustains thinking; for the element of the holy, reminding us that the gods who have been may still be and may again be present, preserves the very possibility of recognizing, even of dealing with, the disappearance of the divine that is the great problem of our destitute time.

In his interpretations of *Oedipus Rex* and *Antigone,* to which I am about to turn, Heidegger offers the unexpected in that he makes larger generalizations than we are accustomed to meeting in literary or dramatic criticism and in that these generalizations arise from his own distinctive understanding of the great issues of life and art as addressed by the early Greeks.

Oedipus Rex: Being, Appearance, and Unconcealment

Oedipus Rex epitomizes Greek Being-there, Heidegger believes, by making manifest the "unity and conflict of Being and appearance" (EM, 80/90) that was foundational for the early Greek thinkers, principally Parmenides and Heraclitus. For Heidegger the movement of the play

> is one struggle between appearance (concealment and distortion) and unconcealment (Being). The city is beset by the secret of the murderer of Laius, the former king. With the passion of a man who stands in the manifestness of glory and is a Greek, Oedipus sets out to reveal this secret. Step by step, he must move into unconcealment, which in the end he can bear only by putting out his own eyes, i.e. by removing himself from all light, by letting the cloak of night fall round him, and, blind, crying out to the people to open all doors in order that a man may be made manifest to them as what he *is.* [EM, 80/90]

Some readers, perhaps, will be put off by the "must" of the final, rhapsodic sentence; but it is a point on which the interpretation insists. Oedipus' true Being, Heidegger holds, is that of a man who murders and commits incest, while everything else—his role as king and savior of the city—belongs to the realm of appearance. The only thing that can "come out," then, the only thing that can be "raised to unconcealment" (EM, 80/90), is that Being.

The source of our trouble, it would seem, is the contrast between the compulsion here portrayed and the idea, defended at length in *Being and Time,* that *Dasein* is free to be free. That entitlement may also be described, however (as noted in my discussion of Heidegger's view of the history of the Being), as the living of a destiny. The burden of the play then falls on a man whose future lies in the revelation of what he has already been and in the sustaining value of this revelation for his people.

This is not to say that Oedipus has a future in the same way as readers of *An Introduction to Metaphysics*. Oedipus is, to use Heidegger's word, an embodiment, and what he embodies is a way of existing in which are gathered the essential decisions a people has made about its collective possibilities. In this sense, Oedipus is the future of Sophocles; he is what Sophocles has decided the epitome of Being-there should turn out to be. And just because he is the epitome, he stands good not only for Sophocles himself but for politicians and priests and for all the others who together made that age what it was, so that Oedipus' destiny becomes nothing less than the destiny of a people as a whole.

That destiny does not impose passivity but requires a passion that is less outer or inner force than it is one's way of living within the totality of beings. That way involves a version of the thrownness described in *Being and Time* but one that no longer delivers Being-there to the everyday world. Quite the opposite: Oedipus is thrown out of all that—or, more precisely, out of its equivalent, his appearance as king and savior. But if he is thrown out, this cannot be merely in order to fall, since an appearance that cannot last is itself a kind of falling; he is in fact thrown out to rise, and what he rises to is the unconcealment, the truth, of what he is. Hence "we cannot regard Oedipus only as the man who meets his downfall; we must see him as the embodiment of Greek Being-there who most radically and wildly asserts its fundamental passion, the passion for disclosure of being *(Seinsenthüllung)*, i.e., the struggle for being itself" (EM, 81/90). Such a passion (Heidegger warns) should not be conceived as Oedipus' subjective desire, nor is it a matter of mood. About the relation between passion and *Dasein* we can make the same statement Heidegger often makes about the relation between language and *Dasein*: the former does not belong to the latter, but the latter to the former.

But what of appearance? Are we satisfied that Oedipus merely seems to be a king and a savior while really being a murderer and perpetrator of incest? Semblance presupposes appearing, as coming to light, because there can be seeming only when there is something to seem like and when that something can be seen. Hence "The essence of appearance ⟨Schein⟩ lives in the appearing ⟨Erscheinen⟩. It is self-manifestation, self-presentation, standing-there, presence" (EM, 85/96). Though this reminds us of the stress on *alētheia* that remains a dominant note in Heidegger's thinking from the time of *Being and Time*, Heidegger is more concerned in the present context with what might be called the dark side of appearance: "The area, as it were, which opens in the interwovenness of Being, unconcealment, and appearance—this area I understand as *error*" (EM, 83/92). To put it another way, *Dasein* is not situated in relation to

Being in such a way that semblance, for example, can be penetrated spontaneously or in such a way that Being can be grasped automatically in appearance. Whether such goals can be achieved with any consistency remains problematic because we are always liable to err: to mistake as identical different ways of appearing or to mistake the anonymous opinion of "they" (*das Man*) for truth and hence to continue "falling" in the everyday world instead of seizing the opportunity—as presented, for example, in moments of dread—of living a more authentic life. With the decision to do one or the other, authentic history begins.

To speak of doing, of course, is off the mark, as my use of quotation marks points out, insofar as it implies individual effort or assertion, which Heidegger—in a parenthetic remark added to the text in the early 1950s—describes as inessential to decision: " . . . decision means here not man's judgment and choice, but a separation in the . . . togetherness of being, unconcealment, appearance, and nonbeing" (EM, 84/93).

But if human beings do not separate—if they do not make the necessary distinctions—who or what does? The answer is suggested in Heraclitus' concept of *polemos*, which is a kind of primordial tension, a struggle of powers that is at once conflict and unity. The *locus classicus* is Fragment 53, which reads, in Heidegger's translation: "Conflict is for all (that is present) the creator that causes to emerge, but (also) for all the dominant preserver. For it makes some to appear as gods, others as men; it creates (shows) some as slaves, others as freemen" (EM, 47/51). Therefore decision, at least in Heidegger's later understanding, transpires as a separation allowing the emergence of everything and anything rather than an effort by individuals in the form of judgment or choice. To look "behind" all this for some prime mover can only force the conception back into the familiar mold of causation and development. In Heidegger's conception, if I am not mistaken, the mover is everything that moves, ultimately answerable to Being itself. At the same time, we must remember that because of the intimate relation of Being to appearance, because the unconcealment of Being can be held back by semblance, deception, illusion, one mode of decision through which *polemos* works is the homelessness we see in Oedipus. I refer in particular to the errancy that follows the time when Oedipus is thrown out of his appearance as king and savior and precedes the time when his status as murderer and sexual violator emerges into unconcealment (a time, incidentally, for which Heidegger does not directly account). It is precisely an example of how error is actually lived and of what it means for decision to unfold. In the *polemos* of the drama Sophocles demonstrates that decision is nothing less than the articulated, unified movement of all conflicting powers, according to which separation occurs so that emergence can.

This being the case, one need not confine oneself, with Heidegger, to the view that *Oedipus Rex* demonstrates the Greek passion for the disclosure of Being. It also demonstrates the passion for *polemos*—the pathos that is the living of separation and emergence—and for the pathos of the need to "reenact" all this through the peculiar unconcealment that is tragedy. It is a need that Heidegger does not explain, but he does attempt through the example of tragedy to elucidate his own reexamination of early Greek thinking:

> The thinking of Parmenides and Heraclitus was still poetic, which in this case means philosophical and not scientific. But because in this poetic thinking the thinking has priority, the thought about man's being follows its own direction and proportions. This poetic thinking forms a body with the contrary aspect *(ihm zugehörigen Gegenseite)*, the thinking poetry of the Greeks and particularly that poetry in which the Being and (closely related) Being-there of the Greeks was in the truest sense created *(stiftete)*: the tragedy. [EM, 110/121–22]

The tragedy to which Heidegger turns is *Antigone*.

Antigone: Being and Thinking

Before following him, however, we must consider both the position that thinking takes in relation to beings and Being and Heraclitus' vision of that relation, for only then shall we see why an interpretation of Antigone should fall, as it does, within the longest subsection in the book and why that section should bear the title "Being and Thinking."

That the position thinking takes in relation to Being is unique becomes clear when we compare it, on the one hand, with the distinction between Being and appearance and, on the other, with the distinction between Being and becoming. In both of these cases, Heidegger points out, what we distinguish from Being comes from some being. The sun that emits sunlight—a genuine appearance, so to speak—and the sun that falsely appears to revolve around the earth are the same sun. As for becoming, we distinguish what sets it apart from Being—namely, moving toward some definite ontic state—on the basis of whatever being is doing the moving. Becoming and appearance are therefore, Heidegger concludes, "on the same plane" as the Being of the being (EM, 83/98). By contrast, in the distinction between Being and thinking, in which "we must discern the fundamental position of the Western spirit, against which our central attack is directed" (EM, 89/99), what is distinguished from Being is utterly different in its nature from appearance or becoming, and, at the same time, the nature of the opposition is utterly different, too.

> Thinking sets itself off against being in such a way that being is
> placed before ⟨vor-gestellt, represented⟩ it and consequently
> stands opposed to it ⟨entgegensteht⟩ as an object ⟨Gegenstand⟩.
> This is not the case in the previous distinctions. Now we see how
> this distinction can achieve a pre-eminence. It predominates be-
> cause it does not situate itself in between and among the other
> three decisions [between and among being, nonbeing, and ap-
> pearance] but represents them all, and thus representing them
> ⟨vorsichstellend⟩, placing them before itself transposes ⟨umstellt⟩
> them, as it were. [EM, 89/98]

The paradigmatic case of representational thinking is logic, which is
rule-dominated, formalistic, and doctrinal. As if to try his hand at a
brief institutional "archeology" of the type to be developed by Michel
Foucault, Heidegger remarks that logic began to develop when Greek
philosophy, losing its original animus, was

> becoming an affair of schools, organization, and technique. It
> began when *eon*, the being of the essent, was represented as *idea*
> and as such became the "object" of *epistēmē*. Logic arose in the
> curriculum of the Platonic-Aristotelian schools. Logic is an inven-
> tion of schoolteachers, not of philosophers. Where philosophers
> took it up it was always under more fundamental impulsions, not
> in the interest of logic. [EM, 92/102]

As a thinker in the same tradition as Leibniz, Hegel, and Kant, Heidegger seeks to overcome the representational thinking of logic, not, of
course, to eliminate thought, and even less to substitute feeling for
thinking, but to effect a "more radical, stricter thinking, a thinking that
is part and parcel of being" (EM, 94/103) and not set over against the
latter as a subject is set over against its object.

Reminding us of logic's derivation from *logos*, Heidegger argues that
the Greek term originally had nothing to do with language. Homer's
use of the predicate form provides one proof:

> Recognizing the slain suitors in the underworld, Agamemnon
> says: "Amphimedo, what disaster has brought you here under the
> black earth, all picked men and year mates? If one were to gather
> *(lexaito)* the best men of a polis, one would make no other choice."
> [*Odyssey*, XXIV. 106]

and the Aristotelian use of the nominal form provides another proof:

> *taxis de pasa logos*, "all order has a character of bringing together."
> [EM, 105/95]

Heidegger likens *logos* to the German *Sammlung*, collection, and *legein*
to the German *lesen*, to gather or collect, understanding the terms as

suggesting "collecting collectedness, the primal gathering principle" (EM, 108/98). How such an organizing principle relates to the seemingly disorganizing principle of *polemos* is suggested by Heraclitus:

"Opposites move back and forth, the one to the other; from out of themselves they gather themselves." The conflict of the opposites is a gathering, rooted in togetherness, it is *logos*. The being of the essents is the supreme radiance, i.e., the greatest beauty, that which is most permanent in itself. What the Greeks meant by "beauty" was restraint. The gathering of the supreme antagonism is *polemos*, struggle (as we have seen above) in the sense of setting apart ⟨Aus-einandersetzung⟩. For us moderns, on the contrary, the beautiful is what reposes and relaxes; it is intended for enjoyment and art is a matter for pastry cooks. [EM, 101/111]

Equally provocative to Heidegger is the Parmenides fragment *to gar auto noein estin te kai einai*, commonly translated "Thinking and Being are the same"; more appropriately translated, in Heidegger's view, this would run: "There is a reciprocal bond between apprehension and Being" (EM, 111/122). To explore the statement, Heidegger steps back in a manner reminiscent of his approach in *Being and Time* when, as noted in chapter 1, he states that an ontological inquiry must inquire into the Being of the being who is conducting the inquiry. To proceed in such a way is not to retreat from the difficulty posed by the fragment but to take a footing (to this extent is Heidegger Cartesian) on what cannot be doubted, and that is the fact that "In one way or another it is man who speaks in this maxim" (EM, 111/122); or perhaps better: "The maxim in one way or another brings man to language *(bringt . . . den Menschen zur Sprache)*." Simple because basic, this idea becomes a motif (Heidegger goes on to speak interchangeably of the "idea of man," "the essence of man," the "notion of man," the "definition of being-human") that brings the interpretation to the threshold of the famous first chorus of *Antigone*, in which Sophocles takes up the problem, first posed by Heidegger in *Being and Time*, of what it means to be human.

In an apparent departure from his way of approaching *Oedipus Rex*, Heidegger examines the text in three phases; but, while it is true that he had stressed what might be called the "character" of that hero, his commentary, however brief, amounted to a statement about the play as a whole; and the same is true of his commentary on *Antigone*. Furthermore, the questioning that underlies each phase of his reading of *Antigone* underlies his reading of *Oedipus*, where they were subsumed into a single brief set of observations. Finally, in choosing this particular chorus, Heidegger has been guided by his desire to collect some of his own thoughts through the mediation of a passage that is already of a collecting type, a passage, that is to say, that is at once statement and synthesis.

In the first phase of interpretation "We seek that which sustains the whole and towers above it" (EM, 113/125), while in the second phase, in which the strophes are considered in sequence, we "hear how the being of man . . . unfolds" (EM, 117/129); the third phase then considers how the last part gathers together the essentials brought out earlier, but in a manner that throws into relief the presence of the interpreter. About this phase Heidegger remarks: "In the third phase we attempt to take our stand in the center of the poem, with a view of judging who man is according to this poetic discourse" (EM, 114/125).

The Strange

Heidegger takes his departure from the chorus's opening pronouncement: "There is much that is strange, but nothing that surpasses man in strangeness" (EM, 114/125). The prominence of the two variant terms that end each clause justifies Heidegger's attempt to consider very closely the range of their meanings. "Strange," *deinon,* can imply both the sense of a power so awful in its force that it compels panic and also a quieter sense, implying awe. It can indicate at the same time one who uses power and who does so, moreover, in a way that accords with Heidegger's theory of interpretation as violence:

> But on the other hand *deinon* means the powerful in the sense of one who uses power, who not only disposes of power ⟨Gewalt⟩ but is violent ⟨gewalt-tätig⟩ insofar as the use of power is the basic trait not only of his action but also of his Being-there. Here we use the word violence in an essential sense extending beyond the common usage of the word, as mere arbitrary brutality. [EM, 115/126]

All entities must be understood, says Heidegger, as the strange in the first sense, the sense of an overpowering power, within which Being-there is exposed; Being-there can be seen as violent in the fashion just described, that is, violent through the exertion of power, which may be taken to mean gathering power in order to make it manifest:

> Man is the violent one, not aside from and along with other attributes but solely in the sense that in his fundamental violence ⟨Gewalt-tätigkeit⟩ he uses power ⟨Gewalt⟩ against the overpowering ⟨Überwaltigende⟩. Because he is twice *deinotaton,* in a sense that is originally one, he is *to deinotaton,* the most powerful: violent in the midst of the overpowering. [EM, 115/126]

Heidegger is as fascinated by the quality of the strange or uncanny, *das Unheimliche*, as Freud had been by its linguistic and psychological variants.[6] Heidegger, of course, makes no attempt to trace the strange to a state of feeling, such as the impression that something awesome might make upon us. Rather, he considers what it means to be deprived of an essential home or *Heim*, that deprivation being itself a function of man's tendency "toward the strange in the sense of the overpowering," such that he continually "surpasses the limit of the familiar ⟨das Heimische⟩" (EM, 116/127).

Heidegger finds confirmation for his emphasis in line 360 of the second strophe, reading *Pantoporos aporos ep' ouden erchetai*: "Everywhere journeying, inexperienced and without issue, he comes to nothingness" (EM, 116/127). By that very process through which man hews paths for himself, he goes beyond all paths, or, as Heidegger prefers to say, echoing *Being and Time* as well as his description of Oedipus, he is thrown out of all paths. Putting the matter thus creates in the reader (it is hoped) a sense of the dynamic nature of human action, combined with a sense that all action is a coming-forth within powerful resistances—as if, notwithstanding the human capacity to decide, the field of possibles (as Sartre would say) were ultimately defined, not by *Dasein* itself, but by the totality within which *Dasein* finds itself. Since all of this is a way of saying in what sense man is the strangest, Heidegger can point out that the complete line, in effect, contains its own interpretation of *deinotaton*—just as, we might add, all the strophes in this chorus amount to an interpretation not merely of *Antigone* but of the very civilization the Sophoclean *Dasein* helped to found. The interpretation, however, is completed only with a phrase, *hypsipolis apolis*, in line 370. As the previously examined and similarly constructed phrase *pantoporos aporos* deprived man of *poros*, of passage, so this line deprives him of *polis*. Although this is, for most of us, a more familiar concept than the concept of *poros*, Heidegger directs attention beyond the usual meaning of city or city-state to the meaning of an essential place, "the there *in* which, *out of* which, and *for* which history happens. To this place and scene of history belong the gods, the temples, the priests, the festivals, the games, the poets, the thinkers, the ruler, the council of elders, the assembly of the people, the army and the fleet" (EM, 117/128). Heidegger brings out the uncertainty that surrounds this series of founding and therefore decisive undertakings; for if the types of persons described are preeminent, they are preeminent because of the work they do, and the true work means always going beyond what

6. "The Uncanny," in Sigmund Freud, *On Creativity and the Unconscious: Papers on the Psychology of Art, Literature, Love, Religion*, ed. Benjamin Nelson, trans. under the supervision of Joan Rivière (New York: Harper & Row/Torchbooks, 1963), pp. 159–62.

is present-at-hand into the unknown; it even means living without *polis:*

> Pre-eminent in the historical place, they become at the same time *apolis,* without city and place, lonely, strange, and alien, without issue amid the essent as a whole, at the same time without statute and limit, without structure and order, because they themselves *as* creators must first create all this. [EM, 117/128]

The Unfolding

In the second phase of interpretation, we recall, Heidegger follows the sequence of strophes in an effort to understand just how it is that the Being of man unfolds. By unfolding Heidegger does not, however, mean developing. While the opening strophe shows man sailing and plowing and the first antistrophe shows him catching birds, hunting in the wilds, fishing, and taming animals, it would be a misinterpretation, in Heidegger's opinion, to read this as an account of progress from a faltering beginning through higher and higher stages. Tacitly challenging the assumptions both of historicism and of psychologism, Heidegger argues that

> The basic fallacy underlying such modes of thought consists in the belief that history begins with the primitive and backward, the weak and helpless. The opposite is true. The beginning is the strangest and mightiest. What comes afterward is not development but the flattening that results from mere spreading out; it is inability to retain the beginning. [EM, 119/130]

It is this persistent desire to locate origins, or at least to delimit areas of time in which seminal events began to occur, that causes scholars such as Paul Friedländer to maintain a skeptical attitude toward Heidegger's commentaries on ancient Greek culture. Friedländer resists, for example, Heidegger's argument that truth as correctness of perception and assertion was first put forward by Plato; it was, Friedländer says, already to be found in earlier epic.[7] From this it does not follow, however, that Heidegger himself falls prey to the developmental fallacy. If he errs, he errs by too neatly reversing the direction of historical development, so that the efforts and events that others see as progressive become regressive. Though neither as schematic as Spengler nor as gloomy, Heidegger does tend, as we have seen, to dwell on the dark side of things (witness his too-ready acceptance of Staiger's sense that the speaker in the Mörike poem is melancholy). One way out of that

---

7. Paul Friedländer, *Plato: An Introduction,* trans. Hans Meyerhof, 2d ed. (Princeton: Princeton University Press, 1969), vol. 1, p. 229.

cul-de-sac is to turn utopian, which Heidegger does not do (though his exertions in behalf of the future attest to his belief that a better future is possible). Another way is to transfer utopia to the past, equating the best with the first—or rather, with the first insofar as it is Greek. For it should be remembered that Heidegger is attempting, in the present interpretation, to discover the true meaning of Greek *Dasein*. That very special phenomenon cannot, in Heidegger's view, be "explained" by historiography; it is not "logical"; like the epiphany in the Mörike poem, it simply happens. One of the enduring problems we must therefore face is the problem of giving articulate voice to what is ineffable without simply invoking what E. R. Curtius calls the *topoi* of inexpressibility,[8] which do little more than demonstrate a writer's or a speaker's inability to handle a large subject. Heidegger strives to keep the largeness—one is tempted to say, the grandeur—before us, underlining its wondrous nature rather than his own stance toward it. The mode of discourse to which such an attitude lends itself is what Heidegger calls mythology:

> If this beginning is inexplicable, it is not because of any deficiency in our knowledge of history. On the contrary, the authenticity and greatness of historical knowledge reside in an understanding of the mysterious character of this beginning. The knowledge of primordial history is not a ferreting out of primitive lore or a collecting of bones. It is neither half nor whole natural science but, if it is anything at all, mythology. [EM, 119/131]

The interpretation unfolding before us, then, may be likened to the unfolding depicted in the chorus, in that both are made up and made for belief. They are, accordingly, less argumentative than suasive, less rationally cognitive than reflectively peripatetic, less like an assertion requiring assent than a path inviting walkers.

In this sequence-oriented phase of interpretation Heidegger notes features methodologically closer to literary criticism than is often the case in his writings. Looking again, for example, at the opening strophe, we see that he focuses upon the manner in which man is depicted as going forth, in the section just following the opening words on strangeness: "The account of this departure concerts with the movement of the prosody; the word *chōrei* in line 336 is situated at the point where the meter shifts: *chōrei*, he abandons the place, he starts out— and ventures into the preponderant power of the placeless waves. The word stands like a pillar in the edifice of these verses" (EM, 118/129). The counterpart of man's excursion upon the sea is his incursion into

8. E. R. Curtius, *European Literature and the Latin Middle Ages*, trans. Willard R. Trask (1958; rpt. New York: Harper & Row/Torchbooks, 1963), pp. 159–62.

the earth, the singularity of these actions appearing to be reinforced in
the following strophe, which seems to attribute to *Dasein* the unique
possession of language.

In Heidegger's translation the second strophe runs:

> And he has found his way
> to the resonance of the word,
> and to wind-swift all-understanding,
> and to the courage of rule over cities.
> He has considered also how to flee
> from exposure to the arrows
> of unpropitious weather and frost.
>   [EM, 113/124]

Heidegger sees language as belonging not merely to *Dasein* but to the
totality of what is—to the overpowering power of sea, earth, and animal
nature. It is a matter of ascertaining "where," as it were, this or that
power operates: "The difference is only that the latter, the power that is
man's environment, sustains, drives, inflames him, while the former
reigns within him as the power which he . . . must take upon himself"
(EM, 119/131). So all-powerful is this differentiated power that it even
accounts for language, which, far from being a human invention, is that
which enables *Dasein* to be in the first place:

> How could man ever have invented the power which pervades
> him, which alone enables him to *be* a man? We shall be wholly
> forgetting that this song speaks of the powerful *(deinon)*, the
> strange and uncanny, if we suppose that the poet makes man in-
> vent such things as building and language. The word *edidaxato*
> does not mean: man invented, but: he found his way to the over-
> powering and therein first found himself: the violent one, the
> wielder of power. [EM, 120/131–32]

If all that is has an environing power of its own, if it thus consistitutes
one of those resistances to which I have referred, nevertheless it could
not be what it is except in that totality in which *Dasein* lays out paths of
its own through violence. Yet even as one recognizes this capacity, one
confronts the limitations set forth near the middle of the chorus:

> Everywhere journeying, inexperienced and without issue,
> he comes to nothingness.
> Through no flight can he resist
> the one assault of death,
> even if he has succeeded in cleverly evading
> painful sickness.
>   [EM, 113/124]

The condition of issuelessness, *Ausweglosigkeit*, resembles the condition depicted in Sartre's *Huis Clos (No Exit)*, in Kafka's fiction, in Beckett's fiction and plays, works which contend that there is no escape from what we do inasmuch as every movement we make is a movement on the path *we* make. Though man can, to be sure, go on somewhere, that somewhere looks to Heidegger suspiciously like nowhere:

> For man, as he journeys everywhere, is not without issue in the external sense that he . . . cannot go on. In one way or another he can always go farther into the etcetera. He is without issue because he is always thrown back on the paths that he himself has laid out: he becomes mired in his paths, caught in the beaten track, and thus caught he compasses the circle of his world, entangles himself in appearance, and so excludes himself from being. [EM, 121/132]

Heidegger's world view is darkened by the shadow of death in a manner alien to the Greeks, a fact of which he is only too aware. Death, the limit of limits, blocks off any escape, and this to Heidegger is a thing at once powerful and strange, a thing which *Dasein* can name but cannot go beyond. Indeed, it is that which sets the ultimate limit on man, a state of affairs reflected in the second antistrophe by the absence of any effort to name any new power; for Heidegger, this is the section in which the powers that have already been named are gathered "into their inner unity" (EM, 121/133). It is not obvious, however, that such is the burden that the lines in question actually sustain. If we apply the technique Heidegger employs in the early part of phase one, we focus on statement and stress—on what is more or less plainly said and the degree of emphasis with which it is said. This yields, it seems to me, a statement "about" three closely related conditions: nothingness, death, sickness. The position of each at the end of a cohesive syntactical period recalls the position of "strange" and "strangeness" in the opening lines, reinforcing the idea, which I now make explicit, that if the antistrophe has any special unity of its own, such unity depends on the force and parallelism of these related conditions, and that the conditions named do not apply equally to all of the powers named. On the contrary, the Being at issue here is specifically human; the afflictions described are not, for example, to be associated with the environing power of the sea or the earth. What Heidegger's observations show, I think, is a kind of premonitory parallelism in his thinking. That is, he sees the lines as more recapitulatory than they really are because his attention is already shifting to the concluding strophe, which does indeed, as he argues, carry us back to the beginning, in that we can understand the concluding choral "reaction" only by reconsidering the original point of departure, which was the meaning of "strange."

The strophe reads:

> Clever indeed, mastering
> the ways of skill beyond all hope,
> he sometimes accomplishes evil,
> sometimes achieves brave deeds.
> He wends his way between the laws of the earth
> and the adjured justice of the gods.
> Rising high above his place,
> he who for the sake of adventure takes
> the nonessent for essent loses
> his place in the end.
>   [EM, 113/124]

Heidegger approaches the meaning of skill by way of the Greek *technē*, which he distinguishes both from the sense of technique and from the notions of art or craft. *Technē* for Heidegger signifies a mode of *ecstasis*, specifically a pattern of looking beyond whatever is already given at any time. When we recall his insistence that beginnings are great and that diminution typically follows, we can appreciate the admiration he feels when he says that such looking out is an event that occurs initially and *persists* in occurring.

Heidegger's high claims for art are rooted in his belief that a work of art is more, vastly more, than an instrument of pleasure. If knowledge is the capacity to discover the Being of anything whatever—in his phraseology, to put such Being to work—then art is knowledge as well as truth. In a statement echoing many passages in *The Origin of the Work of Art*, Heidegger declares:

> The work of art is a work not primarily because it is wrought
> ⟨gewirkt⟩, made, but because it brings about ⟨er-wirkt⟩ being in
> an essent; it brings about the phenomenon in which the emerging
> power, *physis*, comes to shine ⟨scheinen⟩.... Because art in a
> pre-eminent sense stabilizes and manifests being in the work as
> an essent, it may be regarded as the ability, pure and simple, to
> accomplish, to put-into-the-work ⟨ins-Werk-setzen⟩, as *technē*.
> [EM, 122/134]

That process is a struggle, a use of violence, for Being does not come forth on its own; it must be brought forth—almost fought forth—into manifestation. Hence *technē* constitutes a fundamental characteristic of *deinon*.

Equally fundamental is the Greek word *dikē*, which is normally termed "justice," but which Heidegger translates as *Fug*. Manheim notes that because this word occurs in modern German only in the phrase *mit Fug und Recht*, and because "it conveys no precise meaning but suggests 'proper order,' 'fitness,'" Heidegger is free to define it in his own way, which he does not hesitate to do.

Heidegger regards the liberties he takes as necessary, given the fact that *dike* loses its original force when rendered as "justice" or as "norm" rather than as, say, "the overpowering." *Fug,* by contrast, commands a wider range and greater depth of meaning, since it counts not only as "joint and framework ⟨Füge und Gefüge⟩" but as "decree, dispensation, a directive that the overpowering imposes on its reign," and "finally . . . [as] the governing structure ⟨das fügende Gefüge⟩ which compels adaptation ⟨Einfügung⟩ and compliance ⟨Sichfügen⟩" (EM, 123/ 134–35).

The relation between *techne,* or violence, and *dike,* or the overpowering, is a reciprocity, like the Heraclitean unity of conflicting powers in *polemos.* The relation is a kind of striving swirl that can be articulated only in some circular manner, such as the following: "In this confrontation *techne* bursts forth against *dike,* which in turn, as *Fug,* the commanding order, disposes ⟨vergüt⟩ of all *techne.* The reciprocal confrontation *is.* It is only insofar as the strangest thing of all, being-human, is actualized, insofar as man is present as history" (EM, 123/135).

Man is the strangest, *deinotaton,* because of the relation between these two meanings—more actively expressed, because of the interplay between the two ways of exerting power. No matter how hard men work, no matter how much *techne* they carry into the midst of entities in order to bring forth Being, the overpowering order remains always itself, unmastered. Work is ecstatic, and *ecstasis* means venturing forth into the unknown—a dangerous venture in which *Dasein* battles storms of distraction, in which non-Being surrounds and threatens, in which *Dasein* runs the risk of becoming lost in "dispersion, in-stability, disorder, mischief. The higher the summit of historical Being-there, the deeper will be the abyss, the more abrupt the fall into the unhistorical, which merely thrashes around in issueless and placeless confusion" (EM, 123/135).

The Unspoken

The third phase of interpretation, in which Heidegger expresses the concept of "violence" outlined above, takes up where the second phase ends, with the final strophe, the aim being, as we recall, to "show what does not stand in the words and is nevertheless said." Because this requires violence, the resulting interpretation becomes in a sense mimetic, reflecting in its own way the dangerous venturing described above. It is as if the text had become *dike,* the interpretation *techne,* so that the reciprocity we have seen in the relation of the two can be seen equally in the interpreter's approach to what is essentially spoken. Hence, as *Dasein* wrests Being from unconcealment within the totality of what is, interpretation wrests Being from unconcealment within the totality of the text.

The final strophe sounds a catastrophic note as man "loses his place in the end," the disaster reflecting historical destiny, which Heidegger now views from the standpoint of the necessary consequence imposed on human life by the overpowering:

> Man is forced into such a Being-there, hurled into the affliction ⟨Not⟩ of such being, because the overpowering as such, in order to appear in its power, *requires* a place, a scene of disclosure. The essence of being-human opens up to us only when understood through this need compelled by being itself. The Being-there of historical man means: to be posited as the breach into which the preponderant power of being bursts in its appearing, in order that this breach itself should shatter against being. [EM, 124/136–37]

Being means Being itself, *Sein selbst*, which of necessity hurls man forth; but if we focus on *Dasein*, we see a breaking-away from all that is familiar so that Being can break in. The result is disaster because the overpowering against which man ventures can never be mastered and because man must finally come to nothingness; yet, as "the deepest and broadest affirmation of the overpowering" (EM, 125/137), even this disaster is deemed a good. To put it another way: Being is brought about, is put to work in the sense previously described, through the breaching that Being demands of persons and of a people. Hence the reader of Heidegger may come to feel a tension between activity and passivity, between Being-there as violent venturing and Being-there as "mere" opening, an irreconcilable tension that renews our sense of what Heidegger means when he speaks of the historical. "*As history* the overpowering, being, is confirmed in works" (EM, 125/137). That is, human working—as in art—bears witness to the very Being that Being-there serves in bringing beings forth. The Being-there peculiar to pre-Socratic Greek culture, what Heidegger calls "Greek *Dasein*," has nonetheless an originating role, since, if there is any truth to what Heidegger says above about art's capacities, it is proper to hold, as he does, that Greek *Dasein* could not have been were it not for the type of poetic thinking that shines forth in *Antigone:* for in this text "we are dealing with the poetry and thinking that first awakened and established the historical Being-there of a people" (EM, 126/139).

The chorus concludes:

> May such a man never frequent my hearth;
> May my mind never share the presumption
> of him who does this.
>
>   [EM, 113/124]

Although Heidegger acknowledges that these lines furnish some basis
for thinking that the chorus ends by rejecting man, he denies that this is
what they do in fact mean. And indeed the gloss he rejects presupposes
a turnabout in point of view that makes the chorus—to say the least—
inconsistent. But if Heidegger is justified in objecting to such a reading,
his own interpretation drifts rather wide of the mark: "Insofar as the
chorus turns *against* the strangest of all, it says that this manner of being
is *not* that of every day. Such Being-there is not to be found in the usual
bustle and activity" (EM, 126/138). Stating the matter that way, however, merely replaces one type of discontinuity with another: now the
chorus suddenly denies that the things already said truly present *Dasein*
as it is; it merely states what it can be when it somehow transcends the
everyday. But the everyday is a modern notion based on a sense that
mundane life is *merely* mundane, that man has fallen away from an
earlier, pristine condition, and that one can be genuinely human only
rarely, in bursts of transcendence—a perspective that finds its literary
counterparts, to be sure, in Joyce's epiphanies and Virginia Woolf's
heightened moments. But even if one accepts such a view, there is no
reason to suppose it was the view of Sophocles; least of all should
Heidegger fail to see that strangeness is an essential characteristic of
Dasein as such and not a characteristic that appears only when *Dasein*
emerges from the everyday.

Heidegger's difficulty may be traced to his habit of construing a text
as a nexus of leading words or themes adding up to a kind of statement
that he can play off against his own thinking. In the present case this
means overlooking the dramatic structure of the chorus and, in the
same process, overlooking the common-sense meaning of what is said in
the concluding lines. It seems to me that both considerations—the dramatic and the commonsensical—are satisfied when one hears the lines
in relation to the lines that precede them. There, at the end of the third
strophe, man is shown rising higher than he should and making the
grave mistake of confusing what is with what is not, so that he loses his
place in the end.

The closeness of the connection becomes the more or the less evident
as one adopts different formal divisions. The E. F. Watling (Penguin)
translation presents a series of four-line strophes, the last two of which
correspond to what Heidegger distinguishes as strophe three and the
lines with which the chorus ends:

> O wondrous sublety of man, that draws
> To good or evil ways! Great honor is given
> And power to him who upholdeth his country's laws
>   and the justice of heaven.
>
> But he that, too rashly daring, walks in sin
> In solitary pride to his life's end,

> At door of mine shall never enter in
>   To call me friend.[9]

A more recent translation observes a division into two strophes and two antistrophes, the second of which corresponds to the two strophes just quoted and thus to strophe three and the concluding lines in Heidegger's construction.

> Beyond imagining he's wise
> Through labyrinthine ways both good and bad:
> Distinguished in his city when
> He is law-abiding, pious;
> But displaced when he promotes
> Unsavory ambition.
> And then, I want no part with him,
> No parcel of his thoughts.[10]

Both of these translations, taken together with Heidegger's, make it plain that the shift in attitude answers the action that goes immediately before. For however one divides the lines, there comes a point at which man overreaches himself, rises too high, and becomes in a profound sense "displaced"; at that time the chorus says no, I reject such a man. The chorus does not deny that the tendency to err is an aspect of the human condition. On the contrary, it takes its place among all the other aspects dramatized. But when people err in excess, when they aim too high, then one must say so; and this is what the chorus does. If it lacked the capacity so to judge, what Heidegger calls the historical Being-there of the Greeks in their early, great age could not have been what it was.

For perspective, the measure that enables the chorus to speak as it does may be thought of, not only in terms of the *dikē* that Heidegger sees as the overpowering, but in terms of *dikē* as justice. Heidegger, to be sure, regards justice as merely a juridical and moral concept; but within the play the powerful orders that interweave (to use one of Heidegger's own terms) include the orders of *nomos* and of *polis*. Heidegger's "law of the earth" (*Satzung der Erde*) accounts for the former, and he probes as well the meaning of *polis*, bringing out the broad sense of place as well as the sense of the city. A comparable range of meaning is invoked, however, by *nomos*, which also means a musical mode, and by *isonomia*, which means "equilibrium among forces, but also the principle that gives a citizen equal rights in a democracy."[11] *Antigone*

9. *The Theban Plays: King Oedipus, Oedipus at Colonus, Antigone*, trans. E. F. Watling (London: Penguin, 1947), p. 136.

10. *The Oedipus Plays of Sophocles: Oedipus the King, Oedipus at Colonus, Antigone*, trans. Paul Roche (New York: New American Library/Mentor, 1958), p. 177.

11. My argument draws on Albert Cook, *Enactment: Greek Tragedy* (Chicago: Swallow, 1971), pp. 99 ff., although that author cannot be held responsible for my conclusions or for

surely is a play about equilibrium among forces, even as it is a play in which the *polemos* among forces might almost be deemed a force in itself. One of Goethe's generalizations in *Wilhelm Meister* (Book VIII, ch. vii) states that "equilibrium cannot be restored except by contraries," and this applies, it seems to me, to a tragedy that brings disorder back to order, imbalance to balance. Law prevails because justice prevails, but justice itself (e.g., in the teaching of Solon) comes to pass as equilibrium.

If *nomos* was separated from *physis* by Plato, many of the tragedians took it for granted that the two were connected by the unifying tendency that is—paradoxically to the modern mind—inherent in their very opposition.

The "definition" of the human condition that the play embodies evidently allows room for these additional aspects, and probably more. It does not, in any case, lend itself to the sort of elucidating condensation that Heidegger brings to *Oedipus Rex*, which enables him to say that Oedipus embodies the fundamental Greek passion for the disclosure of Being. Even less obliging, it would seem, is *The Odyssey*, which, while it presupposes the constant possibility of unconcealment, and depicts it at crucial junctures, derives much of its strength from the tension that precedes and surrounds those junctures. In other words, it is conceivable that one could, without harm and with potential benefit, turn the direction of poetic thinking toward the idea that in these instances of Greek tragedy and epic we behold a passion for *polemos* as well as a passion for unconcealment, the tension between the two being, possibly, that through which passion itself most dramatically comes forth.

Thinking about Nothing

The state of wonder alluded to in the lecture on Heraclitus makes itself felt not only in the long section on *Antigone* but in other parts of the study, including those that deal with the familiar philosophical question: "Why is there something rather than nothing?" Furthermore, the thinking that ensues seems governed by an admonition, also put forward in "*Aletheia*," to take up wonder as the abode of thought, which means, in temporal terms, dwelling on an issue until one is dwelling in it. That is to speak metaphorically, to be sure. To put it another way, Heidegger constantly returns to the fundamental issue of the meaning of Being, starts again and again from the same question but without answering and hence without ever truly departing from it, and by this

---

my suggestions pertaining to Heidegger. For an interesting observation by Hölderlin on equilibrium in tragedy, in connection with the idea of element, see SG, 172.

circularity creates a region of poetic thinking so consistent and unique that each part of the resulting book resembles every other part in the book, while very little of it much resembles any part of any book by anyone else. Whatever takes place—the reading of *Oedipus* or *Antigone,* which we have followed, or the problem of nothing, to which we are now turning—takes up its place in the manner of the Greek *chōra,* which, we recall, does not signify space or place in the modern sense "but that which is occupied by what stands there. The place belongs to the thing itself. Each of all the various things has its place." So the parts of Heidegger's book have each their place, which helps to explain why, when taken from their peculiar "scene," they resemble discrete items in a museum, worth experiencing but lacking the fullness that inheres in them only when they continue in their own aura and abode.

Some parts, of course, stand up, when out of context, better than others, Heidegger's discussion of nothing and nothingness being a case in point. It stands up, I believe, because the possibility of nothing is ever present and is tangibly experienced (if not explicitly mentioned) when thinking dwells upon the wonder that something, that anything, is; for if something is, it has overcome the possibility that it need not have been. The discussion also stands up because Heidegger gets at the issue by means of art, and art, and more especially poetry, is an omnivalent force from whose continual resurgence the book draws energy and continuity.

The advantage of the question "Why is there something rather than nothing?" lies in the words that follow "something." The question could have been: "Why is there something?" But "rather than nothing" frees questioning to explore the possibility of non-Being, which is to say that it frees us to wonder and to contemplate the source of that wonder. The source is, again, something or anything, but not in the form of something or anything that just happens to be present. Rather, the question holds open a duration in which inquiry feels in the dark for some ground to explain why a given being does not, for example, fall back into non-Being:

> Now the essent is no longer that which just happens to be present; it begins to waver and oscillate, regardless of whether or not we recognize the essent in all certainty, regardless of whether or not we apprehend it in its full scope. Henceforth the essent as such oscillates, insofar as we draw it into the question.... And the search for the why undergoes a parallel change. It does not aim simply at providing an also present ground and explanation for what is present; now a ground is sought which will explain the emergence of the essent over against nothingness, or more pre-

cisely, the ground for the oscillation of the essent, which sustains and unbinds us, half being, half not being, which is also why we can belong entirely to no thing, not even to ourselves. [EM, 21–22/ 23]

This sense of oscillation and emergence resembles the sense of the uncanny that the Heidegger of *Being and Time* regarded as characteristic of dread. Rilke's Malte spoke with alarming eloquence to the latter sense, overwhelmed as he was by dread; thus the value for Heidegger of the passage from Rilke's novel. That passage is very different in tone and tenor, however, from passages Heidegger uses later; and even when he turns to texts in which others see embodied the darker experiences addressed in the writings of the early Heidegger—the poems of Trakl are in this respect paradigmatic—the later Heidegger finds calmness, play, ceremony, the musical, the holy; and when wonder occurs, it is not the amazement of a being in panic but the still fascination that reflection finds in the phenomenon of Being itself. To illustrate the difference, compare the passage from *Malte Laurids Brigge* with the "authentic speaking about nothing" that Heidegger discovers in the third volume of a Knut Hamsun trilogy about a man named August. The novel, entitled *The Road Leads On,*

describes the last years and end of this August, who embodies the uprooted modern man who can do everything equally well yet who cannot lose his ties with the extraordinary, because even in his weakness and despair he remains authentic and superior. In his last days August is alone in the high mountains. And the poet says: "Here he sits between his ears and all he hears is emptiness. An amusing conception, indeed. On the sea there were both motion and sound, something for the ear to feed upon, a chorus of waters. Here nothingness meets nothingness and the result is zero, not even a hole. Enough to make one shake one's head, utterly at a loss." [EM, 20/22]

Poetry as Emergence, Founding, and Bringing-Forth

Although the difference between the two recorded experiences is a difference in mood, to borrow from the language of *Being and Time*, this in turn arises from the fact that poetic thinking no longer dwells on Being-there but on any phenomenon of time or Being that occurs and, beyond these, on the meaning of beings and of Being itself, and, beyond that, on the ground that thinking seeks as a source of fundamental ontological wonder. Poetry (and a novel is poetry in Heidegger's sense) can speak of beings as if they "were being expressed and invoked for the first time. Poetry, like the thinking of the philosopher, has always so much world space to spare that in it each thing—a tree, a mountain, a house, the cry of a bird—loses all indifference and commonplaceness" (EM, 20/22). This is another way of stating that poetry may be compared with *physis*, as the actual emergence of actual trees, mountains, houses, bird cries. Through the qualification "as if" Heidegger glances at the homage art pays to the "real" world by fostering an "illusion" of it; here, the illusion is that each thing is now invoked for the first time. But there is a poetically founded "first time" that is primordial. In poetry, Heidegger says, there is so much world—literally, so much world to spare—that anything can emerge through it; and if "it" refers simultaneously to poetry and the world, so much the better, because the world envisaged here is founded by poetry. It is not, therefore, the world in the sense of *Being and Time*, since in that work thought had not freed itself from constant reference to *Dasein*. By the time of *The Origin of the Work of Art*, which is also the time when *An Introduction to Metaphysics* is first laid out, the world includes *Dasein* but no longer "belongs" to such a being. The world, like Heraclitus' world-fire, now has many meanings, and the context in which it appears is as wide as thinking can make it or, better, as wide as thinking can allow it to be. The emphasis of thinking now falls, not upon the role of *Dasein* in a world drama, but upon that drama. In such a drama are many roles played differently together, like the parts in a dance or a piece of music. One of Heidegger's more interesting attempts to capture this interaction occurs in his discussion of men as the violent ones, the wielders of power, who open up beings—sea, earth, animals—*as* the beings they are.

> [This] happens only insofar as the powers of language, of under-standing, of temperament, and of building are themselves mas-tered ⟨bewältigt⟩ in violence. The violence of poetic speech [*Sagen*], of thinking projection, of building configuration [*bauen-den Bilden*], of the action that creates states is not a function of faculties that man has, but a taming and ordering of powers by virtue of which the essent opens up as such when man moves into it. [EM, 120/132]

Such a view does not differ fundamentally from the view, expressed in *The Origin of the Work of Art*, that a work of art actually works; that through art things are set to work; and that the work of art has the capacity to found. Equally close is the link with Heraclitus' thinking about *alētheia* and the reflections of Parmenides (a frequent topic in *An Introduction to Metaphysics*) on the relation between Being and thinking:

> We know from Heraclitus and Parmenides that the unconceal-ment of being is not simply given. Unconcealment occurs only

when it is achieved by work: the work of the word in poetry, the work of stone in temple and statue, the work of the word in thought, the work of the *polis* as the historical place in which all this is grounded and preserved. [EM, 146/160]

But where, in the achievement of the work, is the worker? In *The Origin of the Work of Art* the artist, we recall, combined with art, audience, and work of art to form a fourfold. Here, by contrast, the work is thought of in relation to the power of *physis*, which, emerging, arises, unfolds, and lingers, coming into unconcealment by achieving itself as world. The latter is not yet the world of the fourfold, which we will encounter in the chapter that follows, though it is already more, as I have indicated, than the world that belongs to Being-there. World now comes about in consequence of a primordial separation, of the type referred to earlier in the present chapter. So fundamental is this struggle that it gives rise to the differentiation of the human and the divine:

It is this conflict that first projects and develops what had hitherto been unheard of, unsaid and unthought. The battle is then sustained by the creators, poets, thinkers, statesmen. Against the overwhelming chaos they set the barrier of their work, and in their work they capture *(bannen)* the world thus opened up. It is with these works that the elemental power, the *physis* first comes to stand. [EM, 47/51]

This is Heidegger's way of enlarging on Heraclitus' fragment, which traces emergence, as well as the persistence of what emerges, to an *ur*-conflict. "This conflict, as Heraclitus thought it, first caused the realm of being to separate into opposites; it first gave rise to position and order and rank. In such separation cleavages, intervals, distances, and joints opened. In the conflict ⟨Auseinandersetzung, setting-apart⟩, a world comes into being" (EM, 47/51). Heidegger does not commit his own thinking, it would appear, to the narrative sequence he attributes to Heraclitus, nor does he delve, in Heraclitus' manner, into the issue of origins. For Heidegger, there is nothing prior to those beginnings in which something emerges through the power of *physis*, in which a collectivity establishes a city-state or in which a poet embodies the passion of an epoch. Nevertheless, by recounting Heraclitus' vision in the form of a story with two crucial phases, Heidegger allows us to infer that the temporal ordering may reflect an order of priority in the sense of rank. In *The Origin of the Work of Art*, we recall, poetry finally enjoyed the highest position in a hierarchical arrangement of the several arts; so the desire to order, in the sense of ranking, is by no means new. The issue, in the present text, is not of course the relative placement of the arts but the relative placement of those who perform work—the poets, thinkers, statesmen, whom Heidegger calls creators. In Heidegger's account of Heraclitus, the work brought forth by the latter looks almost like an epiphenomenon, though this is surely not what Heidegger wishes to imply. What he wishes to imply, it seems to me, is that all phenomena of whatever sort—shoes or a painting of shoes, actual mountains or a poem about mountains—are brought forth through a power involving human effort in only one of its two modes, and that mode not the higher. The point of departure is the idea, set down in *The Symposium* (205b), that *poiēsis* is "calling something into existence that was not there before," as one standard translation has it.[12] For Heidegger that occasion for which "whatever passes over and goes forward into presencing" (VA, III, 11/10) is the true meaning of *poiēsis* (rendered in "The Question Concerning Technology" as bringing forth, *Her-vor-bringen*):

> It is of utmost importance that we think bringing-forth in its full scope and at the same time in the sense in which the Greeks thought it. Not only handcraft manufacture, not only artistic and poetical bringing into appearance and concrete imagery, is a bringing-forth, *poiēsis*. *Physis* also, the arising of something from out of itself, is a bringing-forth, *poiēsis*. *Physis* is indeed *poiēsis* in the highest sense. For what presences by means of *physis* has the bursting-open belonging to bringing-forth, e.g., the bursting of a blossom into bloom, in itself *(en heautōi)*. In contrast, what is brought forth by the artisan or the artist, e.g., the silver chalice, has the bursting-open belonging to bringing-forth not in itself, but in another *(en allōi)*, in the craftsman or artist. [VA, III, 11/10–11]

Such a theory allows for a poetry requiring poets—the works of a Sophocles, a Hölderlin, a Trakl—but also for (so to speak) a poetry without poets—the blooming of a blossom, the coming-out of a butterfly from a cocoon, the plummeting of a waterfall when the snow begins to melt. The last two analogies underline the fact that Heidegger's example is a threshold occasion, a moment of ecstasis when something moves away from its standing as one thing to become another. The bud, too, would therefore exemplify bringing-forth; but if that be allowed, an infinite regress has begun, for the emergence of the bud requires the prior emergence of other sustaining and nourishing parts of the plant, not to mention some ecstasis of germination, without which there could be no further bringing-forth. No one occasion, then,

12. Plato, *The Collected Dialogues*, ed. Edith Hamilton and Huntington Cairns (Princeton: Princeton University Press, 1963), p. 557. The translation of *The Symposium* is by Michael Joyce.

can be regarded as privileged. What is of highest value, in the realm of bringing-forth, is the autonomous process that reminds us of the ecstasis of Being-there, but with the Being-there removed. Separating and ordering, Heidegger thrusts the artist into a prominence never enjoyed, for example, in *The Origin of the Work of Art*, only to show that, for the highest instance of bringing-forth, the artist is not required.

If this does not sit easily with the reader, it is at least in part because one cannot determine from the account the fate of that differentiation, in *An Introduction to Metaphysics*, wherein man as *technē* bursts forth against Being as *dikē*. There, the overpowering power of Being, *physis*, moves equally through man and through all that surrounds him, There, language and building and all that goes with human life belongs with *physis* no less than the sea or the earth or animals. But even in that earlier rendering, the center of interest shifts away from Being-there to Being, which is why Heidegger insists that *physis* is so overpowering that it can never be mastered by the violence of *technē*. The discussion in "The Question Concerning Technology" moves further in the same direction, then, but in a way that seems to elevate one type of bringing-forth at the expense of another. This happens, I believe, because Heidegger does not make, as he could have done, the connection between *poiēsis* and the world that, by the time of "The Question Concerning Technology," has already been worked out. For world has become a totality involving an interplay of regions and that power of saying that works through poetry and at the same time through all other bringing-forth.

Poetry retains a special place befitting its capacity to found. This is expressed in a passage, from *An Introduction to Metaphysics*, that will help to lay the ground for our examination, in chapter 6, of poetic thinking in relation to the fourfold of the world:

> Let us think of the sun. Every day it rises and sets for us. Only a very few astronomers, physicists, philosophers—and even they only on the basis of a specialized approach which may be more or less widespread—experience this state of affairs otherwise, namely as a motion of the earth around the sun. But the appearance in which sun and earth stand, e.g., the early morning landscape, the sea in the evening, the night, is an appearing. This appearance is not nothing. Nor is it untrue. Nor is it a mere appearance of conditions in nature which are really otherwise. This appearance is historical and it is history, discovered *(entdeckt)* and grounded in poetry and myth *(Sage)* and thus an essential area of our world. [EM, 80/89]

Because this text, as already noted, straddles the two main periods with which we are concerned, it is not certain that *Sage* here names saying in the sense established by works such as "The Thing," with which the following section opens. But even if the term speaks ambiguously, even if it means nothing more than myth, the passage still returns to a basic idea that informs the earliest part of the present discussion as well as the previously cited text, "The Question Concerning Technology." The idea is that of unconcealment; specifically, whatever comes to appearance comes that way, insofar as it is brought forth, into unconcealment, whatever the manner of bringing-forth (i.e., whether it "bursts open" in itself as a blossom or in another as a chalice). Heidegger's term, in the technology essay, for that wherein this coming occurs and continues (lingers, if you will) is "revealing" (Entbergen), which plays upon the same root, bergen, that appears in unconcealment (Unverborgenheit) and, as he himself goes on to point out, brings us back to truth as alētheia, the original point of departure in the present chapter.

6

Poetic Thinking and the House of Being:
Rilke and Anaximander

> It is precisely because thinking is not poetry but a primordial saying and speaking of language that it must stay near the poetic.
>
> *What Is Called Thinking?*

"What Are Poets For?", "Letter on Humanism," and "Anaximander's Maxim," three works from 1946, show Heidegger's thought moving in the same general direction as before and on the strength of the same underlying beliefs. Yet each work can be seen to move, for interesting reasons, in its own peculiar way, the first- and last-named pieces being in this respect the furthest apart.

Those already converted to the Heideggerian cause will probably prefer the Anaximander essay, as the more radical, while skeptics will probably feel more comfortable with the Rilke piece, employing, as it does, a more familiar terminology. For me this is a way of saying that Heidegger's approach to the ancient fragment is a demonstration of poetic thinking in a way that his analysis of Rilke, for all its virtues, is not.

Let us consider the two works in turn, beginning with "What Are Poets For?"

Approaching Rilke

The fully stated question, from which the title is drawn, is posed by Hölderlin in the elegy "Bread and Wine": " . . . and what are poets for in a destitute time?" (H, 248/91). Rendered destitute by the absence of gods and the failure of mortals to come into their own essential nature, our own epoch is such a time, and the author of *The Duino Elegies* and the *Sonnets to Orpheus*—these two poetic cycles being the only "valid" poetry Rilke composed—is one of its poets. In practice Heidegger goes outside them, commenting on a piece of occasional verse from a letter, a poem from the early *Book of Hours (Stundenbuch)*, a 1924 lyric on "The Force of Gravity" ("Schwerkraft"), and some other late pieces. In making his selection, Heidegger once more leans on such standard helps as dating and provenience. The improvised verse appears in a letter of August 15, 1924, and "The Force of Gravity," which Heidegger merely describes as "late," was penned on October 5 of the same year. Equally significant, both were written in the Château de Muzot where, in February, 1922, Rilke had composed the *Sonnets* and where, in the same month, he had finished the manuscript of the *Elegies*, begun in 1912. The assumption is that the *Elegies* and the *Sonnets* make up a single large work to which the other productions, at least in part because of the time and place of their composition, also belong. Thus Heidegger slips back—as in *The Origin of the Work of Art* and some of the Hölderlin essays—into that very tradition of received representations and self-justifying procedures that he had undertaken, in *Being and Time*, to "destroy."

It is not at all clear, furthermore, that the improvised poem provides a better way of grasping Rilke's achievement than a work such as "The Panther" ("Der Panther"), which helps establish his fascinating conception of animals and their relation to human beings, and which could be usefully related to his conception of the Open (to which we will turn below). The same applies to "Turning" ("Wendung"), which provides a measure for the inward movement in Rilke that Heidegger discusses at length on the basis of other sources.

It further appears that the status of a poem—whether it is already valid or is merely "on the way" to becoming so—is decided largely on the thematic level. That is, Heidegger tends to prefer a work that is manifestly "about" an issue; and while the same tendency appears in his interpretations of other poets, it is particularly strong here. The advantage of the two late poetic cycles is that they permit such an approach to a much greater extent than, say, the *Dinggedichte*, the poems about things, where the strength lies in concreteness.

The Draft

"The Force of Gravity" hints at what Rilke means by his crucial concept of the draft:

> Mitte, wie du aus allen
> dich ziehst, auch noch aus Fliegenden dich
> wiedergewinnst, Mitte, du Stärkste.
> Stehender: wie ein Trank den Durst
> durchstürzt ihn die Schwerkraft.
> Doch aus dem Schlafenden fällt,
> wie aus lagernder Wolke,
> reichlicher Regen der Schwere.

Center, how you draw yourself
out of all things, regaining yourself
even from things in flight: Center, strongest of all!
Standing man: like a drink through thirst,
gravity plunges through him.
But from the sleeper there falls,
as from low-lying cloud,
a rich rain of weight.

[H, 260/104]

Heidegger does not relate this poetic conception—as might profitably have been done—to the famous remarks on gravity and centeredness in Heinrich von Kleist's essay on the marionette theater. To do so would be to stay in the realm of mere literary history. Nor does he connect this conception, in the manner of a Merleau-Ponty, to Rilke's singular notion of the psychical and corporeal. To do so would be, for Heidegger, to skirt the fundamental question about Being that must always be raised. Heidegger even denies that Rilke's approach to gravity deals with physical gravitation. The center spoken of is deemed to be the same as the "unheard-of center" in the Sonnets (Pt. II, no. xxviii), which is unheard-of because we are less aware of it than of the common middle of some ordinary physical thing.

The center is understood as that which holds all beings together, mediating between them, in a process that Heidegger sees as a "drawing-toward"; it is for this reason that he plays back and forth between his own term Zug—draft, in the sense of drawing or pulling—and Rilke's term Bezug, originally meaning relation or reference, but here endowed with a larger significance. The longer that play continues, the more the draft assimilates the relation, so that Hofstadfter, in his seamless translation, finally lets Bezug become "the draft."

The power of the draft is the power of attraction, for which physical gravity is a mere analogue; the draft, in its mediating pull, gathers everything in such a way that the manner in which each being lets itself be gathered is that being.

Rilke's name for the whole draft is the Open, by which he points to all that is unbounded, unbarring, infinite, and that thereby holds a promise of ultimate release from the limitations of existence. It is not a realm that Heidegger particularly likes. It implies, for one thing, an escape from consciousness, as we learn from Rilke's admiration for the ability of animals to be in the world without seeing that world over against them as an object. But consciousness, for Heidegger, is neither here nor there; nor could it be otherwise in a thinking that, from the period of Being and Time, sees in the philosophy of Descartes the very essence of dualistic, logical, representational, scientific, mechanistic metaphysics.

The Open, despite its name, could not be more different from un-concealment, as defined by Heidegger:

> If we attempted to interpret what Rilke has in mind as the Open in the sense of unconcealedness and what is unconcealed, we would have to say: what Rilke experiences as the Open is pre-cisely what is closed up, unlightened, which draws on in bound-lessness, so that it is incapable of encountering anything unusual, or indeed anything at all. . . . The confinement within the bound-less is established by man's representation. The oppositeness confronting him does not allow man to be directly within the Open. In a certain manner, it excludes man from the world and places him before the world—"world" meaning here all beings as a whole. [H, 262/106–7]

On the other hand, Heidegger is sympathetic toward Rilke's concern over the dramatic diminution, within our epoch, of our capacity to experience things as things. In the Middle Ages, Rilke contends, money was still metal, still beautiful, still wholly and immediately a thing, and not a mere piece of change in which reality appears, at best, as a nostalgia-inspiring residue.

It is only in an epoch of representation, an epoch of calculation and planned production, that things undergo such change: in short, in a destitute time. In the world sustained in such a time, *aisthēsis*—the directly given, vivid immediacy of things—becomes foreign. The will to self-assertion, carried out in technology, forces things into the mold of a calculating control, transforming the world into a ghost of itself.

Rilke offers, as an alternative, the prospect of a release into the Open, not conceived as, for example, the sky or ordinary space, but into a transcendental "orbit" that Rilke seems to have adopted, *mutatis mutandis*, from ancient cosmologies.

Now the circular and the spherical, as quasi-spatial figures broadly expressing realms of experience that are by no means merely spatial, have excited phenomenological interest. Poulet's *Metamorphoses of the Circle* traces the pattern in authors from the earliest times to the twen-tieth century, and Bachelard concludes his *Poetics of Space* with a study of roundness.[1] The interest bespeaks a respect for the integrity of a lived experience, irrespective of its relation to the "objective" spatiotemporal world. With its capacity for suggesting self-completeness, wholeness, and unity, the circle or sphere helps us, in Bachelard's words, to collect and confirm ourselves. His conception of roundness derives from ob-

---

1. Georges Poulet, *The Metamorphoses of the Circle*, trans. Carley Dawson and Elliott Coleman in collaboration with the author (Baltimore: Johns Hopkins University Press, 1967); Gaston Bachelard, *The Poetics of Space*, trans. Maria Jolas (1964; rpt. Boston: Beacon, 1969).

servations like Karl Jaspers' statement: "Every Dasein seems in itself round"[2]—observations that do not arise spontaneously from perceptions but are given only in meditation. Bachelard, of course, is more inclined to the patently spatial than is Heidegger: an important caveat. But the qualification is less true when it comes to roundness, which leads Bachelard to seek "centers of cosmicity,"[3] understood not as physical middles but as that which brings the contradictions of the cosmos together within its own unity. What is more, Bachelard turns to Rilke, whose conception of a round birdcall prompts—without being influenced by—Michelet's sense that the bird's mode of Being is essentially spherical.

Heidegger, in contrast to Bachelard, does not begin from an image or (as in the case of Michelet) a discursive passage but from a word. The meaning of this cannot be construed as variously as its mere lexical range suggests, but it has already been defined (though Heidegger does not say so) by a concern with roundness that recurs throughout Rilke's canon.[4]

If Heidegger ignores the many passages that could make possible a phenomenology of the sphere in Rilke, it is because such an enterprise would leave the central question unasked, and that is the question, not of what Being means in Rilke's spherical conception, which remains within "the language of metaphysics" (H, 277/122), but the question of what Being means when the poetic thinker plays out possibilities that remain unspoken or unthought in the original poetic conception.

> The spherical does not consist in a circuit which then embraces, but in the unconcealing center that, lighting, safeguards present beings. The sphericity of the unifying, and the unifying itself, have the character of unconcealing lighting, within which present beings can be present (*Anwesendes anwesen kann*). This is why Parmenides (Fragment VIII, 42) calls the *eon*, the presence of what is present (*das Anwesen des Anwesenden*), the *eukuklos sphaire*. [H, 278/123]

Such lighting, which in no wise differs from the lighting or clearing of Being, differs markedly from the region within which present beings, in Rilke's vision, transcend themselves; this is an imaginary space, a space within one's own interiority, that is like a poetic version of that subjectivity from which metaphysics regards all beings. It is into this realm that we must enter, according to Rilke, if we are to protect the unshielded condition that springs from our relation to nature:

2. Bachelard, *The Poetics of Space*, p. 232.
3. Ibid., p. 238.
4. Käte Hamburger, "Die phänomenologische Struktur der Dichtung Rilkes," in *Philosophie der Dichter: Novalis, Schiller, Rilke* (Stuttgart: Kohlhammer, 1966), pp. 179–275, esp. pp. 200 ff.

Wie die Natur die Wesen überlässt
dem Wagnis ihrer dumpfen Lust and keins
besonders schützt in Scholle and Geäst,
so sind auch wir dem Urgrund unsres Seins

nicht weiter lieb; es wagt uns. Nur dass wir,
mehr noch als Pflanze oder Tier
mit diesem Wagnis gehn, es wollen, manchmal auch
wagender sind (und nicht aus Eigennutz),
als selbst das Leben ist, um einen Hauch

wagender.... Dies schafft uns, ausserhalb von Schutz,
ein Sichersein, dort, wo die Schwerkraft wirkt
der reinen Kräfte; was uns schliesslich birgt,
ist unser Schutzlossein and dass wirs so
ins Offne wandten, da wirs drohen sahen,

um es, im weitsten Umkreis irgendwo,
wo das Gesetz uns anrührt, zu bejahen.

As Nature gives the other creatures over
to the venture of their dim delight
and in soil and branchwork grants none special cover,
so too our being's pristine ground settles our plight;
we are no dearer to it; it ventures us.
Except that we, more eager than plant or beast,
go *with* this venture, will it, adventurous
more sometimes than Life itself is, more daring
by a breath (and not in the least
from selfishness).... There, outside all caring,
this creates for us a safety—just there,
where the pure forces' gravity rules; in the end,
it is our unshieldedness on which we depend,
and that, when we saw it threaten, we turned it
so into the Open that, in widest orbit somewhere,
where the Law touches us, we may affirm it.

[H, 255/99]

What is the nature of this daring that is more venturesome than life itself?
And what remains to be dared?

The House of Being

In seeking an answer, Heidegger suggests that Rilke leaves unsaid and
unthought the possibility that, if life itself is a daring venture, what is
more adventurous even than life must be more daring also than the
Being of beings in which that life consists. This can only mean: more
daring than Being, which is not bound to particular beings but is the

mode in which all beings are. The difficulty, at this point, is that there seems to be nothing by which Being can be surpassed. To see the question that way, however, is to presuppose that there must be something "other" that can somehow be more than Being. In truth, says Heidegger, restating a position taken in *Being and Time* (SZ, 38/62): "If Being is what is unique to beings, by what can Being still be surpassed? Only by itself, only by its own, and indeed by expressly entering into its own. Then Being would be the unique which wholly surpasses itself (the *transcendens* pure and simple)" (H, 286/131). In transcending, Being does not pass over into something else: unique to itself, it passes itself along in its own way and so comes into its own, satisfied to be its own "more."

In no other modern thinker, perhaps, do we find quite this sense of plenitude. The ontic fullness of which Sartre speaks, for example, is something one aims toward. When one squeezes into a hole, one hopes to occupy it so completely as to establish a plenitude in the world, which Sartre associates with the "spherical plenitude" of Parmenides. One pursues the goal, of course, as a consciousness, through a nothingness whose transcendence is toward Being, whereas for Heidegger Being is transcendence understood as a surpassing of itself by itself. Sartre seems to come nearer to Heidegger in stressing, as we have seen, the generosity of artistic creation, which is a gratuitous gift. But such generosity and such giving remain on the ontic level of inter-subjectivity: the "more" that the artist adds to the natural landscape by imagining it is an intentional object given over to another consciousness. In the process, Being is unveiled (and Sartre's description shows some Heideggerian influence), but always as the act of one discrete being in relation to another. There is a Heideggerian flavor as well in Sartre's account of the way in which man unveils the world. On our way back to Heidegger, we can attempt the experimental variation of reading the following from a Heideggerian perspective:

> Every one of our perceptions is accompanied by the consciousness that human reality is "unveiling," that is to say that, through it, "there is" being, or that man is the means by which things manifest themselves; it is our presence in the world that multiplies relations, it is we who put this tree in relation to this corner of sky; thanks to us, this star, dead for thousands of years, this quarter-moon and this dark river unveil themselves in the unity of a landscape; it is the speed of our automobile, of our airplane, that organizes the great terrestrial masses; with each of our acts the world reveals to us a new face.[5]

5. Jean-Paul Sartre, *Situations, II: Qu'est-ce que la littérature?* (Paris: Gallimard, 1948), pp. 89–90.

The concluding example indicates too much deliberate, objectifying self-assertion for Heidegger. Consciousness or perception no longer interests Heidegger except insofar as each is raised by the Rilkean metaphysics Heidegger wants to go beyond; nor does *Dasein* play the role in Heidegger that it plays here—or that it played, for that matter, in Heidegger's earlier thinking. What remains—and it is important—is the situation of a man within a realm that would not *be* without him. Man is a being who, in going beyond, yet stays "inside," and what he stays inside is indissociable from his going. He is within Being and so dwells in that through which he has his Being.

Sartre goes on in the same passage to say that man is not the producer of Being, while Heidegger sees the problem, again, in terms of daring or venturing. It now develops that the precinct of Being *(Bezirk des Seins)* is what the more daring ones dare. The venture occurs from within, not in the sense of an interiority or an immanence but in the sense that man's going is at all times a going through language.

A useful perspective on this idea is furnished by Kenneth Burke, who reaches by a somewhat different route much the same conclusion Heidegger announces in his notion of language as the house of Being. In "What Are the Signs of What? A Theory of 'Entitlement,'" Burke playfully inverts the relation of words to things, suggesting that the latter may be meaningfully regarded as signs of the former. The premise is that human beings are so immersed in the medium of words that everything is linguistically mediated, the form of mediation varying with the norms of the society in which a particular language is spoken:

> Thus, in mediating between the social realm and the realm of nonverbal nature, words communicate to things the spirit that the society imposes upon the words which have come to be the "names" for them. The things are in effect the visible tangible material embodiments of the spirit that infuses them through the medium of words. And in this sense things become the signs of the genius that resides in words . . .; for man, nature is emblematic of the spirit imposed upon it by man's linguistic genius.[6]

Heidegger expresses himself more radically, and perhaps more poetically, when he states:

> Language is the precinct *(templum)*, that is, the house of Being. . . . It is because language is the house of Being that we reach what is by constantly going through this house. When we go to the well, when we go through the woods, we are always already going through the word "well," through the word "woods," even if we do not speak the words and do not think of anything relating to

6. Kenneth Burke, *Language as Symbolic Action: Essays on Life, Literature, and Method* (Berkeley and Los Angeles: University of California Press, 1966), p. 362.

language. Thinking our way from the temple of Being, we have an intimation of what they dare who are sometimes more daring than the Being of beings. They dare the precinct (*Bezirk*) of Being. They dare language. [H, 286/132]

Since all beings whatever are beings only by virtue of dwelling in this house, that Rilkean inner space in which *Dasein* may seek release can occur there and only there, assuming it can occur at all. It hardly need be said that for Heidegger the genuine transcendence remains the transcendence pure and simple of Being, which, as we have seen, does not go over into something else but only into itself. Heidegger adds: "Being itself traverses this going over and is itself its dimension" (H, 286/131). If that last word carries an echo, it is because we have heard it in that other work of 1946, the "Letter on Humanism," where dimension is the realm vouchsafed to the gods by divinity, which is in turn a realm sustained by the holy. The difference is that the other dimension, that of Being, is with us, before us, around us, through us—and we through it—as we traverse the language that is its house. But, as an earlier part of the "Letter" implies, it is only because Being, in yet another dimension, makes possible the ecstases of *Dasein* that this same dimension can be with us, before us, around us, and through us; for Being is also "the dimension of the ecstasis of ex-istence. The dimension is not, however, the familiar spatial one. Rather, all that is spatial and all spaces of time have their Being in the dimension (*west im Dimensionalen*) which Being itself is" (W, 333–34).

By contrast, the dimension of the holy (W, 351–52) can be identified only by its traces, and it takes someone unusually daring, such as a poet equal to the historical challenges of his epoch, to discover them.

The mark of such poets "is that to them the nature of poetry becomes worthy of questioning, because they are poetically on the track of that which, for them, is what must be said" (H, 294/141).

In Heidegger and Heidegger's Rilke the questioning yields no binding answers, not because language is inadequate but because we are inadequate to language. It is precisely the poets who, recognizing this, yet declining to despair—and Rilke seems one of these—most deeply question poetry.

Two objections may be raised. One is that the criterion for discerning the mark of such poets is too broad. Among modern writers, questioning the nature of art, not to mention its value, is *de rigueur;* and practically every poet has been questioning language since at least as early as 1902, when Hugo von Hofmannsthal, in the *persona* of an English Renaissance courtier, describes in a letter a crisis that has rendered him incapable of speaking or thinking. More and more the uncanny wells up, spilling over into everything he sees and does until the identities of familiar things waver and blur. So uncontrollable does the process become that it threatens the loss of what Heidegger calls "the relation of all relations," namely, language. Hofmannsthal describes the process—which reflects the poet's anxiety about his vocation and about the nature of poetry—as a vertiginous change of perspective recalling the time when a piece of his own skin, examined through a magnifying glass, took on the appearance of a field with furrows and hollows. The experience becomes more and more like the movement of falling characterized in *Being and Time* (SZ, 178/223) as turbulence *(Wirbel)*: "Individual words swam around me; they ran into my eyes, which stared at me, and into which I stared back; a turbulence they were, which made me dizzy when I looked down at them."[7] The difference is that turbulence now arises, not from immersion in the discourse of the "they" depicted in 1927, but from the same questioning so central to the Rilke essay of 1946.

Here, then, in a particularly vivid form, is a fundamental experience of modern poets, of whom Hofmannsthal's fellow Austrian is one, but only one. That is why Heidegger's criterion for discerning the mark of appropriate poets strikes me as too broad.

Possibly too narrow, on the other hand, and hence too confining, is the metaphor of the house of Being. It is, to be sure, an arresting metaphor; and that may be part of the problem. The reader may visualize something all too static, something that looks for all the world like a thing—and one, moreover, that is present-at-hand. The problem is not merely that the metaphor gives a misleading prominence to space; the problem is that it thrusts before consciousness what could almost be called a picture of metaphysics.

The explanation lies in Heidegger's theory of understanding. As *Being and Time* demonstrates, understanding is foundational, which is to say, it provides that wherein anything may be understood:

> With the term "understanding" we have in mind a fundamental *existenziale,* which is neither a definite *species of cognition* distinguished, let us say, from explaining and conceiving, nor any cognition at all in the sense of grasping something thematically. Understanding constitutes rather the Being of the "there" in such a way that, on the basis of such understanding, a *Dasein* can, in existing, develop the different possibilities of sight, of looking around [Sichumsehens], and of just looking. [SZ, 336/385]

In this theory, we note, seeing is not divorced from its foundation but arises from it: just insofar as we are beings who understand do we see

7. Hugo von Hofmannsthal, *Erzählungen und Aufsätze,* ed. Rudolf Hirsch (Frankfurt: Vischer, 1957), vol. 2, pp. 342–43.

and hear. But when we turn to the Leibnizian principle of reason, taken by Heidegger to exemplify the metaphysical position of Western thought, we find two separate realms, one belonging to the senses, another to reason itself. In this conception, it becomes necessary to distinguish between the "mere" perception of phenomena through the senses and the understanding of those phenomena through the nonsensible faculty that is reason. Hence, if we talk about understanding something visually or aurally, we are not really talking about understanding as such but about understanding in a transferred or metaphorical sense. From the perspective Heidegger lays out in *The Principle of Reason*, such a notion is spurious.

> The establishment of this divorce of the sensible and non-sensible, of the physical and the non-physical, is a fundamental trait of what, named metaphysics, gives authoritative determination to Western thought. Once it is recognized that this distinction . . . is insufficient, metaphysics loses the rank of the authoritative determinant for the course of thinking.
>
> Once, then, metaphysics is seen as restricted, the notion of metaphor as authoritative falls as well. In particular it provides the criterion for our notion of the essence of language. Metaphor is so often used in this way as a means for interpreting the works of poetry and the images of art in general. Only within metaphysics is there the metaphorical.[8]

It follows that, when Heidegger seems to use metaphors, he is actually using something else, namely words, which do not operate in relation to the literal because there is no such thing as the literal; there is just whatever the words say. Words operate, for lack of a better term, kinetically, which is why I have so often employed in my discussion the vocabulary of movement and why Ronald Bruzina can state: "By this time we should be ready to recognize that Heidegger is not attempting to formulate a position, but rather to execute a movement. If we realize now that this 'movement' he executes is not always *in language*, but also in a highly original and strange kind of wording, then we are close to seeing that this very *immersion in a wording movement* constitutes thinking."[9]

The house of Being, however, does not exemplify the immersion we find in those later writings in which, significantly, words from the realm of water play an increasingly conspicuous role. The problem with the house of Being, I am suggesting, is that it can easily seem to express

---

8. Ronald Bruzina, "Heidegger on the Metaphor and Philosophy," in *Heidegger and Modern Philosophy* (New Haven: Yale University Press, 1978), p. 187. This entire article, to which I am indebted, rewards close study.

9. Ibid., p. 197.

a formulated position instead of a movement, and this is due at least in part to the fact that, from the viewpoint of metaphysics, it is so plainly metaphorical.

It also has the disadvantage of being tied almost too closely to the criterion of human presence. Not that Heidegger would wish to overlook such presence; but the "Letter on Humanism" announces, with other texts, an increasing concern, as we have seen, with other dimensions, and the house of Being does not reflect these particularly well. When Heidegger has us walking through the woods of words, he is evidently trying to incorporate something from those dimensions (e.g., the emergence of Being, through language, in the mode of thing) and something of the quality of movement so characteristic of the later works. Shifting from the house to the temple is another sign that the "metaphysical metaphor" of the house needs help; and, in a sense, help does come, but only insofar as the reader carries into the temple associations from *The Origin of the Work of Art*, where the sacred edifice draws in the earth and the sky as well as human beings and the gods.

This may explain why, at the end of the "Letter," Heidegger does not round off the essay with another reference to the house—which first appears in the opening paragraph—but steps outside it to speak of sky and earth and mortals:

> The thinking of the future . . . is on a descent into the poverty of its preparatory nature. Thinking gathers language in simple saying (*Sagen*). Language is thus the language of Being, as clouds are the clouds of the sky. With its saying, thinking lays invisible furrows in language. They are still more invisible than the furrows drawn in the field by the farmer's lonely stride. [W, 364]

In light of the theory advanced above, it is relevant to note that the passage moves in two ways: through the tread of the farmer across the field and through the very process of shifting from the clouds to the field. It is also relevant to note the absence of any reference to the gods or even to the holy. Why this should be, one can only guess. My guess is that Heidegger, whether deliberately or not, is holding back as a way of dramatizing the destitute condition of the epoch in which, as he says earlier in the letter, homelessness has become the destiny of the world (W, 339).

It is another kind of destiny and another kind of world that emerge from Heidegger's attempt, through the earliest surviving fragment of Greek thought, to explore the meaning of Being without metaphysics and without metaphor.

Approaching Anaximander

As *Being and Time* seeks, in a measure, to undo the history of metaphysics, so "Anaximander's Maxim" seeks to undo the history of translation. The similarity of purpose accounts for a methodological self-consciousness reminiscent of *Being and Time* but seemingly out of tune with the spirit of other post-1927 writings.

Because of the widespread practice of measuring early thinkers against Plato and Aristotle, translations and interpretations of Anaximander and comparable figures are little more, in Heidegger's eyes, than "classicistic" and anachronistic representations. This means that the texts do not come to us in Greek but, if you will, in a third language, spoken—or rather, written—only by the practitioners of specialized disciplines. The text becomes a kind of palimpsest in which the original meaning can, at best, be glimpsed. The words of that text (in the scholarly reconstruction on which Heidegger leans) are:

> . . . kata to chreeon   didonai gar auto dikēn kai
> tisin allēlois tēs adikias.

> according to necessity; for they pay one another punishment
> and amends for their unfairness. [H, 314]

A translation in a collection of pre-Socratic texts offers the following:

> The Unlimited is the first-principle of things that are. It is that from which the coming-to-be [of things and qualities] takes place, and it is that into which they return when they perish, by moral necessity, giving satisfaction to one another and making reparation for their injustice, according to the order of time.[10]

Compare this with the translation offered by Johann Huizinga and with Huizinga's brief attempt at a gloss:

> "Things must necessarily perish in that same principle from which they arise (i.e. the Infinite). For they have to render expiation to one another and atone for the wrong they did according to the ordinance of time." This utterance can hardly be called exactly lucid. But at any rate it contains the idea of the cosmos having to seek expiation for some primordial wrong. However intended, it gives us a glimpse of a profound thought startlingly reminiscent of Christian doctrine. We have to ask ourselves, though, whether

10. *The Presocratics*, ed. Philip Wheelwright (New York: Odyssey, 1966), p. 54. Cf. the translation by Nietzsche, quoted by Heidegger at the beginning of the essay (H, 296), and the one in Hermann Fränkel, *Early Greek Philosophy: A History of Greek Epic, Lyric, and Prose to the Middle of the Fifth Century*, trans. Moses Hadas and James Hillis (Oxford: Basil Blackwell, 1973), p. 266.

the dictum reflects the already mature stage of Greek thought about statecraft and justice as exemplified in the 5th century B.C. or rather a much older stratum of juridical thinking . . . where the ideas of justice and punishment still mingled with those of sortilege and physical combat, where, in short, the legal process was still a sacred game?[11]

This text—as we will see, once Heidegger's is available for comparison—also falls short of the type of setting-over Heidegger has in mind, though he might have found agreeable Huizinga's description of the "tones of prophecy and rapture" in which the earliest philosophers expressed a view of the universe that was "agonistic" in a peculiarly harmonious, almost symphonic way.[12] When Heidegger argues that primacy belongs both to the language of the text and to the mother language of the translator, to each of which the translator must be bound, he prepares the basis for the subtle, poetic working with words that will enable the reader to think the maxim within the genius of the German language. Though the effort recalls Walter Benjamin's desire, as translator, to transform his mother tongue and thus to participate in its continuing development, Heidegger, for his part, would rather revive it—to return it from within to its own forgotten or heretofore unrealized possibilities.[13]

  Before any setting-over into one's mother tongue comes a setting-over into that which enables what is spoken to come forth. That which enables what is spoken to come forth is thinking, not, of course, as a subjective activity over and against an object (text), but as a movement with the text. Allied with such an approach is a conception of poetry that, not surprisingly, resembles the conception in *The Origin of the Work of Art*. There, we were told, poetry in the narrower sense of the term *(Poesie)* is essentially poetry *(Dichtung)* in the broadest and most fundamental sense. In the case of the Anaximander essay, poesy relates to poetic thinking in the following way:

> The maxim *(Spruch)* of thinking lets itself be set over only in thinking's conversation with that which thinking speaks. Thinking, however, is poetry *(Dichten)*, and not merely a type of poetry in the sense of poesy and song. The thinking of Being is the original way of Being-poetic *(Dichten)*. Only in thinking and before everything does language come to language, which is to say, in its essential nature *(Wesen)*. Thinking says the dictation of the truth

  11. Johann Huizinga, *Homo Ludens: A Study of the Play Element in Culture* (1950; rpt. Boston: Beacon, 1955), p. 117.
  12. Ibid., pp. 116–17.
  13. Schöfer, "Heidegger's Language," in Kockelmans, ed., *Heidegger and Language*, pp. 294–96.

of Being. Thinking is the original *dictare*. Thinking is the *ur*-poetry that precedes all poesy, but also what is poetic in art, insofar as, within the precinct of language, what is poetic in art comes into the work. All poetry *(Dichten)* in this broader and narrower sense of the poetic is, in its ground, a thinking. The poetic nature of thinking preserves the holding-sway of Being's truth. [H, 303]

The substitution of *Dichten* for *Dichtung*, underlining the kinship of poetry and thinking, can be explained in several ways. In the first place, because it can apply equally to the individual poem and to a total body of poems, *Dichtung* is at once too particular and too general. In the second place, *Dichtung*, as the standard term for poetry, has been used for so long, and with so little thought in Heidegger's sense, that it has become a kind of third-language term, spoken only by specialists, in the manner alluded to above. Finally, as a homonym of the infinitive (to compose or write poetry, to invent), *Dichten* supplies a verbal energy for those ecstases of poetic thinking that together make it move.

As in *Being and Time* and the lecture on Heraclitus, *alētheia* plays a leading role in "Anaximander's Maxim," the emphasis falling now upon its necessary dependence on concealment, an emphasis that contrasts with Heidegger's approach to truth in 1927 but is present in his depiction of earth in *The Origin of the Work of Art*.

When we think about the great historical periods and world views, Heidegger argues, we are guided by a "fundamental trait of Being that Being as *alētheia* rather conceals in *lēthē* than discloses" (H, 310). Being has a peculiar way of misleading beings, including human beings, who find themselves led astray in "error." Now error is a mode of forgetfulness to be dissociated from any notion of chronological distance as understood by, say, the discipline of history. Error arises from an inherent tendency in Being that Heidegger calls holding-to-itself, which he endeavors to elucidate through the concept of *epochē* In using this word, Heidegger takes, as Sartre was also to do, a considerable liberty, but one that moves in a different direction. The French philosopher, accepting Husserl's basic definition, makes the word stand, by extension, for the neutralization of the everyday world that is undertaken by literary realism and the Surrealists, this "antiseptic" attitude, as he calls it, being for Sartre a version of the attitude of the ancient Stoics. Himself acknowledging the Stoic origin of *epochē*, Heidegger too looks back to Husserl, but only to alter the meaning of *epochē* even more radically: "This work taken from the linguistic usage of the Stoa does not here name, as in Husserl, the methodology of putting out of action the thetic consciousness in objectification. The *epochē* of Being belongs to itself. It is thought out of the experience of the forgetfulness of Being" (H, 311).

The temporal structures worked out in *Being and Time* are translated into "the epochal essence of Being [which] belongs to the concealed temporal character of Being and characterizes the essence of time thought in Being" (H, 311).

Heidegger tackles the difficult assignment of demonstrating the connection between this time and ecstatic, existential time by doing two things. The first is to suggest a kind of correspondence: "The ecstatic character of *Da-sein*, however, is the correspondence to the epochal character of Being that we mostly experience" (H, 311). What this means is somewhat clarified in the second thing he does, which is to render the lived temporality of the correspondence now as an event, now as a process of enduring: "The epochal essence of Being 'happens'" (*ereignet*) the ecstatic essence of *Da-sein*. The ex-istence of human beings endures the ecstasis and thus preserves the epochal mode of Being (*das Epochale des Seins*) to whose essence the *Da* and consequently the *Da-sein* belongs" (H, 311–12).

Heidegger has already begun the process he will shortly justify in one of those methodological passages that, as in other works we have considered, he distributes throughout his text. This is the process of attempting, prior to any specific interpretation of Anaximander's text as such, to experience the Greek way of thinking.

To this end Heidegger sets himself the task of interpreting Anaximander's words, not according to Platonic or Aristotelian usage, but from the poetry of Homer, in whom they take an earlier, more primordial and original, as well as a less conceptual and less metaphysical form.

> . . . and among them stood up
> Kalchas, Thestor's son, far the best of the bird interpreters,
> who knew all things that were, the things to come and the things
> past,
> who guided into the land of Ilion the ships of the Chaians
> through that seercraft of his own that Phoibos Apollo gave him.
> [*Illiad*, I. 68–72][14]

The *eonta* of line 70, Heidegger observes, belongs, with *eon*, to the archaic vocabulary of Parmenides and Heraclitus, from which the "ontic" and the "ontological" in the later, conceptual vocabulary of Plato and Aristotle are derived. But what is crucial for poetic thinking is that root *e-*, equivalent to the root *es-* in *estin* and the "is" in other languages, such as Latin, German, or English. *On* and *onta*, Heidegger notes, are participial endings lacking their main stems. *On*, for example, means "being," as in the English present participle; but we can

---

14. *The Iliad of Homer*, trans. Richmond Lattimore (Chicago: University of Chicago Press, 1951), p. 61.

immediately see a parallel with the ambiguity disclosed in *eon*, which means both *to be* and *a being:* "In the twofold (*Zwiefalt*) of the participial meaning of *on* is concealed the difference between 'being' (*seiend*) and a 'being' (*Seiende*). That which, thus portrayed, at first looks like grammatical hairsplitting is in truth the riddle of Being" (H, 317).

To Heidegger, the poet's use of the pluperfect "had seen" (which does not survive in the English translation, above), indicates that visionary seeing is a having-seen. Echoing the discussions of the "already" in *Being and Time*, Heidegger remarks: "A seer has always already seen. Having seen in advance, he sees ahead. He sees the future tense out of the perfect tense" (H, 319). Such a vision enacts that unity of the three ecstases that was also delineated in *Being and Time* and that Hölderlin experiences as the "united three" of Heracles, Dionysus, and Christ (H, 248/91). The vision corresponds, furthermore, to the modes of Being that Heidegger uncovers in the fragment by Anaximander; but because these appear only in and through time, it will be necessary to approach them from a basically temporal orientation.

Homer's *ta t'eonta ta t'essomena pro t'eonta*—"what is, will be, or was"—names equally present, past, and future time; hence, any access to one is access to all. Heidegger's analysis pays particular attention, nonetheless, to the role of the present, which denotes not only the "when" of a being but its nature, which is to say its Being. In Heidegger's Anaximander, what is present has accomplished its advent (*Ankunft*) by virtue of emerging in unconcealment; beings that emerge from unconcealment are experienced as present beings, as "what is present" (*Anwesende*), and the Being of such beings is presence (*Anwesen*). In this fragment of ancient Greek thought, in other words, Heidegger discovers a different meaning for the "there" that belongs to beings. The issue is no longer the *Da* of *Dasein*, wherein the "there" denotes the situation into which a particular kind of Being is thrown; the issue is now a "there" indicating that anything is insofar as it is present, has been present, or will be present, for only thus is genuine presence as such achieved. The distinction Heidegger draws between presence and what is present or present beings, is, then, the corollary of the distinction he draws between Being and beings: presence is to Being as Being is to present beings.

Thus we see that Heidegger's descriptions of the three ecstases (he does not employ the term) depends on unconcealment as the *sine qua non* of genuine presence. Hence a certain privilege accrues to a time in which emergence into unconcealment is occurring. Because any being is characterized by presence just because it is a being, such a time cannot be called merely "the present"—the notation would not distinguish it from other times, since all times are at some stage "present time." Such a time Heidegger therefore names the "presently present,"

i.e., it is the mode of Being-present achieved by emerging into unconcealment. (Some flavor of it clings to the progressive tenses employed, for example, in English and Spanish.) When this is not the case,
we encounter times in which such unconcealment was achieved or will
be achieved, the times of the "nonpresently present." That is, these are
still characterized by the quality of presentness, but the presentness
they show is different from the presentness shown by that "presently
present" time just described.

Over the centuries—in Heidegger's account of history—the sense of
the presently present gradually becomes dominant, bespeaking as it
does its nearer relation to unconcealment, so that *eonta* comes to stand
for what is present here and now in the same way that the present-at-
hand (as depicted in *Being and Time*) comes to stand for beings in general. The irony is that in the process we have forgotten the relation that
inspired the dominance in the first place; and to say that we have
forgotten the relation between presence and unconcealment is to say
that we have forgotten to think about the nature of presence, this being
tantamount to saying, again, that we have forgotten Being.

Although the seer's experience of what has been described makes
him, in the common perception, delirious, mad, possessed, this is only
to point to a mode of ecstasis:

> The delirious one *(Rasende)* is beside himself. He is away . . . from
> the mere pressure of what lies there before us *(Vorliegenden)*, of
> the merely-present present beings *(nur gegenwärtig Anwesenden)*
> and at the same time away to what is presently present,
> insofar as this is always only what constitutes the advent *(An-
> künftige)* of what is non-present. [H, 320–21]

In support of this unfamiliar account of presence, Heidegger offers an
interpretation of the fragment's leading words that is at once detailed
and broad, careful and venturesome, clear and obscure, an interpretation that does not yield a product, in the sense of a conceptual resolu-
tion, but presents a process. Because of the central role of this process,
which depends for its success on the very movement of words and
ideas, I will take up salient issues where possible in the same order that
Heidegger himself follows.

Adikia

Like the *a-* in *alētheia*, the *a-* of *adikias*, with which the fragment concludes, is privative. Standard translations set the concept over into the
sphere of morality or law, rendering the companion term *dikē*, for
example, as justice or right. Heidegger, however, prefers the broader

sense of being out of joint or in a state of disjuncture: "The maxim says: what is present is, as what is present, out of juncture (*aus der Fuge*)" (H, 327). Dwelling out of juncture can belong only to what is present, however, because dwelling in juncture belongs to it equally, just as the possibility of speaking the truth belongs to language along with the possibility of speaking falsely. Heidegger connects the idea of the juncture with the idea of the "between" examined in *Being and Time* and *An Introduction to Metaphysics,* though he makes the connection through newly wrought language. The argument can be stated as follows: being finite, what is present is here for a while; one might almost say in a while: "The while is between coming-forth and going-away. Between this twofold absence is the present of all that whiles" (H, 327). The juncture names this while, in which present beings, emerging into unconcealment, come into their own: presence needs a scene for its disclosure, and present beings, in a manner of speaking, provide it. That, I believe, is the drift of the idea Heidegger has in mind when he says that these beings give "*Fuge*" (H, 328).

tisin allēlois

If Heidegger objects to the habit of associating *adikias* and *dikē* with justice, he objects equally to the habit of associating *tisis* with punishment, which is a moralistic rather than an ontological concept. Better is the idea of being ruthless (*ohne Ruch*) and, better still, the old word *ruoche,* which carries overtones of care reminiscent of *Being and Time.* To give another care in the sense of *tisis* as "ruth" is to let the other remain other: hence Heidegger's reminder that the word "rest" (*geruhen*) relates very closely to *Ruch*; as for the giving, that inheres in the nature of those who do the giving:

> *Tisin allēlois* would stand for the basic relationship of the one persistent, *Dasein,* toward the other persistent, the *Seiende,* that makes the presence of the *Seiende* possible by fusing the ecstases to form the thing. The opposite of this care (*Ruch*), the failure to build the thing in all of its authentic dimensions, would be the *Un-fug*—the *a-dikia,* the *Un-ruch,* the care-less.[15]

Finite, present beings—beings that are here "for a while"—live their while by giving care to others, which is to say not only to beings that are like themselves but to those that are not. Such giving is nothing less than the giving of the juncture, though in putting the matter this way

15. Thomas Langan, *The Meaning of Heidegger: A Critical Study of an Existentialist Phenomenology* (London: Routledge & Kegan Paul, 1959), p. 152. Langan's book, which has an especially good section on Anaximander, offers one of the clearest as well as one of the earliest interpretations of Heidegger in English.

one must be careful to avoid implying that human beings "originate" the process. The origin, insofar as one can properly call it that, is the fact that whiling beings exist within "the open realm of unconcealment" (H, 332).

kata to chreeon

Heidegger pays special attention to words of the type known as syncategorematic, words markedly relational in that they can be employed solely in connection with other terms. According to William of Sherwood, logic consists not only of categorematic terms, deployed as subjects or predicates, but also of terms that are "functional" in the sense that they operate only in service to those other, categorematic terms; syncategorematics thus include "every," "both," "neither," "but," "only," and "not."[16]

Concentrating on words of this type means shifting attention away from nominal objects, such as "injustice," to which conventional, third-language translations have lent an aura of unquestioning permanence. To a thinking that improvises and plays, words that, like these, contribute to a sense of dynamic movement and process are therefore especially inviting. Heidegger remarks that the syncategorematic *kata*, meaning "down from above," suggests a descent, or *Gefälle*, involving a consequence, *Gefolge*; hence what is present may be said to fall down along and to follow from presence, so that what is present is "under" that of which it is the consequence. Especially intriguing is the genitive aspect of *kata*, which is said to be "of" *chreeon*; for the genitive

> names a genesis, an origin *(Herkunft)* of present beings from presence. But both the essence of this origin, along with the essence of both [present beings and presence] remains unthought. . . . The essence of presence and with it the difference between the present and present beings remains forgotten. The forgetting of Being is the forgetting of the difference of Being from beings. [H, 335–36]

To chreeon names the relation of presence to present beings and names it, moreover, in a manner closely connected with the notion of giving described above: "*to chreeon* is then the handing-over of presence, which handing-over hands presence over to what is present and thus precisely holds what is present as such in the hand, that is, preserves it in presence" (H, 337). Certain risks go along with speaking of the hand in this way. One is the risk that the reader will associate this process with that of creation, an association made available by any

16. *William of Sherwood's "Treatise on Syncategorematic Words,"* trans. Norman Kretzmann (Minneapolis: University of Minnesota Press, 1968); Alexander Pfänder, "Logik," *Jahrbuch für Philosophie und phänomenologische Forschung* 4 (1921).

number of traditions, images, and works, including Michaelangelo's Sistine Chapel, with its great figure of God touching life into Adam through the hand, or the Rilke story in which human beings fall into their lives from the deity's hands ("The Tale of the Hands of God"). There is also the risk that the reader may associate the process with strictly human, individual endeavor, as in the handing-over of something, such as a birthday gift, in everyday life. Heidegger's concept of the hand, however, encompasses more than human activity in the ordinary sense. Not only does the hand grasp, hold, and press, not only does it reach and hold and bear, but

> the gestures of the hand go everywhere throughout language and indeed most purely when man speaks by keeping silent. For only insofar as man speaks, does man think; and not the other way around, as metaphysics would still have it. Every movement of the hand in every one of its works carries itself through the element, bears itself in the element of thinking. All work of the hand rests in thinking. Therefore thinking itself is the simplest and hence the most difficult hand-work of man. [WHD, 51]

In the language of metaphysics, this states that man is a tool-using animal because he is a symbol-using animal, a formulation that draws too small a distinction between human and nonhuman beings and expresses too narrow a sense of use. The distinction between human and nonhuman is too small because *Dasein* is not a species of the genus "animal" but enjoys its own kind of Being (as *Being and Time* is at pains to prove). The sense of use in the paraphrase is too narrow, on the other hand, first, because use, when poetically understood, embraces the idea of a need as well as the idea of putting something to use (the German *brauchen* meaning both). The sense of use in the paraphrase is too narrow, second, because needful use, as a reciprocity, unites the actors in a relationship as large as, and closely similar to, the relationship that obtains between Being-there and other kinds of Being when the former give in care the juncture through which presence emerges in unconcealment as what is present. A key lies in three lines from Hölderlin's hymn "The Ister":

Es brauchet aber Stiche der Fels
Und Furchen die Erd',
Unwirthbar wär es, ohne Weile; . . .
        [WHD, 117]

It is useful, though, for the rock to have clefts,
And the earth, furrows,
Otherwise it would be inhospitable, without time for staying; . . .

This concept of need does not derive from a sense that present-at-hand things (e.g., rocks) lack, *ab ovo*, what some other kind of thing can supply; nor does it attribute to such things an analogue of human appetite or desire. A rock *qua* rock, as it rests on the ground, is not to be found wanting just because there is nothing to break it open so as to permit the passage of a stream; and the same is true of the earth. On the other hand, if the earth is to be a place of habitation, there need to be water and crops; these once supplied, the earth and rock are useful, and yet not merely so for *Dasein*. They are also useful *for* earth and rock in that both may hand over what can be used because needed, that use and that need being defined by a belonging-together of a unique kind: "'It is useful' says here: an essential to-getherness exists *(bestehen)* between rock and clefts, between furrows and earth, *within* the essential realm that opens with dwelling on the earth" (WHD, 117). Borrowing other terms, we could say, from a slightly different perspective, that it is not the things that belong to the essence of dwelling but what the things give.

Although Heidegger did not express his thinking in quite this way until 1951–52, all the motifs—giving, the hand, presence, the juncture, and use—already converge in "Anaximander's Maxim": "'To use' means accordingly: to let some present thing be present as something present *(etwas Anwesendes als Anwesendes anwesen)*: *frui, bruchen, brauchen, Brauch* mean: to hand over something to its own essence and to hold it as something thus present in the preserving hand" (H, 338–39).

According to Heidegger, Greek offers its own complement of etymological resources, from *hē cheir*, the hand, to *chrao*, "I handle something," which also means to give something into the hand, to hand over,[17] so that Heidegger can connect *to chreon* with the giving previously described as letting-belong: "*to chreon* is then the handing-over of presence, which handing-over hands presence over to present beings and thus precisely holds what is present as such in the hand, that is, preserves it in presence" (H, 337).

Looking back at all three publications of this same year, we may conclude that, the less thinking has to go on, the more poetic it becomes. In the Rilke essay Heidegger has the poet's entire canon to work with and

17. For assistance with the Greek I am grateful to Marsh M. McCall, Jr., of the Stanford Department of Classics. Two other Stanford classicists, A. M. Devine and Lawrence Stephens, judge Heidegger's etymology, in the present instance, to be questionable. As is often the case (and this applies equally to German words), Heidegger, heedless of traditional scholarship, is teasing out "unthought" linguistic possibilities.

in the "Letter on Humanism" he has the entire Western humanistic tradition, while in the essay we have been reading he has a fragment of a single pronouncement. Such bare minimums have long proven provocative, as Shelley demonstrates by recreating a world from the broken statue of Ozymandias and as other writers of the Romantic period demonstrate by letting a fragment grow from seed to orchard (or, in some cases, making up their own fragments in the belief that parts for which wholes must be imagined are more inspirational than pregiven wholes). Such bare minimums are more than enough for a thinking that, like Heidegger's, moves in a spirit of serious-minded play, making the liberties it takes into hermeneutic virtues. Indeed, the very absence of "context" makes it easier for thinking, by founding itself in relation to still "open" texts, to disclose what the latter have left unthought or, at the least, to show the way toward such disclosure.

If Heidegger were in fact a poet in the strict sense, we would not hesitate to describe the wording movement of his thinking as the embodiment of a vision; but it seems to me that the concept of visionary may be legitimately applied to a thinking that moves as Heidegger's does in the present essay, particularly when it approximates, in its own way, the kind of unitary insight that Hölderlin achieves in the united three of Heracles, Dionysus, and Christ. The entire movement, in all its intricacy, cannot be traced here, but we can appreciate its main thrust by seeing what follows from the effort Heidegger makes to affirm that all great thinkers think, ultimately, the same.

Although we have thus far witnessed several times the emergence through which presence is achieved in what is present, another perspective is possible; for when something "whiles" in unconcealment, it can be regarded as having been brought there as something brought forth (*Hervor-Gebrachte*): "It is brought, in that, in unfolding itself, it brings itself forth. It is brought, in that it is set forth, produced (*hergestellt*) by men" (H, 341). To this extent it can be viewed as a manifestation of *ergon*, which means to the Greeks what Heidegger means by the thing brought forth and, by extension, a manifestation, indirect, of the Being of such a thing, which Aristotle understood as *energeia*. By employing this re-thinking strategy on other leading ideas of the ancient thinkers (in a process that I will not attempt to recapitulate here), Heidegger can gather the thinkers together in the following way:

> The *energeia* that Aristotle thinks as the fundamental characteristic of presence, of *eon*, the *idea* that Plato thinks as the fundamental characteristic of presence, the *Logos* that Heraclitus thinks as the fundamental characteristic of presence, the *Moira* that Parmenides thinks as the fundamental characteristic of presence, the *chreeon*

that Anaximander thinks as what is present *(Wesende)* in presence—all name the same. In the hidden richness of the same is
the unity of the unifying one, the *Hen*, thought by every thinker
in his own way. [H, 342]

Plato, Aristotle, Heraclitus, Parmenides, and Anaximander have become Heidegger's "united five," the last-named first because of the
possibilities his poetic thinking open up for the poetic thinking of his
twentieth-century successor.

7

Poetic Thinking and the World

> By ignoring the question concerning the thing and by in-
> sufficiently interpreting a poem, it appears as though
> nothing further happens. One day, perhaps after fifty or a
> hundred years, nevertheless, something has happened.
>
> *What Is a Thing?*

The problem of interpreting things and the problem of interpreting
poems, prominent in these pages from the start, are nowhere more
satisfactorily addressed within Heidegger's canon than in a pair of
lectures given in 1950, the one dealing with a jug and entitled "The
Thing," the other dealing with a poem by Georg Trakl and entitled
"Language."

The Thing

The Heideggerian jug looks, at the start, almost too obvious. The jug is
a container; it has a bottom, not to mention sides; and so on. But a shift
has already been initiated by this thinker who thinks ahead, the better
to make something "happen" in our understanding and hence in our
future. The shift begins with an emphasis, not upon what is so self-
evidently there in the Being of the jug but upon what is not; and what is
not there, in the same way as bottom and sides are there, is emptiness.
We may recall, at this point, Malte's experience of houses from the
inside of their absence, as things that, no longer there in the way they
once were, yet contain life; the worn insides of the peasant shoes with
those openings from which the worker's tread stares forth; and the
Hamsun character who sits between his ears to the sound of nothingness meeting nothingness, producing "not even a hole." So the concern
with emptiness is already, after all, with us, presuming that we have let
something happen by preserving the remembrance of these ways of
Being disclosed by poetic thinking.

The emptiness of the jug is not the void of physical science, subject to
being displaced by something poured into it. Emptiness is rather that
which enables the vessel to receive what is poured into it and to persist
in, hence to preserve, that receiving. I put the matter this way to stress,

early on, the temporal aspect of the thing, which is eventually stressed by Heidegger himself when he connects the jug's capacity to pour with the process of giving. In *The Origin of the Work of Art*, we recall, the art work was regarded as a superabundance with a "more" to give; in the present text Heidegger is more concerned with a giving that, for want of a better term, comes through a thing by virtue not of its own overflowing but by virtue of the totality of the world understood as the fourfold of earth and sky, mortals and gods. Only through its inherence in the fourfold does the jug fully accomplish, in its outpouring, what the water that is given is prepared to give:

> The spring stays on in the water of the gift. In the spring the rock dwells, and in the rock dwells the dark slumber of the earth, which receives the rain and dew of the sky. In the water of the spring dwells the marriage of sky and earth. It stays in the wine given by the fruit of the vine, the fruit in which the earth's nourishment and the sky's sun are betrothed to one another. In the gift of water, in the gift of wine, sky and earth dwell. But the gift of the outpouring is what makes the jug a jug. In the jugness of the jug, sky and earth dwell. [VA, II, 44–45/172]

The description, which emphasizes only two regions of the fourfold world, is, one is inclined to say, anthropomorphic: the act of dwelling carries with it connotations of human occupancy, to say nothing of the betrothal of sky and earth in the fruit or marriage of sky and earth in the spring. Now a properly Heideggerian description is supposed to let things be, yet here we seem to witness an intervention, an intrusion of metaphysics and metaphor. We may then be permitted to ask why such an intervention should be tolerated while the intervention of the representational, objectifying consciousness is not. What we actually see in the present instance, however, is more like a negative intervention, a decision—complete with its enabling act—to let the thing be as it is in a way that science, for example, refuses to do. Science views the thing as an entity existing over against consciousness and therefore liable to measurement and manipulation. It is not that such measurements and manipulations have nothing human about them: scientists and technologists belong to the same species as Martin Heidegger. But there are different ways of existing as *Dasein* and, more particularly, different ways of so existing in respect to things; and the way poetic thinking favors is a rather more basic way of living with things in a common world, a way so ordinary that it is extraordinary that it ever came to seem *extra*ordinary. According to this way of living, things belong with mortals even as things and mortals belong with language. If language is fundamentally poetic, then all that it capacitates will be poetic too, whether jug or water or heaven or earth or the cosmos itself.

This is the best defense I can presently make for the phase of Heidegger's evocation of the world that takes us into two of its regions, that of sky and that of earth. But I recognize that this is not a complete defense, and the reason it is not complete is that Heidegger's approach does not exhaust the field of possibles. For it is possible to live with things in a manner less harmonious and benign than the later Heidegger seems to allow, a manner more reminiscent of the interpretation of *Antigone* in *An Introduction to Metaphysics;* and it is possible to do this, it seems to me, without manipulating them in the way that technology manipulates the natural world. Rain, for example, is not always something welcomed, along with dew, into the slumbering earth. Rain is also tempest and discomfort and damage, an event that ruins crops, drowns human beings, sweeps away their homes—a case of superabundance that is hardly a demonstration of generosity. At another extreme, water may be notable for its absence; and surely a spring that dries up no longer purveys the gift of water. The earth, for its part, is equally subject to extremes—to earthquakes or profound climatic changes or to the gradual loss (as through poor methods of tilling) of its ability to nourish and hence to be a giving region of the world.[1] Going further, we may note that in the world that most of us know and in Heidegger's encounter with the painting by Van Gogh, mortals work the earth, whereas, for the Heidegger of "The Thing," the earth appears to be passive, the sky active. Indeed, the ingredients in Heidegger's account seem to gain some of their almost sexual resonance by association with the ancient beliefs pertaining to an earth mother; and a feminist analyzing this phase of Heideggerian thinking might well detect in the relation of sky and earth an analogue to the relation of man to woman as it has come to be understood in the Western tradition.

Returning to the text, we find mortals playing, through the mediation of the jug, a role quite different from the ones I have just described.

> The gift of the pouring out is drink for mortals. It quenches their thirst. It refreshes their leisure. It enlivens their conviviality. But the jug's gift is at times also given for consecration. If the pouring is for consecration, then it does not still a thirst. It stills and elevates the celebration of the feast. The gift of the pouring now is neither given in an inn nor is the poured gift a drink for mortals. The outpouring is the libation poured out for the immortal gods. [VA, II, 45/172–73]

The very use of the designation "mortals" implies "immortals" or some variant as its counterterm, thus preparing the way for the transition

1. See Wilhelm Perpeet, "Heideggers Kunstlehre," in *Heidegger: Perspektiven zur Deutung seines Werks,* ed. Otto Pöggeler (Cologne and Berlin: Kiepenheuer & Witsch, 1969), p. 238.

from the realm of the human to that of the gods. At the same time, the actions performed by these mortals differ from the actions performed by the human beings in my discussion above. Although nothing specifically excludes the possibility that a drink that quenched was prompted by labor, these mortals are not shown working; leisure, on the other hand, is specified, as is sociability, a linkage that is raised to a higher power when the mortal characters perform the central, devotional act of the scene. Here, then, as in other treatments by Heidegger, the world, while constituted by four coequal regions, depends for much of its force on the least-secular region, that of the gods. It is also the most problematic region, as Heidegger himself suggests by the word "also": "But the jug's gift is at times also given for consecration." This acknowledges that, while a drink *always* allays thirst, it does *not* always serve the aims of consecration, an acknowledgment that burdens a passage that then goes on to place special emphasis on just those aims. Whether a reader is receptive to such an emphasis will depend on the extent to which Heidegger is seen to be (he would not accept the term) anthropological. That is to say, we may ask whether Heidegger is describing a phenomenon to be observed in most if not all cultures or whether he is building up a case for a new or revived religious spirit. If I leave the question standing, it is only because it deserves closer treatment than considerations of space allow me to give it here. Heidegger has in any case succeeded, in my view, in demonstrating the manner in which one type of thing invokes through its very nature the relation of all regions of the fourfold. The jug, like anything else in the four-part cosmos, "has being only when considered from the perspective of language and the meaning of the entity named as thing by the word," it being understood that any such entity "emerges as an interplay or reciprocity of the fourfold's four sectors, an interplay constituted in part by the word naming the entity as thing."[2]

And yet one may draw a distinction between the question of "the thing," which the present lecture is ostensibly about, and one *type* of thing, which it is really about. The jug works as well as it does in the present context for much the same reason that the temple worked in an earlier context: it embodies the transcendental motive that tends to animate Heidegger's poetic thinking about Being. The difference is that the temple was wholly a religious edifice, whereas the jug has religious significance "also" or "sometimes." That second term is not inconsequential, given the temporal concern that permeates the lecture, a concern expressed, for example, in the idea of dwelling. Related to this, we may note, is the kind of duration we experience in certain cultural occasions—here, a marriage and a festival. In other words, human prac-

2. White, *Heidegger and the Language of Poetry*, pp. 34, 35.

tices are "also" or "sometimes" directed to devotional or consecrational ends, even as things, such as jugs, are also or sometimes devoted to such ends. In a reflection embracing both the former and the latter, poetic thinking discovers the paradigmatic cultural occasion, the ceremony, which here takes the form, first, of a marriage, then of a festival or feast.

This appears to come about through a shift from the figurative to the literal, the marriage amounting to a trope connoting the relation of earth and heaven, the festival constituting an actual ceremony. Such a shift could also be charted as a movement from language to fact. But neither formulation means much to a poetic thinking in which all things and all occasions are so grounded in language that they would not be if language were not. On such a view, metaphor loses its privileged status and assumes its place among the many ways of being metaphysical, which is to say (as suggested above),[3] that a metaphor posits a state of affairs deemed literal in order for that very metaphor to have something to stand over against or, to put it another way, in order for that metaphor to be different. But what if there is no literal state of affairs? What if there is nothing that does not somehow come about except through language? Then the trope of heaven marrying earth is no trope; then it is no more figurative than the festival. Or, to reverse the process, it would be no less figurative to speak in a "scientific," "referential" manner of the "relation" of earth and sky. Both ways, all ways, are manners of speaking.

If such is the role of language in this approach to the fourfold through the thing, what is the role of time? In the first place, a ceremony like the one envisaged in "The Thing" is no more confined to a discrete present moment than any other human undertaking. We cannot say with precision, for example, when the festival occurs. While one can, to be sure, point to a datable occasion when the celebrants gather, the occasion takes place only because it constitutes an activity of a generic type that has acquired its typicality by repetition. Hence it possesses the character, at once, of transpiring in the "present" and the character of having-been: indeed, it is meaningful now only by virtue of having been previously meaningful. At the same time, just because it is a phase in a continuity, it is a renewal, a preservation of the type through its enactment in a present pointing toward a future in which the enactment will again be renewed.

Paradoxically, this way of stating the case gives the ceremony a certain aura of timelessness, and yet we would not wish, I think, to label it supratemporal. Supertemporal is almost nearer the mark, in that the ceremony has such a rare power, stands out so much from routine, that

3. Bruzina, "Heidegger on the Metaphor and Philosophy," pp. 193 ff.

we are tempted to speak not merely of ecstasis but of its being somehow (if that were possible) "more ecstatic." I cannot go further than this, and I will attempt no logical proof of what I suggest, but I believe the drift of what I am saying is related to the drift of poetic thinking, with its transcendental motive, its desire to move from the region of the human to a totality of regions in which the gods, though theoretically coequal, sometimes have the look of first among equals. In this connection it is worth noting the role, in Heidegger's later writings, of the mystic Meister Eckhart and the Catholic poet Angelus Silesius; the use he makes, in a work like *The Principle of Reason*, not only of the latter poet but of reflections on God recorded by Novalis, Goethe, Leibniz, and Mozart; and the manner in which, in the same book, he connects the emergence of world with God and play.

It is also worth noting that as early as 1943, the year of the lecture on Heraclitus, *alētheia*, and the world-fire, Heidegger interprets the ceremony of the wedding feast in Hölderlin's "Remembrance" as a paradigmatic occasion for the confirmation of the "between" where poets dwell, for the preservation by the latter of the holy, for consecration, and for origin:

> *The wedding feast* is the meeting of those men and gods from
> which originates the birth of those who stand between men and
> gods and endure this "between." They are the *half-gods* . . . who *must
> become signs.* . . . These who show signs are the poets. The day of
> the *wedding feast, the wedding day*, defines the birthday of the
> poet, that is, the dawning in light of which the open brightens, so
> that the poet sees coming what his word must say: *the holy*.
> [E, 103]

Heidegger's fourfold world is characterized throughout by the air of beneficence that permeates his thinking about world harmony. Indeed, the concept of world that emerges in "The Thing" is closer to the latter type of all-embracing totality than to Heidegger's earlier arrangement, which saw world and earth in opposition. By the time of "The Thing" the world has become synonymous, as I have said, with the fourfold, which is the totality that is, has been, and will be: "This appropriating mirror-play of the simple onefold of earth and sky, divinities and mortals, we call the world" (VA, II, 52/179). Some of the words used here are sufficiently strange to require explanation. It should be said, first, that they are all ways of evoking a sense of unity without surrendering the distinctiveness of the regions that Heidegger sees as the necessary condition of that unity. It is as if he were to say: only different things can come together; and in effect he does say this, though in different terms. One term, the "fold," suggests the capacity to be multiple and single,

somewhat as a fan becomes itself both by arching out through its se-
quenced spines and by gathering them to contraction, or it suggests the
capacity to gather and be gathered, as in the folding of a garment. As a
tactical matter, reference to the cosmic totality as a onefold insures
against the danger of hypostatizing the regions as separate and distinct.

The fold is connected intimately and intricately with the notion of
play and with the "image" of the mirror, which, through the changes
wrought in it by play, becomes a different sort of thing. A mirror can
reflect what is presented to its surface because the mirror is other than
what is presented; but Heidegger's poetized mirror *is the totality itself*,
so that what is reflected is *each and all of the regions* (whether regarded
as fourfold or onefold). Further, it is that totality *at play*, which means
that the reflections are not bound as a mirrored configuration is bound
by what it flashes back. Heidegger's mirror is not in fact a mirror, which
is to say an object, but is something more like a process. It is as if to the
question "What does the fourfold do?" one heard the reply: "It mirror-
plays."

Gone is the strife of the *Antigone* interpretation and *The Origin of the
Work of Art*, where earth was shown struggling with world. The harmonious aura that now envelops Heidegger's thinking about the fourfold, whose mirror-play he once again associates with the idea of betrothal (VA, 53), is already familiar to the reader from the letter to
Staiger in chapter 3, in which Heidegger emphasized the festive aspect
of the Mörike poem, which included a reference to the round dance;
that letter, not coincidentally, is contemporaneous with the present
lecture, which, by giving new prominence to the round dance in the
present context, also prepares the way for the full development the
motif will receive in "Hölderlin's Heaven and Earth" (1959–60).

The following passage contains a striking formulation of the process
to which I have referred, to its manifestation as *Ereignis*, and to the
relation of the latter to occasion, world, and play.

> The four, the unity of the four, presences as the appropriating
> mirror-play of the betrothed, each to the other in simple oneness.
> The fouring presences as the worlding of world. The mirror-play of
> world is the round dance of appropriating. Therefore, the round
> dance does not encompass the four like a hoop. The round dance
> is the ring that joins while it plays as mirroring. [VA, II. 53/180]

As Hofstadter has shown, an adequate understanding of appropriation
requires more than the sense of occurrence that the term *Ereignis* normally denotes, because Heidegger brings out the sense of "its own" in a
cognate term, *eigen*, even as he stresses the evidentiary nature of appropriating, its function as clarification and revelation:

... instead of "appropriate" in the sense of one's own appropriating of something for oneself ... Heidegger wants to speak of an
activity or process by which nothing "selfish" occurs, but rather
by which the different members of the world are brought into
belonging to and with one another and are helped to realize themselves and each other in realizing this belonging.[4]

While Heidegger employs the verb *ereignen* in his early writings in
conventional senses, such as "to happen" or "to occur," the variant
forms that weave in and out of his later, more poetic thinking suggest a
process that is itself as complex and interrelated as the fourfold:

Thus *ereignen* comes to mean ... the joint process by which the
four of the fourfold are able, first, to come out into the light and
clearing of truth, and thus each to exist in its own truthful way,
and secondly, to exist in appropriation of and to each other, belonging together in the round dance of their being; and what is
more, this mutual appropriation becomes the very process by
which the emergence into the light and clearing occurs, for it
happens through the sublimely simple play of their mutual
mirroring.[5]

At least one purpose of "The Thing," then, is to demonstrate
concretely—partly by argument and partly by evocation—the way in
which the jug, as an instance of the thing, relates to the process just
described; and to a considerable extent, it seems to me, the purpose is
achieved. By showing how heaven and earth come into the jug,
Heidegger shows how the jug comes part way into its own, and he
completes the way, as it were, by showing that what comes out of the
jug, and how it comes out, lets the jug come into its own not only in the
human realm but sometimes in the realm of the immortals. But because
this series of perspectives does not necessarily apply to other things,
any more than the perspectives on the temple necessarily apply to other
works of art, the lecture remains a less-than-comprehensive achievement that needs to be examined in relation to the other inquiry into the
thing that Heidegger calls "Building Dwelling Thinking" (1951), which
explores the Being of a bridge in a manner nearly as suggestive as his
exploration of the jug. Since my concern at this point is with the other
problem announced at the start of the chapter, I will not take up the
latter work but will proceed to the problem of interpreting poems by
way of some remarks that Heidegger makes in "The Nature of
Language," a series of three lectures (1957–58) on Stefan George
brought together for publication as a single piece.

4. Hofstadter, *Poetry, Language, Thought,* p. xx.
5. Ibid., p. xxi.

The Poem

Heidegger's point of departure is the conclusion of a poem entitled "The Word":

So lernt ich traurig den verzicht;
Kein ding sei wo das wort gebricht.

Sadly did I thus the renunciation learn:
Where the word breaks no thing may be.
[U, 163]

To answer this newly posed "question concerning the thing," one needs something to which one can at least provisionally refer, something to put in a kind of holding pattern so that one may get on with the seeking without predetermining what is sought. Heidegger offers the rewording: "No thing is where the word is missing" (U, 191). Then the question becomes: where is this "is," and in what does it consist? It is itself no thing; and yet it "is" every time I encounter, let us say, a rock or a tool. Our difficulty, though Heidegger does not express it so, is that we need to carry into the present context our understanding of a giving that emerges in a manner appropriate to the Being that is presenting the gift, an understanding that Heidegger can only hope the reader has arrived at through "The Thing." Recalling this, and recalling the founding role of language as primordial poetry, we may come to recognize "that the word itself gives. The word: the giver. What then does it give? According to poetic experience and the oldest tradition of thinking the word gives: 'Being'" (U, 193).

If the thing is and if the word gives Being, it is plain that there can be no thing where the word breaks off. Clearly we can learn at least this much from the experience the poem makes possible. But in another way we are back where we started from, still needing to think the meaning of "is" and what it means for a thing to be. Although Heidegger does not attempt to explain away this relapse, he does suggest that the matter may be stated in a way that brings new light. For example, if the relation between "is" and the word can be said to play in poetic experience, then the breaking-off of the word presumably leaves a residue: there is still that "is," that mysterious power given by the word. Heidegger paraphrases thus: "An 'is' arises where the word breaks up." That is to say, with the silencing of the word, what is left—the manner in which a thing can be—comes forth. The term "silencing," of course, is not quite right, and neither is "breaking-off," which is probably why Heidegger shifts to "breaking-up." The moment at issue is not in any case one in which the word ceases altogether but one in which it is, as it were, quieted. "The sounded word returns to . . . the place from which it was

granted: in the sound of the stillness which, as saying, moves the regions of the world's fourfold into their nearness" (U, 216).

The passage tells us that the decisive consideration in saying is not
speech in the sense of vocalization but the articulation of essential language, poetry, as that through which each of the world's regions comes
into its own as what it is for itself and for the others. I use "articulation"
here (cf. SZ, 161 ff. and passim) to denote a process of emerging into
order and understanding, for which the nearest analogy would be
communication or expression, and at the same time the mode and act
we encounter when a joint frees movement within the limit of its own
sway, limit being understood as a boundary attained in coming to
fulfillment. This makes saying "extralinguistic," by the ordinary definition of language, since it capacitates all that dwells in each and every
realm.

Terms like "free" and "realm" belong to the understanding of
another key concept, movement, which Heidegger explores at length in
the George essay, his point of departure being the notion that his interpretation moves within the relation of poetry and thinking addressed in
"Anaximander's Maxim" (chapter 6). To the verb *bewegen,* to move,
corresponds the noun *Weg,* way, which is not a provision for getting
from spot to spot but is more like a means for attaining the emergence
appropriate to a realm; hence the way belongs to a given realm, which
is itself nothing less than the lighting *(Lichtung)* in which the beings
that belong to it come into their emergence through the articulation of
the world.

As Heidegger moves further and further from traditional views of
classical thought, uncovering what Paul de Man would call the blind-
ness of its insight, he moves closer and closer to the very different
"classicism" of the East. It is not a trivial matter, then, when he turns to
Lao-tze, describes the latter's reflections as poetic thinking (U, 198), and
adopts the Chinese master's Tao as effectively conveying his own
understanding of way. Inevitably, Heidegger rejects all of the conventional equivalents for Tao—reason, spirit, meaning, and the like—
just as he rejects the conventional equivalents for the leading words of
ancient Greek thought. For Heidegger, Tao, like saying, is a kind of vast
capacitating power, and, like saying, it is foundational inasmuch as it
constitutes that through which—the means, the manner, the mode, in
short, the way—that reason, spirit, meaning come to be. In a glancing
remark one wishes he had expanded, Heidegger speculates that the
widespread interest in methodology is the wastewater flowing from the
hidden stream of the way. In other words, the fascination with methods
recognizes, indirectly and imperfectly, a more primordial phenomenon

before methods (i.e., "before" in the sense of taking precedence over them).

As befits the idea of a way, the attainment to which I have referred is equally an arriving *(gelangen)*; and since arriving occurs only when it is prepared for, Heidegger, employing the umlaut in a manner common to Schwabish and Alemannic dialects, can state that "waying" *(Wëgen)* prepares the way, while moving *(Be-wëgen)* is the way that lets what is on the way arrive. Heidegger locates both ways, the way as preparing and as letting-arrive, in the same realm as three verbs of similar sound and similar sense, *wiegen, wagen,* and *wogen.* In other words, both particular ways belong somewhere in the same manner as way in the less differentiated meaning, though this somewhere is not a region of the fourfold but rather the "watery" realm of a source, spring, or fountainhead *(Quell),* of stream or flow *(Strom).* While this conception, so characteristic of the later Heidegger, points back to my discussion of elemental thinking, it also points forward to the motif of the wave, to be discussed in the next section. The radiations go even beyond these, for the first verb, *wiegen,* meaning "to sway, to move gently, or to cradle," recalls the use of the Matthias Claudius lullaby *(Wiegenlied)* in chapter 2; *wagen* is rich with overtones from Heidegger's analysis of venturing and daring in the Rilke essay; and *wogen,* meaning "to surge, fluctuate, or undulate" and, even more pertinently, "to wave," anticipates the *Woge,* "wave" (also to be discussed in the next section).

"In the word 'way,' Tao, there may be hidden what is most secret in the saying that thinks, in the event that we let this name return to the unspoken" (U, 198). The saying that thinks is not, as one might infer from the remark, a new phenomenon but a newly worded way of looking at the same one; for in Heidegger's understanding, saying thinks by definition, even as it constitutes the poetic: "Poetry *(Dichten)* and thinking are manners of saying" (U, 199).

What, in the meantime, has happened to language? What has happened to language is what has happened to saying, since it is precisely as saying that language capacitates the world: "Language, as the saying of the fourfold world, is no longer something whereby we human beings who speak have a relation in the sense of a connection obtaining between human beings and language. As the world-moving saying, language is the relation of all relations" (U, 214). What language capacitates and how it does so are already suggested by the statement, quoted above, that saying moves the regions of the world's fourfold. I use the word "suggested" advisedly, since the statement hardly amounts to a detailed definition; from it we nonetheless infer that nearness means a closer relation of each region to Being and to the other regions without requiring that Being merge with a region's beings, obliterating the ontological difference, or that the regions merge with one another, losing their respective identities. When Heidegger described the betrothal of the regions in the appropriating mirror-play of all, it was such "Being-apart-together" that he seems to have had in mind.

Almost inevitably, we approach this sort of formulation from the long and rich tradition of the world as theater, a metaphor as familiar to Renaissance England (all the world's a stage) as to Golden Age Spain, with the sacramental world dramas of Calderón, or the courtly celebrations that persisted in European theater productions until late in the eighteenth century, which Hofmannsthal, in our own time, went some way toward reviving. From Heidegger's point of view, all such resonances need to be resisted, however, just because they belong to metaphor and because, as the reader will recall, metaphor belongs to metaphysics. Heidegger's project, in other words, means eliminating, as much as he can, one kind of association while fashioning another, struggling constantly against the temptation to settle on some concise and conclusive expression. His solution, partial as it remains, is to keep on the move, playing variations on themes, adding nuance to nuance, now circling through familiar words, now releasing strange ones to encircle the ones we already know, showing in the process that the quality of superabundance characterizes thinking quite as much as it characterizes art. Such movement, were it totally unbounded, would lead to total disorientation, but in fact we recognize the movement, and are able to follow it, because it remains in its own way regionalized, much as a dancer's movement is regionalized both by the articulation of joints and by the articulation of the total spatial and temporal dancescape—as it were—that the articulation aims to realize.

The idea of play becomes even richer when Heidegger describes the world itself as play, *Weltspiel,* through its manifestation as time and space. As in *Being and Time* and subsequent treatments of the subject, time denotes the unity of the three temporal ecstases, while space is that which makes way for and takes up temporality as space-time:

> Space itself, in its total nature, does not move, but remains still. Time, moving away and bringing, and space, clearing, ordering, granting, and setting free *(das einräumend-zulassend-Entlassende),* belong together in the same, the play of stillness *(Spiel der Stille),* which we are not now able to reflect upon further. The same, which holds space and time gathered together in their nature, can be called play's space of time *(Zeit-Spiel-Raum).* By timing, clearing, and ordering, the same of playing's space of time moves the

four world regions, earth and sky, god and man, over against each
other, [and this is] the play of the world *(Weltspiel)*. [U, 214]

To hold that space and time can accomplish all this is not to hold that they
enjoy the same capacitating power as saying. Heidegger's space of time
is foundational, one might say, only to the extent that language is more
so. Language is the relation of relations; that is to say, it founds the very
relation that the world play's space of time is seen to move. Such a
distinction does not mean that there are two independent movements;
it bears witness, rather, to the same ecstatic unity we find in Heideggerian temporality. Thus, while space-time sustains emergence in the
manner appropriate to each region, moving the regions in their relation
to one another, saying makes that moving possible.

If the specific nature of the fourfold world still remains vague, it is at
least in part because Heidegger has not provided a sufficiently concrete
experience of language. He has not provided this, it seems to me, partly
because the text he focuses on is more illustrative than paradigmatic
and partly because there is too little of it. The opposite is the case in the
first Trakl lecture, which explores at length a complete major poem, and
in the second, which is an interpretation of passages from throughout
the canon.

The World through Poetry: Bread and Wine

The context for both pieces is provided by Heidegger's ongoing attempt
to destroy the metaphysics that for him comes to its term in the work of
Nietzsche and, beyond that, his attempt to discover a ground for language (U, 13; E, 85; H, 333), without which no authentic experience of
things or of the world may be attained. The problem is that language
cannot be grounded in something other than itself because "Language
languages" (U, 12) just as "World worlds." Even to Heidegger the formulation seems strange; to reflect on such a tautology, he warns, is to
open an abyss over which the sentences leave us to hover *(schweben)*—a
term that now plays a key role in a complex of words involving patterns
of movement in poetic thinking. In exploring this pattern below, we
will take account of a change of nuance whereby this hovering emerges
in a more affirmative light. The change has already begun to the extent
that the present discussion attempts to eliminate what is abysmal in the
abyss by arguing that when we are plunged into this type of emptiness
we do not, after all, fall into a void but into a kind of affirmative depth,
which is to say that affirmative possibilities may open up when we risk
moving ecstatically or (the same thing) thinking poetically. Therefore
Heidegger can speak of this depth as in its own way a height and can

envisage height and depth relating in such a way that they "span a realm *(Ortschaft)* in which we would like to become at home, so as to find a residence, a dwelling place for the life of man" (U, 13/192), that is to say, an essential place, *chōra*, as described in my discussion of *The Origin of the Work of Art*.

Equally arresting is another formulation: "To discuss language, to place it, means to bring to its place of being not so much language as ourselves: our own gathering into the disclosure of appropriation *(Ereignis)*" (H, 12/190). Here we encounter another way of approaching the issues developed in "The Thing," but one made more complex by the fact that it builds on the already complex meaning of disclosure of appropriation, with its relevance to the truthfulness in which its region belongs to itself in belonging to the others in the round dance of their Being, the mirroring of their play. If the reader can bear this summary restatement in mind and at the same time consider what has just been said of place, the present crux may begin to appear less forbidding.

The crux involves a tacit play on words that remains concealed in the English term "discuss." The original *erörtern* gains in resonance from the qualities that *Ereignis* draws from *ereignen*, suggesting both a happening and the sense that it is a region's "own" happening, and from *eräugnen*, which implies placing before the eye *(Auge)*.[6] Since the prefix *er-* entails both the idea of beginning a process and the idea of bringing it to a successful end, Heidegger's deployment of the verb tends to erase the difference between starting toward the desired place and actually getting there.

A further perspective on the meaning of place is provided by the following:

> Originally the name "place" signifies the tip of the spear. In it everything runs together. . . . That which gathers penetrates through and is present through *(durchwest)* everything. The place, that which gathers, gathers into itself, preserves what is gathered in, not like a separate capsule, but in such a way that it shines and irradiates through what is gathered and thereby frees it into its essence. [U, 37]

The description is so brief and slips so smoothly into the rest of the passage that we must take the liberty of lingering a moment in what Heidegger himself leaves unspoken. The function of a bladed instrument—a hatchet, say—is to cut. When you work with it, everything runs to the blade: in that sharp edge all force is brought to bear. Wield a spear, and in that wielding force is now brought to bear in the point: if all that runs through the spear did not streak forward, if ev-

6. Ibid., p. xx.

erything did not run into the tip, if the tip did not gather it all, the spear would be no spear. These are my words, but I believe they reflect something of the range of actions that may flash across the reader's mind and that in a sense "complete" Heidegger's assertions, which otherwise may remain obscure.

This is as good a time as any to remind ourselves that what I have called Heidegger's metaphors of place and spear are not metaphors as Heidegger understands the term (for the reasons stated in chapter 6). Gottfried Benn had objected that Hölderlin's phrase "words, like flowers" constituted a break in vision and combined with other merely comparative locutions to make up a vast "herbarium." Heidegger of course rejects the complaint (while acknowledging its validity from Benn's point of view) but tacitly accepts the notion of metaphor as an attempt to bridge a gap. That the example from Hölderlin is, strictly speaking, a simile makes no difference, since a simile makes the same effort as a metaphor, though by virtue of the linking term it makes it more conspicuously. Let us therefore compromise and call the place, the spear, and the other nominal designations we will encounter below "figures of speech," admitting that this also smacks too much of the rhetorical.

Trakl's paradigmatic text—for the aims of poetic thinking, as they presently emerge—is "A Winter Evening."

EIN WINTERABEND

> Wenn der Schnee ans Fenster fällt,
> Lang die Abendglocke läutet,
> Vielen ist der Tisch bereitet
> Und das Haus ist wohlbestellt.
>
> Mancher auf der Wanderschaft
> Kommt ans Tor auf dunklen Pfaden.
> Golden blüht der Baum der Gnaden
> Aus der Erde kühlem Saft.
>
> Wanderer tritt still herein;
> Schmerz versteinerte die Schwelle.
> Da erglänzt in reiner Helle
> Auf dem Tische Brot und Wein.

A WINTER EVENING

> Window with falling snow is arrayed,
> Long tolls the vesper bell,
> The house is provided well,
> The table is for many laid.

Wandering ones, more than a few,
Come to the door on darksome courses.
Golden blooms the tree of graces
Drawing up the earth's cool dew.

Wanderer quietly steps within;
Pain has turned the threshold to stone.
There lie, in limpid brightness shown,
Upon the table bread and wine.
[U, 17/194–95]

To Heidegger the poem is a call (*Ruf*), a term that no longer designates,
as in *Being and Time*, a mode of discourse but a more intervolved—and
more ambiguous—process. The falling snow and the tolling of the bell
are made present through the call, which is to say that the words let
them linger with the other called things, such as the table and the bread
and the wine, that are there in a fuller, more gathering way, a way more
closely related to the disclosure of appropriation that occurs when language's essential place is "discussed." All of this together further
suggests what Heidegger means when he speaks of an essential place,
whether it be the place of the poem or of language itself. Such a place
occurs somewhere: in this sequence of words, this text, around which
gravitates a text of Heidegger; and it occurs sometime: in the words that
were once spoken and that, as a text, speak to us still. If the poem has
therefore a time and a space, it is one that is not discrete and measur-
able but one that stretches beyond the here and now in the same way
that the calling it carries out lingers beyond particular utterance into the
process it begins. Saying the poem lingers is saying the poem gathers,
is saying the poems calls; and what it calls is the gathering of the
fourfold: "The snowfall brings men under the sky that is darkening into
night. The tolling of the evening bell brings them, as mortals, before the
divine. House and table join mortals to the earth. The things that were
named, thus called, gather to themselves sky and earth, mortals and
divinities" (U, 22/199).

This is the best demonstration thus far in Heidegger's work of the
capacity of a poem to accomplish what the temple accomplishes in *The
Origin of the Work of Art*, what the jug accomplishes in "The Thing." I
do not suggest that Heidegger came to the demonstration after developing his thinking about the temple and the jug. It seems more likely,
given his early belief in the primacy of language and the grounding of
language in poetry, that the study of poems, chiefly Hölderlin's, sustained his thinking as he worked out his approach to the fourfold and
his approach to the thing and that his attention to twentieth-century
writing in *On the Way to Language* is a return to the spring at least as

much as it is a breaking of new ground. What is new is the rendering—more specific than anything in the Hölderlin essays, except for "Hölderlin's Earth and Heaven," to which I will return—of the enactment of cosmic totality through a particular poem.

Since that totality, as the reader will recall, has become synonymous with world, Heidegger is the more easily able to infer that "more than a few" in the first strophe does not mean "many people." If we could imagine a Trakl acquainted with the fourfold, I suspect that this is just the sense he would point out and that "many" would hence apply to mortals. Heidegger states rather that the strophe names the world, which can mean only that the many refers to the four regions of his cosmology. Speaking of the world rather than the fourfold makes the poem, at this early stage of its unfolding, look like a thing made to order for interpretative libertarianism. World sounds comfortably compatible with something in the vein of "all people," so that stating that the table is ready is like stating that it is open to all comers. The efficacy of Heidegger's demonstration depends even more, however, upon his handling of later strophes, especially those dealing with the tree of grace, the threshold, and the bread and wine.

The Tree of Grace

The second strophe, in Heidegger's view, speaks in a different mode:

> Wandering ones, more than a few,
> Come to the door on darksome courses.
> Golden blooms the tree of graces
> Drawing up the earth's cool dew.

In a distinction that strikes me as somewhat misleading, Heidegger says that the first two lines do not expressly call world because they merely name things, i.e., door (or gate) and courses (or paths); yet he has just shown how things called into presence by the poem "bear" the world in a sense of bearing-with and in the sense of bearing as gesture (*Gebärde*), as when we speak of a person's bearing (U, 22). The crucial phrase is "not expressly," which points to the fact that the opening lines of the strophe deal, not with the many—who, as we have just seen, come to stand for the world—but only with "more than a few," which means something on the order of "quite a few," and only a narrowly qualified few at that: "Not all mortals are called, not the many of the first stanza, but only 'more than a few'—those who wander the dark courses" (U, 23/200). Inasmuch as mortals are nonetheless named in those lines, and inasmuch as Heidegger goes on to acknowledge the copresence of all four regions in the naming of any of them, there must be

something extra in the strophe's concluding lines to justify its claim to
name the world expressly: "Golden blooms the tree of graces / Drawing
up the earth's cool dew." "Suddenly," says Heidegger, these verses
"name something wholly different" (U, 23/201). In the lectures grouped
later in the volume as "The Word," the experience of learning what renunciation means in a particular poem will be, similarly, a sudden experience. That words of like meaning appear so often elsewhere in these
pages attests to the event of surprise, discussed above in relation to
Bachelard. The pattern indicates at the same time the poetic thinker's
continuing concern for the dynamic, lived movement of the poem. But
what really commands Heidegger's admiration is the way in which the
tree, like the jar in "The Thing," flourishes in the intersection, so to
speak, of the world's regions. How this can be unfolds as soon as one
begins to think about the tree *qua* tree and at the same time about the
Being of the tree called into presence by this poem. The one way of thinking reveals what characterizes the thing we call a tree, and this includes
the fact that it is rooted in the earth and draws benefit from the sky. The
other way of thinking reveals what is characteristic of this poetic tree,
and this includes the distinctive manner in which it relates to earth and
sky together. It is the second way that dominates Heidegger's approach
to the poem:

> The tree roots soundly in the earth. Thus it is sound and
> flourishes into a blooming that opens itself to heaven's blessing.
> The tree's flowering has been called. It spans both the ecstasy
> (*Rausch*) of flowering and the soberness (*Nüchternheit*) of the
> nourishing sap. . . . The poem names the tree of graces. Its sound
> blossoming harbors the fruit that falls to us unearned—holy,
> saving, loving toward mortals. In the golden blossoming tree
> there prevail earth and sky, divinities and mortals. [U, 23/201]

Here the play of poetic thinking is guided by the view that any connection between the tree and any region of the fourfold involves a
connection between the tree and all other regions and a connection
among those regions as well, the one to the other and to the whole.
Though I can think of no precise model for such a view, I believe it expresses in its own way the cofounding previously discussed; it may also
be permissible to draw an analogy with music, or at least with a music-
like harmony, in which the sounding of a tone is taken up by other tones,
each of which blends with the others while its own sonority remains
distinctly heard. I will return to the question of musicality below.

If the analogy is acceptable, then Heidegger's procedure may be
further likened, though still with a sense of tentativeness, to the im-
provising of variations, the theme being the identification of the tree as

the tree of grace. Rather than speaking, say, of rain or dew from above, Heidegger can therefore speak of a blessing. He can also create a verbal echo by indirectly alluding to the great lyric "The Middle of Life," in which Hölderlin applies to the water of a lake the neologism *heilig-nüchtern,* an untranslatable epithet connoting a soberness so pure as to be deemed holy. In Heidegger's description, two nouns, *sobriety* (*Nüchternheit*) and the *holy* (*Heilige*), carry the burden of resonance in a way that permits the reader to remember not only that Hölderlin powerfully influenced the Austrian poet but that Hölderlin's "Bread and Wine" may be audible in the background of the later poem. For the reader who makes such a connection, Trakl's verse may seem to draw inspiration from the piety of Hölderlin's, in which, though the gods are flown, there remains a redeeming vision of human beings as the children of gods.

This general direction is obviously favorable to Heidegger's own case for the poem as a way of calling the world to enactment and hence for his desire to employ it as a word-created duration in which to linger in the realm of the holy. On the other hand, the variant text removes the epiphany that occurs in the final version, with the bread and wine climactically and radiantly present, substituting a much more problematic finish, in which the suffering wanderer yearns but does not attain. The introduction of the variant text in any case works to Heidegger's advantage, first, because it tends to increase the resonance gained by the echoes from Hölderlin and thus adds legitimacy to what might be called Heidegger's sacralizing diction; second, because the darker ending was rejected by the poet himself in favor of the more optimistic climax, which in turn accords with Heidegger's habit of construing Trakl's verse as affirmatively as possible. The one remaining problem is that the downplaying of the sacred or Christian elements appears to make the final version less oriented toward the question of the holy and hence less susceptible to Heidegger's approach. The answer, I believe, is that the final version still points sufficiently in the same direction to furnish Heidegger with the warrant he needs. Certainly he does not force "consecration" on the poem any more arbitrarily than he forces consecration on the jug; for if the text does not require, it at least permits a reading that relates the type of presence achieved by the things in the poem both to the world and to the divine.

Besides this possibly present text, Heidegger makes actually present—and with, I believe, a similar aim—a variant text in which Trakl substitutes the following verses for the last half of the second strophe and the whole of the third:

Seine Wunde voller Gnaden
Pflegt der Liebe sanfte Kraft.

O! des Menschen blosse Pein.
Der mit Engeln stumm gerungen,
Langt, von heiligem Schmerz bezwungen,
Still nach Gottes Brot und Wein.

Love's tender power,
Binds up his wounds anew.

O! man's naked hurt condign.
Wrestler with angels mutely held,
Craves, by holy pain compelled,
Silently God's bread and wine.
                                           [U, 17/195]

The verses suggest a more patently "religious" meaning, and if we see
Christ in the man with wounds and the Eucharist in the bread and the
wine, the meaning can even be Christian or have Christian overtones (I
personally believe that the case for overtones is stronger here than
elsewhere, though not decisively so, given Trakl's mercurial moods and
almost defiant ambiguities).

The Threshold

A threshold, by making it possible to move from one area to another,
may be said to carry the relation of those areas, the inside and the
outside, the one to the other. In Heidegger's view, it is not that the
threshold divides the area but that it sustains the "between" through
which outside and inside, even as the world and things, go through
each other. Hence it is not enough to regard the threshold as transi-
tional; it must also be relational.

"Pain turned the threshold to stone" appears at first sight to be the
darkest utterance in the poem and hence a carryover from the variant
text. But Heidegger interprets pain affirmatively, suggesting that,
though pain tears asunder and parts, it does so in a gathering way. This
is because pain belongs to the order of things, to the order of the
world—with neither of which it should, however, be identified. Indeed, for Heidegger, pain is the very difference between the thing and
the world; lacking that difference, there could be no relation between
them or, by implication, between or among any other regions of the
fourfold. There is, we might say, no healing without a wound, no dance
without a separation of the partners that their dancing yet overcomes,
no passage between outside and inside without some sustaining relation between them, without some between, some threshold—some
pain.

Although the threshold has so far appeared in a predominantly spatial aspect, it is temporal as well; this is made apparent by the fact that

the line in which the threshold is named is the only line in a past tense. Such an abrupt departure from the traditional lyric present that prevails throughout the poem may be construed in at least three ways. It could be the case, first, that the line stops the pain at the threshold—or, more precisely, in it—by implying that the threshold took the pain associated with the solitary wanderer into itself. The association of pain with the wanderer is supported by the fact that the petrifaction occurs in a sentence that the action of the wanderer begins. A second interpretation, building on the first, would shift attention to the lines that follow, so that the petrifying prepares for the splendid radiance of a denouement that, by placing the prior, negative moment further into the past, effectively overcomes it. According to a third and more strenuous interpretation—Heidegger's—the past denoted is neither a time that is over and done with nor one specifically associated with the wanderer. It is a time that has been already and, what is more, *still* is: a lingering time, in short, which preserves the ecstases of temporality in seamless unity.

By sustaining a pain synonymous with the difference between world and thing, the threshold holds difference open; and it is this, the sustaining of difference, that allows the bread and wine to come into their own radiance. The relation between threshold and radiance becomes a mirroring play in which each reflects itself toward and into the other, a process that reduces the risk of seeing the bread and the wine as the "cause" of the radiance.

The ambiguity in Heidegger's description of the process results from the fact that he concentrates now on one phase of the interaction, now on another. Thus it appears as if everything depended on the bread and wine, which radiate—and yet the threshold retains its centrality because that is where the radiance occurs; it also appears that this is all a way of rendering, imperfectly, the way in which the world—the totality of the fourfold—comes into its own; and at the same time it appears that the bread and wine, after all, do unto the world as the world does unto bread and wine: "Bread and wine are gifts from the divinities to mortals. Bread and wine gather these four to themselves from the simple unity of their fourfoldness. . . . Such things have their sufficiency in letting the world's fourfold stay with them" (U, 28/205).

Looking back from this perspective at the appearances just described, it will be seen that all reflect some part or phase of the process but that only the process as a whole attains sufficiency, this whole constituting precisely the world of the fourfold, itself the very process enacted through the poem.

Nowhere else in Heidegger's poetic thinking can one find an encounter with a poem that provides a more satisfactory demonstration of crucial themes and approaches than this encounter with Trakl's "A

Winter Evening." The merit of the demonstration has much to do with the selection, which is appropriate to the aims of poetic thinking to roughly the same degree as the jar and the temple: the rich possibilities suggested by the powerful presence of the bread and the wine—with all their traditional resonance—are almost enough in themselves to provide a place in which poetic thinking can carry out its suggestive, provocative, ambiguous, serious play.

Some large issues remain unresolved, however, including the relation among a number of "linguistic" phenomena that appear throughout Heidegger's text—principally, speaking, naming, and saying; and while these could be explored here, the difficulty of that undertaking may be reduced if we take them up where Heidegger takes them up, namely, in his second piece on Trakl.

Language in the Poem:
A Discussion of Georg Trakl's Poetic Work

To Heidegger a poem is not a particular work in verse but all of a poet's works taken together. The earlier Heidegger would have applied to such a whole the omnibus term *Dichtung*, meaning poetry in general, a particular work, or body of works. By contrast, the Heidegger of the 1952 essay, into which the lecture on "Language" conveniently leads, applies the term only to discrete works, the entire canon now constituting simply one poem or poetic work (the term *Gedicht*, which he here employs, having both senses).

The relative unfamiliarity of the designation makes it easier to assign to it a new terrain, the terrain of the poem's place (in the sense of the term unfolded in the previous section). The aim of poetic thinking is to explore that place, not, I think, as a background but as a kind of horizon, which, though projected by the poet, the poet never quite reaches.

> The poem of a poet remains unspoken. Neither the individual poems nor all of them together says everything. Yet every poem *(Dichtung)* speaks from the totality of one poem *(Gedicht)* and this is what it says every time. From the place of the poem flows the wave that at each moment moves the saying as poetic saying. But rather than leaving the place of the poem, the flowing lets saying's every movement *(alles Bewegen der Sage)* flow back into the everhidden origin. The poem's place conceals as the source of the moving wave the essence of what can appear to metaphysical-aesthetic representation as rhythm. [U, 38]

The term *Sage* has the advantage of bringing along with it little or none of the baggage that accompanies words like *glossa, lingua,* or *language*. By avoiding such terminology, Heidegger tries to let the path of his thinking find its way in the nameless. Saying is not to be understood as a speaking-out from some interiority or as a pregiven communication through which the mind discovers a past intention. To avoid such associations, Heidegger bypasses the verb *sagen* (to say, speak, tell) in favor of the substantive *die Sage,* meaning saga and also legend, fable, tradition, or myth. As if to suggest that he does not quite mean all of these meanings, he brackets the phrase with quotation marks: *"die Sage."* But it is just this afterimage of the phenomenological bracket that brings *Sage* into a wider field of play. *Sage* says "more" than *sagen* because we are unable, by tying it to metaphysical presuppositions, to make it say less: "Language, as the saying of the fourfold of the world, is no longer merely something wherein we—human beings who speak—have a relation in the sense of a connection existing between man and language. Language, as the saying that moves the world, is the relation of all relations" (U, 215). This is the strongest possible way of stating that saying is foundational—that it capacitates all regions and all relations. Saying designates what must be in order for anything to be, including the totality of the world. But if that is the case, then saying must somehow reach beyond what we normally think of as linguistic (though of course without ceasing to encompass the linguistic). In the first place, it presumably includes whatever conditions there may be that mortals do not know about and therefore cannot affect. Would this include, say, gravity? Such questions Heidegger leaves unanswered, if not unasked. All we may state with confidence is, to quote White's excellent summation: "Saying (plus, of course, the unsaid) describes the total ontological conditions requisite for language—the fourfold, its spatio-temporal continuum, the disposition of an entity in the fourfold to become represented in the naming of language."[7] It is only because saying is foundational in this way that Heidegger can distinguish as he does between language and language as saying; for in the passage quoted above he holds that language is the relation of all relations not *as language* but *as saying.* Conceding that Heidegger may be right when he elsewhere suggests that nothing is harder to think than the relation of two ideas, entities, or any other phenomena whatever, and admitting that "as" embodies such a relation, it is clear that language cannot be entirely different. This is because language embraces all the activities dealt with by poetic thinking—for instance, speaking, naming, remaining silent—but not all of the activities are related in the same way to the fourfold of the world and thus to Being. But inasmuch as saying *is* always so related, deeming language-as-saying to be the relation of relations deems language to be founded in saying.

7. White, *Heidegger and the Language of Poetry,* pp. 45–46.

All of the activities embraced by language will therefore be seen as in some sort partial or incomplete. In naming, for example, we find an act that, far from disclosing Being, is carried out solely on the basis of what naming finds already before it, for, as White reminds us, names "present what already is to the act of representation."[8] Through such presentment an entity becomes a thing—a thing, moreover, to be used. What names never present is Being; yet, though Being remains absent, *showing it* to be absent (in contrast with the named thing's presence) indirectly shows it to be.

If language as saying contrasts with naming, it contrasts also with speaking. "Speaking (and the unspoken) describes the partial epistemic limitations on the extent to which language can divulge the being of the entities named representationally in language."[9] The unspoken is included with the spoken because the latter is informed both with utterances past and with utterances future; for some aspects of what one is speaking now may be assimilated from aspects of speaking already done, even as some aspects of what one is speaking now prepare for future speaking, which, though unspoken, yet influences "futurally" one's speaking now. On the more negative side, limited, as it apparently is, to what can be represented linguistically, speaking lacks the capacity of saying that alone relates fundamentally to the world and hence to Being. Speaking, if you will, is to beings as saying is to Being. Speaking and saying thus apply to much that is "nonlinguistic"—to the ontological conditions necessary for the fourfold of the world, to the fourfold's space-time, to the representational function of naming; and if that is to strain the use of the terms, "for Heidegger's purposes, to realize the need for such strain is precisely the point. Only if language is taken back to its roots in Being (the notion of saying) and to how Being is apprehended as the representation of named entities (the notion of speaking) can the relation between language and being become accessible."[10]

As an explanation of Heidegger's general argument about the question of Being and language, the account just presented possesses the integrity of a self-consistent analysis and is not without elegance; for these reasons, and also because it renders much of Heidegger's argument in philosophical terms that are helpful and clear, I have given it considerable space (though White gives much more space to these issues, which are the heart of his enterprise). But when we move back toward Heidegger's thinking about poems, one begins to feel that, in a sense, too

8. Ibid., p. 24.
9. Ibid., p. 46.
10. Ibid.

much has been explained. Although Heidegger's argument may have become more lucid from a philosophical point of view, the main things that happen when Heidegger thinks are in a rather different mode; which is to say that going back to the texts means a return to the peculiar dynamic experience that is poetic thinking. Thereupon some distinctions become problematic. Consider, for example, that, in the first Trakl piece, naming is carried out by speaking (U, 20), by saying (U, 24), by a particular verse (U, 26), by a particular strophe (U, 26), and by calling (U, 24). So far, so good: naming, after all, presents what already is to representation, and it is not nearly so rare and precious as the experience of saying. But Heidegger goes so far as to state that naming "calls"—calling amounting to a crucial step toward the gathering of the fourfold through things—so that naming becomes a more fundamental act than the mere representation of beings that already are:

> What is this naming? Does it merely drape representable, known objects and events—snow, bell, window, fall, ring—with the words of a language? No. Naming does not hand out titles, utilize words, but calls into word. Naming calls. Calling brings nearer what is called. [U, 21]

The nearness Heidegger has in mind should not be identified with physical contiguity. It has to do, rather, with a more basic condition, such as exists when, for example, we find that with certain individuals we feel remote—estranged, let us say, or bored—precisely when we are physically nearby and that somehow we are closer to them when removed from them. Or we find that we are closer to someone living a mile away than to a next-door neighbor or that the people in our neighborhood are so much on the run that we rarely see them, and, when we do, we see them as strangers (cf. U, 210). Although these are, to be sure, excessively "empirical" illustrations, they may suggest something of the interplay between different ways of Being-present. Roughly, the difference attests to the degree of nearness attained by naming, which means the degree to which a thing is brought into relation with the world and, with this, into relation with Being. "Therefore the first strophe does not merely name things. At the same time it names world. It calls the 'many' who, as mortals, belong to the world" (U, 22). If calling and naming, then, are the same, naming moves from its modest status in the hierarchy of "linguistic" acts toward a status nearer that of saying. Far from being stranded in the representational, and thus cut off from saying, naming draws upon saying, quite in the manner of calling, as its primordial source. And this is just what happens in the passage on the movement of saying and the wave. Speaking and saying are there used as synonyms, though not with the aim of rendering them identical; the point seems rather to achieve by connotative instead of denotative means the sense of saying's susceptibility to coming near. Hence the motif of the wave, which moves both intransitively and transitively—moving along and at the same time moving the world— and which moves in its flowing back to its origin. In the wave, poetic thinking seeks a return to the foundation of Being by mirroring the play of difference—the intimacy, as may be said—between speaking and saying in such a way that the very movement of the thinking is itself the mirroring and the play.

Paul Ricoeur writes: "Our loves and hatreds are the revocable figures of love derived from the undifferentiated substance of narcissism: like the waves of the sea, these figures may be effaced without alteration of the substrate."[11] The distinctness of the waves is underlined by Ricoeur's conformity to a natural model, so that the waves are a motion that occurs above the sea-floor without affecting it. Heidegger thinks a different relation. Poetic thinking cannot afford a *sub*strate, which posits a substantial difference from anything *super*. Nor can it afford waves in the plural, for the innocent *s* immediately suggests exactly those natural motions on which Ricoeur's analogy depends. Heidegger's wave is in the singular but is discrete only in the sense that it has been disconnected from representational conceptions. What remains is a movement that cannot be determined with relation to any fixed point. In this respect the wave resembles emergence, emergence being neither completely in nor completely out but a coming-forth that is still coming. So the wave remains indefinite, vague (and it may not be accidental that *vague* in French signifies both "vagueness" and "wave"). Husserl defended vague descriptions arising from everyday experience as more appropriate to lived reality than the exact representations of scientific discourse. Because a wave is vague, one cannot be sure how far to think it or in what direction or mode. At what point does the wave begin or end? Does it in fact go anywhere? Does it have phases? If so, some "parts" of it must be later than others—but how can the wave be later than itself? Is it not equally plausible to suggest that the wave is at all times the extension of itself and that, at any time, it belongs as much as ever to its own origin? Heidegger imagines that the flowing-forth of his wave is such that it never really leaves its place. Once we start thinking temporally, however, the contradiction begins to sound less contradictory. A duration, for example, need not be thought of as going away from its beginning or toward any end. A duration may be thought of as that through which occurrences occur. One can go a step further and cease to think of duration at all, insofar as duration, as a span with a beginning and an end, carries traces of something other from which it derives, by contrast, its own identity. Heidegger thinks of a different time, immeasurable, whose continuing presence seems nonetheless to recur. That sounds like a type of rhythm, but Heidegger, we remember, says not (U, 38). Heidegger seems to be thinking, in some sense, musically; though, given his concern to show that the wave has never left the place from which it flows, it is unlikely that he would now simply turn to another special discipline and its metaphysics, let alone one that thinks in terms of intervals, that representationally measures differences and increments, and that finds a substrate in rhythm, conceived as a more or less regular recurrence. Heidegger's is a more ambiguous music, a music of singing and harmony that is as hard to capture as the Heraclitean fire.

In the contemporaneous *What Is Called Thinking?* (1951–52) Heidegger, by turning away from a concern for the matter of discourse to a concern for its manner, and by redefining what is entailed by the concept of manner, has this to say about the function of musicality:

> The manner *(Weise)* in which our assertion speaks is only indicated adequately when we are able to consider what the assertion actually says. . . . Therefore we must now attend to the question which the assertion puts to us when we reflect upon the manner in which it is said. We understand manner as other than ways and means, other than *modus.* Manner is here to be understood as melody, as timbre and tone, which does not mean merely how the saying sounds. The manner of saying is the tone from which and to which what it says is attuned. [WHD, 13–14]

In the tuning-to and tuning-from we find a counterpart to the wave's flowing and flowing back, a reciprocity that resembles as well the dynamic reciprocities of mirror-play. We find a counterpart, also, to the way, which harmonizes both with the manner of articulation appropriate to its region and with the manner in which all the regions are moved to relation. The passage suggests an accord between Heidegger's thinking and Pater's belief that "All art constantly aspires towards the condition of music." It suggests at the same time a continuing affection for the theme of world harmony, at which we have more than once looked, a desire for a unity not the less simple for embracing many voices. We find the same sense of harmony, of simplicity, in the water examined in my discussion of elemental thinking, that circumambient medium where meanings are manifold, in which thinking is yet at ease; we find it even nearer, of course, in the passage on the wave, which demonstrates concretely what the passage last quoted states in rather more general terms. Sympathetically experienced, Heidegger's discourse, like that of Sir Thomas Browne, moves on the borders of silence, where some have said that music moves, where "the silent note" of love is "far sweeter than the sound of any instrument; for there is a music wherever there is a harmony, order, or proportion; and thus far we may maintain the music of the spheres" (*Religio Medici*, Part II, Sec. ix).

8

Conclusion:
The Play of the World

All our heart's courage is the
echoing response to the
first call of Being which
gathers our thinking into the
play of the world.
From the Experience of Thinking

The shape of the present chapter reflects, to an extent, the prospective tendency that not infrequently characterizes conclusions of books on difficult and ambiguous themes. I am not sure how it could be otherwise, given Heidegger's insistence on the primacy of the future and on the open-ended nature of questioning and play. But in acknowledging this fact, one must resist the temptation to regard time as a linear sequence of discrete periods no one of which can ever coexist with another except in some privileged "moment" or some privileged "mind." The ecstases of temporality cannot be severed from one another, since, as we saw in chapter 1, they constitute a unity. To paraphrase somewhat a formulation in *Being and Time* discussed in those pages, the so-called present is released from the future in the process of becoming what has-been. Hence what emerges in time emerges in much the same way as the cloud and sky poetry, in the Hölderlin poem examined in chapter 4, which does not come from the cloud but comes over it as what it lingers against. It is in order to capture this nuance that the later Heidegger sometimes separates the compound *Gegenwart*, "the present," into *Gegen*, from *gegen* in the sense of "against," and *wart*, from *warten*, meaning "to wait" or "to be on the lookout for"; the resulting term, *Gegen-wart*, suggests that the future, as the ecstasis waited against, looms toward the "here and now" of the present even as it draws the latter to itself.

The practical consequence of these considerations is that a prospective approach can forgo the retrospective as little as it can neglect the process by which it is itself becoming what has-been—and this quite apart form the issue of whether such recognition is explicit. On the practical side, again, one also recognizes the need to make, for purposes of discussion, some reasonable match between Heidegger's essential ontological conception and the particulars of "mere" history. For one

cannot talk about everything at once any more than one can give everything equal emphasis. Moreover, the future is a problematic
phenomenon. We do not know what it "is" because it "is" not, and, if it
"is" not, what observations can we make about it? The question is
rhetorical with a vengeance, since the future does not manifest itself as
a present being, it simply works, and among its workings is the influence it brings to bear through what I am bringing to bear on this very
issue, even now, in this very discourse. The future "is" not something
to be specified or a focus of reflection; rather, it unfolds through the
manifestation of other phenomena that *are* a focus of reflection, even
including, for the moment—as I have said—the present discourse.

These other phenomena, all within the purview of comparatively
recent thought and criticism, are ideas and themes deriving from or
otherwise related to Heidegger's enterprise. Because they are increasingly numerous and increasingly complex, an exhaustive treatment of them is beyond the scope of the present volume; but it will be
possible to look briefly at the form these ideas and themes have taken in
the writings of Hans-Georg Gadamer, Jacques Derrida, Claude Lévi-
Strauss, and Michel Foucault. At the same time, in order to avoid a
pernicious "presentism" (to borrow a term from the historians), and in
the interest of perspective, it will be necessary to glance at some additional texts by Heidegger and to review some patterns already traced.
Through this process we will engage, more closely than before, the
meaning of Heidegger's growing concern with music, with dance, with
the language of gesture, with Eastern modes of thinking and presentation. What tends to unite that concern with the issues treated by the
other writers just named is the theme discussed at the close of the
preceding chapter, namely, the theme of play.

Play, for Gadamer, is "the clue for ontological explanation" because
the peculiar mode of Being of a work of art invites attention to all of the
issues that must be addressed in order to define anything in any mode
or manifestation. In this, Gadamer follows Heidegger's lead, though
with comparatively little concern for the distinction between art work
and thing and with much greater concern for the history of ideas, particularly in its Greek and German form. Especially pertinent, in light of
Heideggerian emphasis and practice, is his interest in movement (also
treated at length by Huizinga):

> The movement which is play has no goal which brings it to an
> end; rather it renews itself in constant repetition. The movement
> backwards and forwards is obviously so central for the definition
> of a game that it is not important who or what performs this
> movement. The movement of play as such has, as it were, no sub-
> strate. It is the game that is played—it is irrelevant whether or not

there is a subject who plays. The play is the performance of the movement as such. Thus we speak of the play of colours and do not mean only that there is one colour, that plays against another, but that there is one process or sight, in which one can see a changing variety of colours.[1]

There is nothing in this, it would appear, with which Heidegger would disagree; the account, indeed, is compatible with the dynamic character of many Heideggerian passages (e.g., the description of the wave in the preceding chapter), and it brings out that totalizing character of play to which we will see Heidegger allude, below, when he speaks of the *Satz*, the movement, period, or phrase, in music.

Equally Heideggerian, at least in its general tone, is Gadamer's notion of the transformative nature of art. What is transformed amounts, for Gadamer, to the very Being of the person experiencing the work; what he calls transformation into structure is a way of saying this, but it is also a way of saying that what the transformation achieves is enduring and true:

> The transformation is a transformation into the true. It is not enchantment in the sense of a bewitchment that waits for the redeeming word that will transform things to what they were, but it is itself redemption and transformation back into true being. In the representation of play, what is emerges. In it is produced and brought to the light what otherwise is constantly hidden and withdrawn.[2]

With this passage difficulties arise, though there is heuristic value, happily, in meeting them. In the first place, redemption implies a condition different from the condition that Heidegger has in mind when, in *Being and Time*, he states that *Dasein* falls by losing itself in its world, by becoming mired in semblance and the opinions of "they," a state in no wise as dire as it sounds, for the world can manifest itself as covered up, hidden, or disguised only because it can equally manifest itself as unconcealed. Gadamer's "redemption," by contrast, has overtones of culpability, and imparts to the transformation the status of a phenomenon occurring in a creation—and, quite likely, in one that is specifically Christian.

Second, if art transforms back, then the statement means that things are made to be what they previously were, before the work; if that is the case, art does not bring them to emergence, for, if it did, Gadamer would have to hold that art simply transforms them. Rather, they have

1. Hans-Georg Gadamer, *Truth and Method*, trans. Garrett Barden and John Cumming (New York: Seabury, 1975), p. 93.
2. Ibid., p. 101.

already emerged, only to *lose* their Being, whereupon art somehow *restores* it to them or, better, them to it. The difficulty is not removed, from a Heideggerian point of view, if transformation is interpreted intransitively, as a movement without a something-moved; for with this we are still faced with a return "into true being," whereas, for Heidegger, art (one can substitute language or poetry or saying) is a way of making emergence possible. And indeed, transformation is itself emergence insofar as you cannot "change your life," in Rilke's phrase, without the art through which Being is given.

Third, emergence does not transpire, for Heidegger, through representation. Representation in all forms belongs to the language of metaphysics, the language that makes metaphor a parasite of the literal, that arranges, tabulates, and labels phenomena according to the precepts of logic, the categories of formal philosophy, the initiatives of technology. Representation could never picture the world or anything in it—or, what is the same thing, could *only* picture it—since a picture (as Heidegger demonstrates in the lecture "The Age of the World Picture") is a conceptual construction arising from the same logical-philosophical-technological nexus of precepts, categories, and protocols.

Fourth, the description of producing and bringing to light is incompatible with the Heideggerian view insofar as it sees light in oppositional terms, i.e., as something counter to the absence of illumination. For Heidegger, concealment is not something shed like a coat or left behind like the darkness of the tunnel when the train comes forth; rather, it adheres to what emerges as a condition of emergence, and it persists as the future possibility of a return to concealment.

Thus, notwithstanding his debt to Heidegger, Gadamer does not place himself—does not, for the most part, even attempt to place himself—among (in Derrida's phrase) "the great destroyers," Heidegger, Freud, and Nietzsche, each of whom struggles without surcease against a tradition committed to nothing so much as its own unexamined perpetuation.

Derrida, more emphatic even that Gadamer about the centrality of play, follows Heidegger to the extent that he detects presence as its paramount distinguishing characteristic, a characteristic shared, in his view, by all ideas and terms denoting first principles, grounds, fundamentals, or—to use the term he favors in this context—centers. For Derrida, all thought has historically based its structures on some organizing principle, some point of origin, aimed at keeping the total structure of thought on track and in balance so that it may better alter its own content or terminology through substitutions, permutations, transformations—in short, through what Derrida, following Lévi-

Strauss, calls a surplus or superabundance of signifiers. To hold that a system of thought does this is to hold that it plays; but because its playing is governed by constant reference to a center, its "freeplay," as Derrida calls it, is never entirely free. At any time the very presence that constitutes the center of the structure transcends it, its governing power being a power over an enterprise different in all ways from itself; hence, that which makes freeplay possible is necessarily out of play.

With Heidegger, Derrida insists that the substitutions, permutations, transformations, and repetitions within a structure of thought are—though Derrida does not employ the terms—epochal; that is, they carry meanings appropriate to the historical Being-there that belongs to a period and a people. But within our own epoch, which evidently begins later for Derrida than for Heidegger, the belief in a normative, centered structure has suffered a rupture, forcing us to recognize that no center can be either fixed law or fixed locus but must be something more like a function within a limited field. While unwilling to date this "event," Derrida gives much credit for it to Nietzsche, who substituted play, interpretation, and the dominance of the sign for traditional concepts of Being and truth; to Freud, who eliminated self-presence in its manifestation as consciousness (and, one might add, gave further legitimacy, in the process, to Nietzschean substitutions, whose operations are the mainstay both of psychoanalytic interpretative practice and of the dreamworld to which it is engaged); and to Heidegger, whose destruction of metaphysics undermines the doctrine of Being as presence.

All three "destroyers" nonetheless fall short, in Derrida's eyes, insofar as metaphysics, by providing an object of attack, clings to their thinking at all times. This is, of course, the objection that Heidegger himself makes against Nietzsche and against every other attempt, including his own, to carry out that destruction, which must remain a destruction from within. It is in the face of this dilemma that Heidegger brings about a rupture in his own thinking, a turning, which sees him abandon his plan to finish *Being and Time*, a decision largely influenced by his extended inquiry, from 1936 to 1940, into Nietzsche's thought. Finding in the latter's will-to-power the fruition of a nihilism, Heidegger can see the futility of his own early quest to overcome tradition—can see that when he called Prometheus the foremost of philosophers (in an address of 1933), he was himself animated by the same self-assertive, aggressive, *Dasein*-centered drive that powers the machines of modern technology no less than the machines of Cartesian rationalism.

> The realization that in his own philosophy, deliberately seeking to "overcome" metaphysics, this will... was still a powerful driving force, standing between him and Being—the goal of his entire

quest—seems to have led to the collapse of this will and to a complete surrender to the "Voice of Being." It is of this supreme renunciation of the metaphysical will by thought that he speaks in the *Feldweg.* "Renunciation does not take. Renunciation gives. It gives the inexhaustible power of the simple." This is the sacrifice, the offering of thankfulness and homage for the grace of Being, of which Heidegger speaks in the postscript to "What Is Metaphysics?" This is not the failure of the courage to think but an acknowledgment that it follows, not from the assertive will of man but through a demand of Being itself. The dominant mood now is not anxiety in the face of Nothingness but one of tranquil detachment (*Gelassenheit*).[3]

Derrida's way of living the decentering rupture resembles Heidegger's when it is stated in general terms. Opting for affirmation, Derrida endorses a mode of poetic thinking that "tries to pass beyond man and humanism, the name man being the name of that being who, throughout the history of metaphysics or of ontotheology—in other words, through the history of all of his history—has dreamed of full presence, the reassuring foundation, the origin and the end of the game."[4] This is, once again, the message in "Letter on Humanism," in the postscript to *What Is Metaphysics?*, in Heidegger's readings of "A Winter Evening" and "On a Lamp" and Hölderlin's elegies and hymns; it is contained as well in "The Age of the World Picture," where Heidegger examines some of the forms of knowledge and power that eventually attract the notice not only of Derrida but of Michel Foucault.

More interesting is the manner in which Derrida, through his version of play, carries out his own turning. The field in which the playing is carried out is, as I have said, a limited field,

> a field of infinite substitutions in the closure of a finite ensemble. This field permits these infinite substitutions only because it is finite, that is to say, because instead of being too large, there is something missing from it: a center which arrests and founds the freeplay of substitutions. One could say . . . that this movement of

3. J. L. Mehta, *Martin Heidegger: The Way and the Vision,* rev. ed. (Honolulu: University of Hawaii Press, 1976), p. 337.

4. Jacques Derrida, "Structure, Sign, and Play in the Discourse of the Human Sciences," in *The Languages of Criticism and the Sciences of Man: The Structuralist Controversy,* ed. Richard Macksey and Eugenio Donato (Baltimore: Johns Hopkins University Press, 1970), p. 264. This lecture, on which I focus for convenience, becomes a chapter in Derrida's *Writing and Difference,* pp. 278–93. In the same volume Derrida views Heidegger (who remains for the French thinker a seminal influence) through the prism of Emmanuel Levinas' *magnum opus, Totality and Infinity.* The reader may wish to compare this approach with the chapter on Heidegger in Derrida's *Marges de la philosophie* (Paris: Editions de Minuit, 1972), pp. 31–78. Derrida's even more playful, post Mallarméan *Glas* is analyzed by Geoffrey Hartman in "Monsieur Teste: On Jacques Derrida, His *Glas,*" *Georgia Review* 29 (1978): 739–97; 30 (1976): 169–209.

the freeplay, permitted by the lack, the absence of a center or origin, is the movement of *supplementarity*. One cannot determine the center, the sign which *supplements* it, which takes its place in its absence—because the sign adds itself, occurs in addition, over and above, comes as a *supplement*. The movement of signification adds something, which results in the fact that there is always more, but this addition is a floating one because it comes to perform a vicarious function, to supplement a lack on the part of the signified.[5]

A sign, according to such a theory, no longer entails the alliance of signifier and signified delineated by Saussure, because the signified has disappeared. It does not merely exhibit a lack, as the passage just quoted implies; it is entirely missing. For Derrida, the structure of thinking does nonetheless possess a center, though only in the sense that, when playing occurs, the "something" that makes it possible is available for signification—one can say all kinds of things about it—but without possessing any determinate Being in its own right.

The problem, for me, is that this flow of signification may finally dispossess the dispossession, that is, may fill the absence with a new virtual presence constituted by application to it of signifiers. The "power of the sign" that Derrida desires to escape, instead of yielding to absence, risks becoming newly endowed with presence by every phrase of discourse that attempts self-consciously to escape it. An alternative escape route is available through recourse to nothingness, as Heidegger has defined it for us; but the trouble with nothingness is that it *is*, quite as much as Being is—is indeed an aspect of Being if not a substitute signifier for Being itself, as Hegel believed when he pronounced the two, Being and nothingness, to be the same.

Derrida should be taken at his word when he describes his orientation as classical and his goals as modest: "Here or there I have used the word *déconstruction*, which has nothing to do with destruction. That is to say, it is simply a question of (and this is a necessity of criticism in the classical sense of the word) being alert to the implications, to the historical sedimentation of the language which we use—and that is not destruction."[6] What is more, "I didn't say that there was no center, that we could get along without the center. I believe that the center is a function, not a being—a reality, but a function. And this function is absolutely indispensable."[7] From a Heideggerian point of view the statement is traditional indeed, for the crucial premise is one that Heidegger refutes as early as *Being and Time*, the premise, namely, that

5. Derrida, "Structure, Sign, and Play," pp. 260–61.
6. Ibid., p. 271.
7. Ibid.

an ontological inquiry can get anywhere by orienting itself toward a being, *Seiendes,* as the source of definition; and Derrida's "a being" is a *Seiendes,* pure and simple. The statement may prompt an objection: "But Derrida states that the center is not a being." He does, and that is the point: Derrida situates his center, says what it is, in the terminology of metaphysics: saying "not a being" defers to that being as the *sine qua non* of what the new "something" is. Furthermore, the author of *Being and Time* would object that no thought is given to the kind of Being that a function is. It *has* one, because the power of the sign gives it; immediately, without fail, compellingly, the statement that "the center is a function, not a being" says that the kind of Being this something has is other than the kind of Being a being has; that the Being it has is the Being of a function; that this absent center is not absent after all but is present as this signified something whose absolutely indispensable presence the absolutely indispensable signifier absolutely guarantees.

Derrida's concept of supplementary signification derives from the venerable idea of the plenitude of Being by way of Lévi-Strauss. According to the French ethnologist, a culture maintains its own coherence, insofar as that coherence is reinforced by symbolic thought, through a complementarity between signifier and signified. Without stating the thesis in as many words, Lévi-Strauss imagines a world constituted of entities that are, in their own Being, just what they are (an animal, the sky, a tree) but at the same time receive whatever "content" a culture imparts to them (any entity may take on any sort of value). Because human beings, as distributors of symbols, can do much more with a tree, let us say, than simply call it a tree, Lévi-Strauss contends that they always have at their disposal a supplementary supply of signification from which to draw. They have thus, at any time, somewhere to turn in order to sustain a complementary alignment between the pregiven world and the invented world of culture. In the phenomenon of *mana* (Lévi-Strauss suggests) we have the case of an entity that, already "loaded" with a certain signification, takes on additional content unlimited in nature and scope: as the very exemplification of plenitude, *mana* can assume whatever meaning is assigned to it:

> At one and the same time force and action, quality and state,
> substantive and verb; abstract and concrete, omnipresent and
> localized—*mana* is in effect all these things. But is it not precisely
> because it is none of these things that *mana* is a simple form, or
> more exactly, a symbol in the pure state, and therefore capable of
> becoming charged with any sort of symbolic content whatever? In
> the system of symbols constituted by all cosmologies, *mana* would
> simply be . . . a sign marking the necessity of a symbolic content

supplementary [Derrida's italics] to that with which the signified is already loaded, but which can take on any value required.[8]

Although Lévi-Strauss's distinction between a content and a carrier of content belongs to the schematism of metaphysics, he is not far, in his basic understanding of the *mana* representation, from a Heidegger-ian perspective. The anthropologist does not see the *mana* representation as something present-at-hand, like a material object; that is, he sees it, to use the words Heidegger employs in a little-known discussion of Ernst Cassirer, not "as a being among other beings but as the 'how' of all the mythic real, i.e., as the Being of beings." Lévi-Strauss, moreover, stresses the nonobjectifying, unifying nature of the thinking that animates acts of magic:

> The magical judgment implied in the act of producing smoke in order to summon clouds and rain is not founded on a primitive distinction between smoke and cloud that appeals to *mana* so as to bring them together, but on the fact that a deeper project of thinking identifies smoke and cloud, that the one is in a certain respect the same as the other.[9]

The discussion of Cassirer, published in 1928, one year after *Being and Time*, suggests the possibility of an even deeper unity connecting the manner in which "mythic *Dasein*" lives with its intuitions and forms of thought. Heidegger does not mean by this that "primitive" peoples differ fundamentally from "modern" peoples; he means rather that a phenomenon like *mana* can be understood only within the specific to-tality of a people's lived world. He does concede, however, if only implicitly, a certain advantage to mythic *Dasein*, because it avoids identifying Being with a being present-at-hand. Hence mythic *Dasein* may be supposed to experience time more primordially, without the need to break down the partitioning of present and future. We may further suppose that the distinction between the metaphorical and the literal does not arise and hence need not be overcome. To this extent it would not be extravagant to compare the general tenor of poetic think-ing with the thinking of mythic *Dasein*.

> In "thrownness" mythic *Dasein*, in its manner of being-in-the-world, is delivered up to the world in such a way that it is overwhelmed by that to which it is delivered up. . . . *Dasein* is

8. Claude Lévi-Strauss, "Introduction à l'oeuvre de Marcel Mauss," in Marcel Mauss, *Sociologie et anthropologie* (Paris: Presses Universitaires de France, 1964), p. L. The English translation appears in Derrida's "Structure, Sign, and Play," p. 261, and in *Writing and Difference*, p. 290.

9. "Introduction à l'oeuvre de Marcel Mauss," pp. xlvi–xlvii.

captivated and can experience itself only as belonging to and related with this reality. In thrownness, accordingly, all disclosed
beings have the ontological feature of overwhelmingness
(*mana*). . . . In thrownness there is a unique case of being-driven
in which there is an openness for whatever may be surprisingly
extraordinary.[10]

Without this predisposition, the system-building that constitutes for *la
pensée sauvage* "the science of the concrete" would not be necessary,
indeed would not be possible. More to the point, from a Heideggerian
perspective such openness accounts for "the play element" in mythic
Dasein's culture, with its floating signifiers that are unaware of themselves; that have no "why"; that signify just because they *do*.

In contrast with Heidegger, who often begins with an inquiry into
the concrete particularity and essence of things, Lévi-Strauss does not
develop an ontology that could account for the Being of those beings in
"nature" that carry symbolic values. But if one allowed the problem of
mana to continue in a Heideggerian direction, one would discover that,
in at least one important respect, *mana* relates to the thing in much the
same way as art does. As Heidegger demonstrates in *The Origin of the
Work of Art*, the work possesses a thingly character—it is always at least,
on one level, grainy wood or sound waves or colored shapes—yet it is
more than a thing. So, too, *mana* is a thing and more than a thing:
"Things endowed with *mana* present themselves as having a power and
density which enable them to be detached from their thingly context . . . and to pack within themselves the full sense of world as, e.g.,
sacred stones, trees, bread, etc."[11] However different may be its sources
and motivations, the visionary poetry of a Trakl, with its incantatory
intensity, has more than a little of this sensible-sensuous fullness, and
the same applies *mutatis mutandis* to Hölderlin. The difference between
their poetry and "pure" magic consists in the fact that each confronted
the overwhelming at a time when mythic *Dasein* as a widespread mode
of Being had leaked away through the rupture of rationalism, leaving
each with the fear that the overwhelming was a burden to be borne
alone.

With Lévi-Strauss, whose floating signifiers can settle wherever
mythic *Dasein* wants them to, Huizinga recognizes the signifying
function of play; it is predicated for the historian, furthermore, on a
distinction parallel to Lévi-Strauss's distinction between nature and

10. Heidegger, "Ernst Cassirer's Mythical Thought," in *The Piety of Thinking: Essays by
Martin Heidegger*, trans., with notes and commentary, by James G. Hart and John C.
Maraldo (Bloomington: Indiana University Press, 1976), p. 43. See SZ, 490, n. xi, for
Heidegger's comment on the relation of his approach to Cassirer's.
11. *The Piety of Thinking*, p. 123.

culture, between the "animal" level and the level of meaning: "It goes beyond the confines of purely physical or purely biological activity. It is a *significant* function—that is to say, there is some sense to it. In play there is something 'at play' which transcends the immediate needs of life and imparts meaning to the action. All play means something."[12]

Transcendence, however, entails a "toward which" not to be found in the Derridean conception of play. What Derrida offers is, if you will, an "away from": thought becomes an activity that can move in any direction except the direction leading back to presence. One is always therefore on guard, in reading Derrida, for fear that some series of substitutions, permutations, or transformations may, in its superabundance, flow over from a "finite ensemble" and spill out a meaning. I have already raised the possibility, of course, that Derrida's dedication to avoidance (as it might be called) defines his activity from the standpoint of presence, as the one thing to be avoided, and hence guarantees its presence in the mode of absence.

Like Derrida, Heidegger is traditional in his own way but is even more oriented toward the future; or better: he is more concerned to "let be" the prophetic strain in thinking's practice of play, the better to stay ready for whatever is to come. This latter phenomenon, itself dependent in part on the readiness sustained by thinking, will not be the product of some tomorrow that will eventually materialize if only we have the patience to wait it out. For all we know, it may emerge as a reconstitution of what has already been, making newly real what currently abides in the mode of remembrance. Meanwhile, all manner of notice and calling—hints, signs, intimations—disclose themselves in the poetic thinking and thinking poetry that come to us from different epochs, including our own—epochs in which saying, though made manifest in different ways, can yet capacitate in us such apprehension as is required to bring it usefully near our more immediate experience: •

> When thinking lets what has-been retain its own essence and does not . . . disturb its sway, then we experience, through remembrance, the return of what has-been as it turns around and comes toward us from the future. Suddenly remembrance must think of what has-been as what has not yet unfolded. [E, 100]

What is yet to come would not have the interest that it does were we not disposed, through our own thrown ecstasis, which never ceases until life itself ceases, to a kind of healthy presentism. I mean the tendency to consider where we are going "later" in relation to where we are going "now," a tendency that merely casts in a different terminology

12. Huizinga, *Homo Ludens*, p. 1.

Heidegger's insistence (in the early works) on a readiness for existential decision and (in the later works) on a releasement toward what is yet to come.

It is a desire shared by Michel Foucault, who places himself in a "family" of thinkers whose lineage can be traced to the Kantian question "What is the Enlightenment?" The importance of the question is that Kant thought to ask it at a time when "Enlightenment" stood for an epochal movement of Being that was still in progress; hence Kant inaugurates a tradition that brings attention to bear, in an unprecedented way, on contemporary problems. The family thus founded includes, in Foucault's view, Heidegger, Nietzsche, and the members of the Frankfurt School, the latter group being closest to Foucault's own historical analysis of discourse. The concept of discourse, it should be said, is not in essence linguistic in the narrow sense (neither, for that matter, is Heidegger's *Rede*) but is constituted by a nexus of concrete practices that find expression in language. In pursuit of his project, Foucault retains some of the playfulness characteristic of earlier undertakings, such as *The Order of Things (Les Mots et les choses)*, a playfulness similar in its seriousness and rigor to Heidegger's; perhaps more significant, however, is the fact that in his exploration of knowledge and power, of *epistēmai* and institutions, Foucault carries out an undertaking for which the Heideggerian analytic not only leaves room but for which "The Age of the World Picture," among other works, provides a preliminary outline.[13]

I have emphasized the manner in which Heidegger presents his thinking because Heidegger suffers more than most writers from being paraphrased; because the manner of presentation is what enables the reader to experience this thinking as Tao, understanding that word as way in the sense defined in chapter 7; and because a thinking that moves needs to be followed in the very act of moving, even if this means the occultation of "meaning" through nonlogical mergings wherein the discourse approximates now the condition of music, now the element of water. In *What Is Called Thinking?*, a work on which I would like to dwell for a time, the pathos of this thinking may be experienced more clearly, perhaps more poignantly, than is normally the case. After exploring a fragment of Parmenides, Heidegger underlines the need to reflect on what is said so as to keep on the way that the exploration has opened up:

> But today, when we know too much and mean too quickly, when
> we calculate and arrange everything at a moment's notice . . . today

13. This analysis is based in part on comments made by Foucault during a meeting (October 18, 1979) of the Stanford Faculty Seminar on Interpretation.

there is no longer the slightest place for confidence in the ability
that the presentation *(Darstellung)* of a matter could be powerful
enough in itself, by showing the matter itself, to bring a
thinking-together along on the way. [WHD, 165–66]

Let us note, first, the role of time; for what prompts the lamentation is
the tempo, not of the presentation, but of the reader's anticipated engagement with it. In the terminology of Lévy-Strauss, the issue is one of
complementarity, though not of the type posited by the anthropologist.
For Lévi-Strauss, complementarity is required for the intelligibility of
symbolic systems, and it actually occurs, whereas for Heidegger, complementarity would bring closer the end of the rupture, and it does not
occur. Moreover, it is temporal, inasmuch as it is possible only when
ecstatic temporality is lived in the manner of "whiling" or lingering.
Heidegger in fact says "the same" as Keats in the famous letter of 1817:

> . . . several things dove-tailed in my mind, and at once it struck
> me what quality went to form a Man of Achievement especially in
> Literature and which Shakespeare possessed so enormously—I
> mean *Negative Capability*, that is, when a man is capable of being
> in uncertainties, mysteries, doubts, without any irritable reaching
> after fact and reason. . . . This pursued through volumes would
> perhaps take us no further than this, that with a great poet the
> sense of Beauty overcomes every other consideration, or rather
> obliterates all consideration.[14]

Heidegger says the same as Keats because the releasement that is *Gelassenheit*, forgoing assertion in favor of letting-be, is the thinker's
capability—and not only Heidegger's, for Wittgenstein in the post-
humous writings makes a turn closely resembling Heidegger's in that
he gives up answering in favor of questioning, accepting the rupture,
increasing it even, and learning to linger without irritable reaching. The
rupture, it should be said, is another name for a phenomenon brought
to attention through Heidegger's reading of Hölderlin: it is the destitute
time writ large, indeed, writ epochally.

We have seen its inscription (to borrow a Derridean term) in the
poetic crisis of a Hofmannsthal, and, if the scope of the present work
allowed it, we could trace it through the fabling *Angst* of Kafka, whose
"In the Penal Colony" at once parodies and exalts the office of language,
incarnate and lethal as it is there shown to be, not only to itself but to
the colonial (read Western) historical tradition. It is not in any case
accidental, perhaps, that when Heidegger makes a presentation come
face to face with a missing complementarity, he raises to prominence

14. *The Selected Letters of John Keats,* ed. Lionel Trilling (New York: Doubleday/Anchor,
1956), pp. 103–4.

one of the most powerful of Kafka's favored words, *Verlegenheit*, a word
brought to attention on the opening page of my Introduction.

The presentation takes the form, initially, of a question, and returns
near the end to the interrogative mode:

> Is the saying "The moon has risen," in the first line of the "Eve-
> ning Song" by Matthias Claudius, an assertion and even a propo-
> sition? What is the essence of this saying? I do not know. I do not
> trust myself to explore the question. The assurance that the saying
> "The moon is risen" belongs to the poem and is poetry rather
> than thinking does not help us out of our perplexity *(Verlegenheit)*.
> The correct observation that this saying is a line of poetry and not
> a proposition does not help very much as long as we remain in the
> dark as to what it means for saying to gather into a poem. Pre-
> sumably we can never properly consider what poetry is as long as
> we have not sufficiently asked: "What is called thinking?"
> [WHD, 163]

It is hard to imagine a more lingering, circular, redundant book than the
one that carries that question in its title, for the same question is posed
repeatedly, and the same or similar themes and motifs weave constantly
in and out. This can be explained in part by the fact that Heidegger gave
the lectures in intervals of a week or more and so provided summaries
and transitions for continuity. But given the frequency with which
Heidegger revised texts over the years, one must suppose that he regarded the presentation as sufficiently representative; and it may be
further supposed that he found it so, first, because the dominance in it of
a single hushed tone, its *da capo* structure, and its simple *largo* movements (if the musical terminology may be allowed) combine to make it
qualitatively appropriate as *Darstellung*. The second reason is that open-
ended questioning is not conducive to linear design, incremental ad-
vancement, or climactic closure. Such questioning leads rather to circularity and overlapping periods, in which attention is sustained long
enough for the reader to experience the strangely pleasant strain of
lingering as the discourse doubles back on itself in a manner similar to
the manner in which poetry and thinking that have been in the "past"
come forward from the future, rediscovering, in permutations of the
question of Being, considerations not yet thought.

As for the beauty of which Keats speaks, a counterpart in Heidegger is
the vision conveyed by his understanding of the Mörike poem (chapter
2)—in particular, of the concluding lines: "But what is beautiful shines
blissfully in itself"—and by his understanding of a Hölderlin poem, in
two strophes, on Socrates and Alcibiades.

SOKRATES UND ALKIBIADES

'Warum huldigest du, heiliger Sokrates,
  Diesem Jünglinge stets? Kennest du Grösseres nicht?
Warum siehet mit Liebe,
  Wie auf Götter, dein Aug' auf ihn?'

Wer das Tiefste gedacht, liebt das Lebendigste,
  Hohe Jugend versteht, wer in die Welt geblickt,
    Und es neigen die Weisen
      Oft am Ende zu Schönem sich.

"Why, holy Socrates, dost thou pay homage always
  To this youth? Dost thou not know any greater?
    Why does thine eye,
      As though at gods, look at him with love?

He who has most deeply thought loves what is most alive,
  Who has looked upon the world understands youth at its height,
    And the wise often incline,
      In the end, to the beautiful.

[WHD, 9]

To Heidegger's way of thinking, verbs are privileged, from a negative point of view, because they do not lend themselves to hypostasis as readily as nouns (they are presumably less readily assimilated to the present-at-hand); and they are privileged, from an affirmative point of view, because of their temporal character. They are, in short, the words that authentically say, and hence it is not surprising that Heidegger locates a crux, within "Sokrates und Alkibiades," not in the role of the beautiful but in the jointure (to use an old term) of the two predicates in the opening line of the second strophe: "He who has most deeply *thought loves* what is most alive." The reader may well be caught off guard, however, by the evident transition that finds Heidegger saying, immediately after noting the contiguity: "Inclination rests (*ruht*) in thinking. A strange rationalism, that grounds love in thinking" (WHD, 9). It is of course, in Heidegger's eye, no rationalism at all, let alone a strange one, any more than the earlier concept of *Dasein* and mood was a theory of affectivity. The latter is worth mentioning in the present context if only to underline how far Heidegger has come since 1927. Analogies to care and to other features of *Being and Time* continue to appear from time to time, as we have observed, but everything, where mortals are concerned, hinges now on thinking the play of the world. This applies to all work, even the hand-work (*Handwerk*) of handicrafts, which takes the place, in Heidegger's inquiry, of the art work in earlier writings and in this sense is complementary to the emphasis on the jug in "The Thing." Still concerned with equipment, Heidegger, setting aside the technical language of 1927, speaks simply of the readiness *(Fertigkeit)* of the tool (WHD, 49). If we compare the example he now employs (a carpenter teaching an apprentice) with the example he employs in *The Fundamental Problems of Phenomenology,* we note a closer focus on the maker of the thing. Like the artisan in Book X of *The Republic,* Heidegger's craftsman is a viaticum for determining what constitutes the essence of making:

> The hand holds. The hand carries. The hand sketches and signs *(zeichnet)*, probably because man is a sign. Hands enfold themselves, when this gesture means bearing man in the great onefold. All of this is the hand, is the authentic hand-work. In it rests everything that we normally recognize as hand-work; and normally we leave it at that. But the gestures of the hand go everywhere throughout language and are at their purest when man speaks by being silent. For after all, it is only insofar as man speaks that he thinks; and not the other way around, as metaphysics would still have it. Every movement of the hand in every one of its works carries itself *(trägt sich)* through the element, bears itself *(gebärdet sich)* through the element of thinking. All work of the hand rests in thinking. [WHD, 51]

This passage requires clarification on three counts. First, whereas Heidegger previously employed the term *ruhen,* which includes the sense "based upon," he now employs the term *beruhen,* which denotes precisely that sense. Second, the statement that thinking bears itself (which seems to me more felicitous than the more correct "behaves") points to the playful possibilities in the noun form, meaning gesture or bearing, which is close in sound and meaning to the word for bearing, as in carrying a child toward birth—possibilities developed in a passage to which I will turn below. Third, though Heidegger remains silent on the issue, what he says of the hand-work applies to the work of art as well. We know this (as noted in chapter 2) from the complementary interpretation of *poiēsis* spelled out in "The Question Concerning Technology," which groups poetry, other types of art, and handicrafts within the same order because what is brought forth in them comes not through itself, as in the *physis* that Heidegger regards as *poiēsis* in the highest sense, but through another, namely, the poet, artist, or artisan.

If the relation of love to thinking remains unexplored, this does not mean that nothing remains to be said. In Heidegger's reading of the Hölderlin poem, thinking grounds loving, which is directed toward the beauty of youth; and Heidegger leaves the matter there. But youth is a time, as is the old age of those wise ones of whom the poet speaks. The aging wise Socrates, the poem suggests, embodies the concern with *thanatos*, the Being-toward-death of *Being and Time*, which faces everyone "in the end," and the appeal of *erōs* embodied in a beauty that is *poiēsis* in the highest sense because it is brought forth in itself. The beauty of youth is the beauty of a bearing nearer the bringing-forth of birth and further from the going-away of death, so that those who have lingered long in thought may love, through it, the unity of what has-been with the promise of what is to come. Of this overlooked aspect of Heidegger's thinking Octavio Paz observes:

> Although he has never developed his affirmation, it is noteworthy that the German philosopher confirms what we all know with an obscure and prior knowledge: love, the joy of love, is a revelation of being. Like man's every movement, love is a "going to the encounter." In the wait our whole being leans forward. It is a yearning, a reaching out toward something that is still not present and is a possibility that *can* not be produced: the apparition of woman. The waiting keeps us in the air, that is, suspended, outside ourselves.[15]

Love need not be erotic in the narrow sense or even in the sense of avid desire *(Gier)*, which, temporally, implies rapid pace and hastiness and which Heidegger therefore opposes (without making the connection I am attempting here) as a danger to the mission of questioning (WHD, 19). Neither does Heidegger make a connection between the passage on Socrates and a later passage on the relation of mother and child; yet love sustains both figures, even as thinking sustains their love; at the same time, it sustains those others, the youth loved by Socrates and the child loved by the mother, through the bond of devotion, obedience, piety. It is not coincidental, then, that the mother is depicted in a Socratic role, namely, as a teacher attempting to bring a person younger than herself into understanding (a task made feasible by the fundamental capacity for hearing that is the essence of good dialogue, as it is of good teaching).

Piety comes into consideration, on the one hand, through the resonance that carries from the passage on Matthias Claudius's "Evening Song," which Heidegger's German auditors would recognize as a lyrical prayer for divine beneficence. It comes into consideration, on the other hand, through the relation between thinking and thanking *(Danken)*, the latter term appearing in the Epilogue to *What Is Metaphysics?* and reappearing prominently in *What Is Called Thinking?* in a passage recalling prior discussions of remembrance and memory as well as the Hölderlin text in which love appears as inclination. The passage

15. Octavio Paz, *The Bow and the Lyre*, p. 135.

depends for its effect on the manner in which Heidegger plays with
Gedanc, an old word for thought, with connections to thanking. Remembrance *(Gedächtnis)* and thanking are both based on *(beruhen)* this
Gedanc, which is not a mere retention of the past but a gathering of
what has-been through our waiting against what is to come.

> In the *Gedanc,* a "beginning" word, the primordial essence of
> remembrance holds sway: the gathering of the incessant, loving
> intent *(Meinen)* for all that the heart allows to presence *(anwesen
> lässt).* Intent is here understood in the sense of *minne:* the in-
> clination... of the heart as it thinks in the innermost way upon
> the beings that are *(Wesenden).* [WHD, 91]

Such inclination is a gift from Being, given because Being needs a scene
for its own disclosure; hence, when we give ourselves through love,
through intent, through inclination, we give the given. The same
applies to thinking, an event in Being which needs mortals who remain
receptive through the expectant openness of their own questioning.[16]
    In such a relation, causality in the four modes of metaphysics (mate-
rial, formal, final, and efficient) plays no part because each mode removes capacitation, as it were, to another time, another place: the
"why" of the event is set outside the event and made prior. As though
to break down this notion, which ultimately leads to the problem of the
fundamental ground, two lines from a poem by Angelus Silesius are
woven like a leitmotiv through the pages of *The Principle of Reason:*

> Die Ros ist ohn warum; sie blühet, weil sie blühet,
> Sie ach't nicht ihrer selbst, fragt nicht, ob man sie siehet.

> The rose is without a why; it blooms because it blooms,
> It cares not for itself, asks not if anyone sees it.
>
>   [SG, 68]

Gertrude Stein puts the matter a little more radically, perhaps, when
she says that "A rose is a rose is a rose"; but she says the same.
    The concept that most nearly corresponds to this way of thinking is
the Greek *aition,* "that to which something else is indebted," to which
Heidegger turns in "The Question Concerning Technology." Seen in
this light, the traditional modes of causation are simply "the ways, all
belonging to each other, of being responsible for something else" (VA,
III, 8/7). Even in this form the ways do not tell us much about the
manner in which the rose is brought forth from itself as *physis* or about
the manner in which it is brought forth through another—the artist—in

---

16. Joseph J. Kockelmans, "Thanks-giving: The Completion of Thought," in *Heidegger
and the Quest for Truth,* ed. Manfred S. Frings (Chicago: Quadrangle, 1968), p. 167.

the poem; or rather, they do not tell us more than we already know from the treatment of *poiēsis* in the two modes investigated in the same pages.

They become more helpful if extended (an undertaking Heidegger does not attempt) to complex cases. In the performance of a symphony, for example, responsibility may be seen in the interconnecting indebtedness of each constituent: the musicians, as users of equipment (instruments, chairs, music stands, and the like), together with their skills; the artisans responsible for the preparation of the equipment; the members of the audience, together with their capacity to hear and to sustain attention; the score, a being with a thingly character that allies it with equipment even as it carries an already constituted inclination (the totality of the composer's notations); the composer, as one who brings forth within the same order as the artisan; that artisan who is the printer of the score; the manner (in the sense of melody, timbre, tone) of the score as performed; the space of time in which that manner emerges through the concerted composure of performance; the space of time of the tradition without which the music could not move into its own articulation—without which, as the temporal structure that preserves the reciprocal responsibility of all the constituents, it would not be music; and finally, the space of time which is the world play's manner of moving, through all that is thus indebted, to its own disclosure.

Movement as a musical term in German is *Satz*, meaning also period, passage, or phrase, a repertoire that enables Heidegger to deconstruct, as Derrida would say, the centrality of the notion of *Satz* as the principle of reason *(Satz vom Grund)*. He does so with the aid of a passage by Bettina von Arnim:

> One speaks of a movement in music and of how it is carried out, or of the accompaniment of an instrument and of the under- standing with which it is handled, but I mean just the opposite, namely, that the movement carries out the musician, that the movement so often displays itself, develops, concentrates, until spirit and essence *(Geist)* coincide with it. [SG, 151]

Rimbaud says the same when he declares, "It is false to say: I think. One ought to say: I am thought"; Montaigne says the same when he declares, "I did not make my book any more than my book made me." On the other hand, Kierkegaard does not say the same when he states that "Everywhere that language ceases, I meet the musical." Yet he too shares, with these other writers, an admiration for a manner of art that so composedly baffles reflection, that embodies so fully the *aisthēsis* of immediacy. Music is so seamless, so fused, so at one with itself, that it seems indebted to, responsible for, only itself. In Heidegger's vision, of course, that cannot be; language does not cease where the musical begins, since music, as art, is founded in language as the saying of the play of the world. And yet music, together with dance, bids fair in Heidegger's total "style" of thought and discourse to carry language to a higher realization. The closer discourse comes to the musical, the more readily does one accept von Arnim's reversal and the more readily does one yield to the assimilation of the movement of discourse to the movement of music. To the musical one gives oneself in negative capability. Music becomes surrender, flow; one rides with its waves, flickers with its flame: thus the musicality of the text intensifies the strain of passivity in hermeneutic tradition—in Heidegger's words, the strain of letting-be.

Of poetic making Yeats observes:

> It is indeed only those things which seem useless or very feeble
> that have any power. And all those things that seem useful or
> strong, armies, moving wheels, modes of architecture, modes of
> government, speculations of the reason, would have been a little
> different if some mind long ago had not given itself to some emo-
> tion, as woman gives herself to her lover, and shaped sounds or
> colors or forms, or all of these, into a musical relation. . . . A little
> lyric evokes an emotion, and this emotion gathers others about it
> and melts into their being in the making of some great epic; and
> at last, needing an always less delicate body, or symbol, as it
> grows more powerful, it flows out, with all it has gathered, among
> the blind instincts of daily life, where it moves a power within
> powers, as one sees ring within ring in the stem of a tree.[17]

The organic terminology misleads to the extent that it implies a likeness between poetry and things as the mimetic tradition understands likeness. It is, of course, just such an understanding that Yeats rejects when he turns to the Japanese Nō theater, whose dance-plays, so moving and so motionless, so eloquent and so still, constitute a presentation powerful enough in itself to bring a thinking-with along on its way, holding open in its peculiar playing a space of time in which ecstatic temporality seems to stand forth in rare visibility. Even so, Yeats does not neglect to remind us that the inclination to the beautiful is also required, though in the manner of a gift and not as something forced. In the figure of the dancer Yeats finds not only the embodiment of unified time but also the unity of the sensible and the nonsensible,

---

17. William Butler Yeats, "The Symbolism of Poetry" in *Critical Theory since Plato*, ed. Hazard Adams (New York: Harcourt Brace Jovanovich, 1971), p. 723. Cf. Valéry's description of the way in which everyday phenomena become musicalized, in *The Collected Works of Paul Valéry*, vol. 1: *The Art of Poetry*, trans. Denise Folliot (Princeton: Princeton University Press, 1958), pp. 52–81.

which, though a given for Heidegger, is sundered by metaphysics and its metaphors.

> Labour is a blossoming or dancing where
> The body is not bruised to pleasure soul,
> Nor beauty born out of its own despair,
> Nor blear-eyed wisdom out of midnight oil.
> O chestnut tree, great-rooted blossomer,
> Are you the leaf, the blossom or the bole?
> O body swayed to music, O brightening glance,
> How can we know the dancer from the dance?

Yeats's poetic instinct enables him to see the implicit togetherness of the mortal, the dancer, and the thing, the tree, and the labor that entails a bearing, both in the sense of carriage and in the sense of bringing to term, in playing's space of time. Yeats's lines, in Heidegger's language, call things to arrive so as to bear upon those who bring them to bear, in turn, through their participation in the play of the world:

> The things let the fourfold of the world stay with them. This gathering, assembling, letting-stay is the thinging of things. The unitary fourfold of sky and earth, mortals and divinities, which is stayed in the thinging of things, we call—the world. In the naming, the things named are called into their thinging. Thinging, they unfold world, in which things abide and so are the abiding ones. By thinging, things carry out world. Our old language calls such carrying *bern, bären*—Old High German *beran*—to bear; hence the words *gebären*, to carry, gestate, give birth, and *Gebärde*, bearing, gesture. Thinging, things are things. Thinging, they gesture—gestate—world. [U, 22/199–200]

In "A Dialogue on Language" Heidegger essays a presentation, soberly playful and evocative, that will embody a unitary vision free from centered, presence-based, metaphorical metaphysics. The theme of the dialogue, at the point where we take it up, is the same Nō theater that attracted Yeats. Now, by Western standards, Nō plays are remarkable for their omissions. They have little to offer in the way of *dramatis personae*, they display slight action, and they are wanting in conflict. As Jerzy Grotowski would say, they are not discursive; that is, they do not develop in the manner of argumentation, narrative, or, for that matter, digression. To this extent are they "poor," even as Grotowski's theater, stripped of stagey sedimentations, is poor. The same trait characterizes the process by which the philosopher strips away layers of received wisdom to disclose what is irreducible, hence essential. In this way Descartes finds apodictic certainty in his own act of thinking, an act of profound, because foundational, simplicity. In his own way, and in the same epoch, Corneille, as though determined to eliminate accidentals, leaving only essentials, produces a dramaturgy sinewy and spare, inaugurating the splendid poverty of the French classical theater.

Striving for a tradition that will be more than the modern equivalent of this "rational" classicism, a theater less logocentric and more gestural, Artaud, like Yeats, turns to the East, discovering in a still older tradition of acting and dancing "a sort of spiritual architecture, created out of gesture and mime but also out of the evocative power of a system, the musical quality of a physical movement, the parallel and admirably fused harmony of a tone."[18] It is not very difficult, then, to imagine the appeal that this tradition, quite as splendidly poor (if not more so) than its European "counterpart," must possess for a Heidegger; for it is Heidegger who announces, in the aftermath of the devastation wrought by the Second World War, that "The thinking of the future ... is on a descent into the poverty of its preliminary nature" (W, 364).

Drawn on by the power of the simple (das Einfache), which reveals itself only at the expense either of rigorous analysis or of resolute releasement, the thinking of the future—which is nothing less than poetic thinking—already has, itself, an admirably fused harmony of a tone parallel to the fundamental tone that characterizes each Nō play;[19] thus the readiness that informs Heidegger's response to everything his Eastern visitor tells or shows him.

To give Heidegger (called Q for Questioner) a flavor of what he could experience fully by attending a Nō play, the visitor (called J for Japanese) first portrays in words, then acts out, the relation between gesture and the emptiness of the Japanese stage:

Q: This emptiness necessitates an extraordinary gathering (Sammlung).
J: Thanks to which only a slight gesture of the player lets what is powerful appear.
Q: What do you mean by that?
J: When for example a mountainous landscape is to appear, the player slowly lifts his open hand and holds it still at eyebrow level over his eyes. May I show you?
Q: Please do.
    (The Japanese lifts and holds his hand in the manner described.)

                                                              [U, 107]

This gesture of the hand is hand-work, not in contrast with play but precisely because it belongs to the total play of the world. By thus

18. Antonin Artaud, The Theater and Its Double, trans. Mary Caroline Richards (New York: Grove, 1958), p. 55.
19. See Twenty Plays of the Nō Theatre, ed. Donald Keene (New York and London: Columbia University Press, 1970), p. 12.

refusing to set work apart from play, Heidegger follows a path also taken by Freud, who beheld in the dreamer a world fairly bursting with the play of transformation, transposition, merger, improvisation—and called the activity dreamwork. As hand-work, then, the gesture participates in the play of the world by bearing, a word, as we have seen, with rich overtones, including that of gestation. This last notion may be meant to forestall any association with bearing in the sense of something that is endowed with traits "added on" to it in accordance with its nature. Gestation also suggests a process of emergence that transpires in due time, through itself, like the blossoming of a flower, rather than a process controlled by application of will. It is, like thinking, a place through which Being is disclosed: "The dialogue between Being and man, in which Being manifests to man its need for a place of disclosure, and man devotes himself completely to his task of giving Being that place of disclosure in the midst of things, takes place in thought."[20]

In gesture, language is neither absent nor present, that dichotomy being as inappropriate as the dichotomy between play and work or between the sensible and the nonsensible. Because thinking is unthinkable without language, and because the gestures of the hand move always through the element of thinking, they move equally through language, as the play of the world itself made manifest through the capacitation of saying. Now saying works at its play irrespective of the speaking that goes on, as we see in the case of the unspoken, which poetic thinking inclines toward on its way to the saying that wells around and through speech. Silence too, then, is a way of saying, as is emptiness, which constitutes a kind of ground for the essence of gesture, as indicated by the following response to the question, "Where would we look, then, for what is essential in the gesture you showed me?"

> J: In a beholding that is itself invisible and that, thus gathered,
>   so bears itself toward the emptiness that in it and through
>   it the mountains appear.
> Q: The emptiness, then, is the same as nothingness, that kind of
>   Being, namely, that we try to think as other than all present
>   and absent beings (An- und Abwesenden).

[U, 108]

From the time of What Is Metaphysics? and the lectures that become An Introduction to Metaphysics, Heidegger insists that poetry is capable of speaking authentically about nothing; hence the quotation from Hamsun on the sound of nothingness, and hence the observation that, when the poet speaks, it is as if the things thus revealed were invoked for the first time: "Poetry, like the thinking of the philosopher, has always so

20. Kockelmans, "Thanks-giving," p. 130.

much world space to spare that in it each thing—a tree, a mountain, a house, the cry of a bird—loses all indifference and commonplaceness." Like the poet, the actor in the Nō play—or the partner in the dialogue—lets things appear, as if for the first time, from this emptiness that suddenly becomes, thereby, a ground, itself invisible, through which there comes to visibility that which a beholding, also invisible, can for the first time see.

But isn't this interplay of the visible and the invisible simply the displacement, to a new field of discourse, of other, abandoned dichotomies? Merleau-Ponty tells us why the answer must be no.

> No one has gone further than Proust in fixing the relations between the visible and the invisible, in describing an idea that is not the contrary of the sensible, that is its lining and its depth. For what he says of musical ideas he says of all cultural beings, such as *The Princess of Cleves* and *René*, and also of the essence of love which "the little phrase" not only makes present to Swann, but communicable to all who hear it. . . . He says it in general of many other notions which are, like music itself "without equivalents," "the notions of light, of sound, of relief, of physical voluptuousness. . . . Literature, music, the passions, but also the experience of the visible world are—no less than is the science of Lavoisier and Ampère—the exploration of an invisible and the disclosure of a universe of ideas. The difference is simply that this invisible, these ideas, unlike those of that science, cannot be detached from the sensible appearances."[21]

Gesture is incarnate, though never material in a mechanical sense: for if movement occurs, something, some body, must be moving. This is not, admittedly, an idea that Heidegger says much about; it is perhaps only partially thought, but it is everywhere powerfully presupposed, not least in the rejection of the dichotomy of sensible and nonsensible that is at the heart of his quarrel with metaphors and metaphysics. It is presupposed, as well, in the analysis of hand-work, which is said to rest in thinking, whereas no such basis is ascribed to the relation of thinking to the hand as such. The silent distinction may be traced to that linkage of indebtedness and responsibility with which Heidegger replaces traditional causality. If such is indeed the case, then there may be small risk in viewing thinking and corporeality as mutually indebted and mutually responsible, such that each, without being interchangeable, requires and sustains the other.

In his performance the visitor enacts anew an aspect of Eastern theater and articulates the dance-like meaning of gesture's practice in the

21. Maurice Merleau-Ponty, *The Visible and the Invisible*, ed. Claude Lefort, trans. Alphonse Lingis (Evanston: Northwestern University Press, 1968), p. 149.

play of the world. As a *particular* reenactment, the gesture inscribes itself in the occasion, the self-presentation of the dialogue as such. This means: gathering what is futural toward an experience that, foreign to metaphysics, yet appears homely to a thinking with the time to remain properly, openly, givingly, poetic.

Such gathering finds embodiment in ceremony and celebration, as we know already from Heidegger's vision of the unity of the world through the round dance of mirroring play: "The round dance is the ring that joins while it plays as mirroring. Appropriating, it lightens the four into the radiance of their simple oneness." This thinking informs Heidegger's interpretation of Mörike's lamp, with its ring of dancers, and his interpretation of the dancing performed in the wedding of earth and sky of which Hölderlin speaks. For Heidegger—and, Heidegger believes, for the poet—the round dance is the same as the Greek dance, with singing in honor of the gods, called *chorois timan Dionuson* (e.g., in Euripides' *Bacchae*), a connection that accounts for the Dionysian over-tones in Heidegger's description of the dance-encircled lamp. In the round dance, the gods themselves celebrate, but not for themselves alone, for the dancing evokes the essence of the wedding as a world occasion: "The wedding is the totality of the unity of: earth and sky, men and gods" (E, 173).

The sky could justly be called the heavens, since this is the only English word that approximates the ability of the German *Himmel* to mean either sky or heaven or, as in the present case, both. The relation of earth to the heavenly sky is a version of the "between" phenomenon, described in another lecture on Heidegger's favorite poet as the dimension through which mortals measure themselves: "Man... has always measured himself by something, and by something heavenly. Even Lucifer comes from heaven.... 'Man measures himself... by divinity.' It is 'the measure' with which man measures out his dwelling, his stay on earth beneath the sky" (VA, II, 69).

Such a measure is itself measured by the end that comes to mortals dancing and singing (the musical resonance of measure is not to be overlooked) in their ceremonies and celebrations.

> Should the essence of play be determined from the standpoint of Being as ground [as reason], or must we think Being and ground—Being as groundless *(Ab-Grund)*—through the essence of play, and indeed of the play which we mortals are brought into, mortal because we dwell in proximity to death, which, as the ultimate possibility of Being-there, capacitates the utmost illumination *(Lichtung)* of Being and its truth? Death is the still unthought measure of the immeasurable, that is, of the highest play, into which man as something earthly is brought, into which he is placed. [SG, 186–87]

By alluding to Being-there Heidegger quietly contrasts the stark mood of *Being and Time* with the releasement brought about through participation in the world play; mortals are no longer seen as thrown but as brought and placed, death itself being placed in a kind of emptiness from which measures may be taken, gestures made, dancing danced, without any irritable reaching after fact and reason.

In *The Principle of Reason,* reason all but disappears in favor of play, in the sense suggested above and in a yet fuller sense, developed when, near the very end, Heidegger turns, for an enrichment of his vision of the fourfold world, to Heraclitus' four leading words, *physis, cosmos, logos,* and *aiōn.* From earlier inquiries we recognize in *physis* that through which emergence occurs from its own unfolding, as in the blossoming of a flower or human birth. *Cosmos,* Heidegger says, names the manner in which the world comes to radiant appearance in its own order and splendor.

> . . . finally Heraclitus names that which addresses itself to him as *logos,* as the same as Being and ground: *aion.* The word is difficult to translate. One says: world time. It is the world which worlds and temporalizes *(zeitigt)* in that, as *cosmos* (Fragment 30), it brings the jointure *(Fügung)* of Being to glowing gleaming. In that which the names *logos, physis, cosmos,* and *aiōn* say we may hear that unsaid which we name the destiny of Being. [SG, 187]

This world time is further elucidated by Heidegger's translation of another fragment in which the word occurs: "The destiny of Being is a child playing, playing a board game" (SG, 188).[22] Like all events in Being, like all the giving that so intrigues and perplexes poetic thinking, such playing—gratuitous, abundant, uncaused—resembles the rose of Angelus Silesius that blooms because it blooms, the rose of Stein that is a rose and over again a rose.

> The "because" is swallowed up in play. The play is without a "why." It plays as long as it plays. It remains just play.
> But this "just" is everything, the one, the only.

[SG, 188]

22. Cf. Eugen Fink, *Spiel als Weltsymbol* (Stuttgart: Kohlhammer, 1960), p. 241; Caputo, *The Mystical Element in Heidegger's Thought,* p. 82.

Index

102, 166; and founding, 85, 86, 105,
196; Greek passion for disclosure
of, 125; history of, 79; house of,
152–58; human, at issue, 133; identified with a being present-at-
hand, 207; illumination of, 223; of
inquirer, 127; at issue for *Dasein*,
33; is transcendence, 153; itself,
136; and its truth, 223; and man,
82, 83, 221; man within, 154;
meaning of, 117, 139; nearness of,
102; nearness to, 112; need of, for
scene, 95; never presented by
names, 194; nothing can surpass,
153; nothingness as aspect of, 205;
overpowering power of, 145; passion for disclosure of, 100, 139;
plenitude of, 206; poetic thinking
about, 174; precinct of, 154; as
presence, 203; question of, 3, 4,
101, 115, 212; relation between, and
beings, 106; roots of language in,
194; round dance of, 184; set into
work, 49; story of, 80; in struggle,
97; as synonym for the holy, 95; of
"there" constituted by understanding, 156; things lose, 202; and
thinking, 113, 125–28, 142; thinking
of, 160; time as horizon of, 95;
transcendence of, 155; true, of
Oedipus, 122; in unconcealing capacity, 120; unveiled, 153; wrested
from unconcealment, 136
Being-in-the-world: *a priori*, 8; as
Being-with-others, 10; existence as,
11
Being-there, 79, 82, 84, 137, 223;
ecstasis of, 145; Greek, 123;
grounding of, 84; historical, 135,
203; historical, of people, 136;
interest shifts from, to Being, 145;
ultimate possibility of, 223; violent,
128, 136
Being-toward-death, 215
Being-with-others. *See* Being-there
Benjamin, Walter, 31, 107, 160
Benn, Gottfried, 185
"Between," 165, 176, 223
Biedermeier period, 66
Bringing-forth, 141, 169
Browne, Sir Thomas, 198

Bruzina, Ronald, 157
Buddeberg, Else, 83, 95
Burckhardt, Sigurd, 86
Burke, Kenneth, 57, 154; "What Are
the Signs of What? A Theory of En-
titlement," 154

Calderón de la Barca, Pedro, 182
Call *(Ruf)*, 186, 189, 195
Care, 17, 90, 103, 109
Cassirer, Ernst, 207, 208 n.10
Center, 205, 206; of cosmicity, 151;
Derrida on, 202, 203; not a being,
206; in Rilke, 149
Ceremony, 175, 223
Chōra, 140
Christ, 83, 163
Christian: creation, 201; elements,
189; experience, Heidegger's early
concern for, 71; meaning in Trakl,
190; tradition of harmony, 105
Circle, Bachelard on, 150. *See also*
Hermeneutic circle
Circumspection *(Umsicht)*, 6, 7
Classicism, 66, 72, 79, 85, 220
Claudius, Matthias, 61, 181, 215;
"Evening Song," 212, 215; "Lul-
laby, A," 181; "Lullaby by Moon-
light," 61–62
Clearing, 42. *See also* Lighting
Coleridge, Samuel Taylor, 90
Communication, 10
Complementarity, 211
Concealment *(Verbergung)*, 43, 44,
202; *alētheia* depends on, 161;
Greek experience of, 117, 118, 119
Concern, 17
Conflict. *See* Polemos
Consciousness, 149, 153, 172
Consecration, 174, 176, 180
Cook, Albert, 138 n.11
Corneille, Pierre, 220
Cosmos, 119, 224; four-part, 174; po-
etic, 172
Creation, 47; Christian, 201; poetic,
172
Curtius, E. R., 151

Dance, 142, 218, 224; Greek, 223;
Heidegger's concern with, 200;
round, 67, 184, 223